Freeway Birding

San Francisco to Seattle

Harry G. Fuller

To Dan Murphy and Rich Stallcup (1944-2012),
two great California birders who taught me much and
invited me into their open fraternity.

1st Printing February 2013
Kindle ebook edition February 2014
2nd Printing, with corrections and additions April 2014

ISBN 978-0-9768321-3-3

Text by Harry G. Fuller
Maps by Jill F. Livingston, © Living Gold Press
Cover design and author photo by Kathryn G. Maloof
Front cover photo © Peter Thiemann
Back cover & p. 352 photos © Dan Elster www.elsterphotography.com
Illustrations © Irene Brady, Natureworks Press
Book design by Living Gold Press

Library of Congress Cataloging-in-Publication Data

Fuller, Harry.

 Freeway birding, San Francisco to Seattle / Harry G. Fuller.

   pages cm

 Includes bibliographical references and index.

 ISBN 978-0-9768321-3-3 (alk. paper)

 1. Bird watching--California, Northern--Guidebooks. 2. Bird watching--Oregon--Guide-

books. 3. Bird watching--Washington (State)--Guidebooks. 4. California, Northern-

-Guidebooks. 5. Oregon--Guidebooks. 6. Washington (State)--Guidebooks. I. Title.

 QL684.C2F85 2013

 598.072'3479461--dc23   2012042161

LIVING GOLD PRESS

PO Box 2
Klamath River,
CA 96050

www.LivingGoldPress.com
www.FreewayBirding.com

Table of Contents

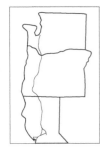

List of Maps

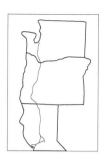

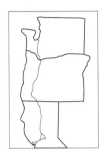

Introduction

I don't leave home without my binoculars. Almost never. I know there are other travelers as fascinated by birds as I am. In fact, I've met some. We watch roadside fences for Kingbird, Kestrel or Meadowlark. We check passing treetops for a Red-tailed Hawk or Raven. Perhaps we even note the swirl of Rock Pigeons or Brewer's Blackbirds while pulling into a large parking lot. We scan roadside breeding platforms for Canada Goose or Osprey.

This book is designed for my fellow fence post watchers.

Surely there are also more casual birders who long for sights beyond the inevitable mileage signs and eighteen-wheelers when they travel the Interstates of this expansive land, folks who crave a few minutes in a shaded rest stop with something interesting to watch. Or perhaps a half hour's respite at a park just off the highway: a river, an Osprey fishing, swallows hawking bugs. Maybe a picnic in some birdy spot. Replenished, these nomadic birders return to the freeway for another three-hour stretch.

This book is for them, too.

There are many who travel Interstate 5 between Central California and Seattle on business, on vacation, hitting the road in the RV, or going to visit some family member along the route. There are lots of rest stops along the way, and tantalizing wildlife signs. Travelers may wonder if there's a good place to stop, maybe to see a bird they've never seen – or not seen for years? While the traffic swirls by at high speeds, what's going on at a slower pace just off the highway? What birds are around here at this time of year?

This book is for those travelers as well.

Freeway Birding covers the major routes you might drive between San Francisco and Seattle, a driving distance of approximately 800 miles. Through most of this book, we will be "moving" along the Pacific Slope's great north-south freeway, Interstate 5. "Eye Five," as we locals call it, runs from the Mexican border roughly north to Seattle and thence to Vancouver B.C. This book deals with the portion of the highway between San Francisco and Sacramento on the south—that is, more specifically, the highways that connect the San Francisco Bay Area to I-5 further inland in California—and thence northward on I-5 through Oregon and Washington up to Seattle. It notes good birding spots right next to the highway, and those within a 20-minute drive off the freeway along the route.

If you're staying in a major city at either end of the route covered by *Freeway Birding*, there's plenty of birding information available already. Seattle and San Francisco are large cities with parks, coastal areas, and freshwater ponds and lakes. Both cities offer numerous good birding sites. Sacramento is on a major river. Birding in these cities can be wonderfully rewarding. Local Audubon chapters have good information online about where and when to bird, so I have listed only some of the easier-to-find birding spots in Sacramento, San Francisco and Seattle.

If you drive the entire length of highway covered by this book you'll pass more than fifteen National Wildlife Refuge units and a national Wilderness Area. There are at least two National Monuments and a National Recreation Area. Along this route are six National Forests, and more than a dozen B.L.M. and Corps of Engineers properties with public access. Further, there are dozens of city, county and state parks and wildlife areas. There are a handful of properties controlled by Nature Conservancy or various Audubon societies.

In California alone, freeways from San Francisco to the northern California border near Ashland, OR, pass near more than a dozen Important Bird Areas that have been recognized by the National Audubon Society. In Oregon there are a score of Important Bird Areas easily reached from I-5. Northward, in Washington State, another half dozen can be found along this interstate. Important Bird Areas are noted in the text, abbreviated IBA. Then there are the highway rest stops.

In some areas there are some bird-rich side roads worthy of a birder's time away from freeway monotony. I give only passing mention to any birding area more than 20 minutes one-way from an I-5 interchange. In researching this book I had to go birding, a lot. I visited drab parking lots as well as fascinating parks, and I drove plenty of inviting gravel roads. Sometimes I found the best birding in an area of privately owned land bordering an otherwise unremarkable byway or in a seemingly nondescript portion of a national forest. Thousands of drivers might pass the same spot, unaware of the avian riches along the road.

This book is to share what I've enjoyed discovering along the way.

Online Resources

As most birders know, there are now myriad regional and statewide email services that alert the world to most bird sightings of interest as soon as they happen. On our website, www.FreewayBirding. com, the author and publisher provide a list of links to useful sources for anyone birding along this stretch of I-5. I did not put URLs into the text of this book because I find about 10% of all links, even those found in an "updated" search engine, turn out to be dead. Thus I frequently had to begin a general search to find a specific piece of information or map. Online, the author has a shot at keeping URLs updated.

Digital cameras, GPS, rare bird alerts (online or by phone), email groups for specific regions, portable devices with birding apps — all these can help any birder visiting a new location. Local Audubon societies often offer free bird walks and have information on local hotspots. Visitors are always welcome on Audubon outings. Some local parks, Audubon centers and National Wildlife Refuges conduct nature walks as well.

In putting together this book, I've been able to check my own observations with those of thousands of other birders by using eBird, Backyard Bird Count, FeederWatch, over a century's worth of Christmas Bird Count records, and public photo albums on Flickr, Smugmug and similar photo-sharing sites. Citizen science endeavors like these have produced a mountain of good data, often with images as evidence. In addition, Point Reyes Bird Observatory and Klamath Bird Observatory (headquartered in Ashland, OR) are actively researching avian populations in California and Southern Oregon. In Seattle there's the Puget Sound Bird Observatory. The Golden Gate Raptor Observatory does an annual fall migration count in the San Francisco area.

I urge all birders to participate in citizen science bird counts whenever possible. The eBird project is most inclusive and flexible for amateurs like me. The data can be from anywhere, anytime, and the data can be entered at any time. You can enter records from birding you did twenty years ago. You can enter data from your trip to Florida or Costa Rica. Some of the places mentioned in this book have attracted faithful eBird data contributors. Other sites, perhaps equally rich in actual birds, have eBird data that is sparse or nil. The more we birders contribute, the better our shared database will be.

I do not include complete lists of every likely or even every common species for every location. Widespread and common species such as Canada Goose, Mallard, Wild Turkey (introduced), Double-crested Cormorant, Mourning Dove, Great Blue Heron, Turkey Vulture, Cooper's Hawk, Red-tailed Hawk, American Kestrel, American Coot, American Crow, Common Raven, Tree Swallow, Cliff Swallow, Barn Swallow, European Starling, Red-winged Blackbird, Song Sparrow and American Robin can be expected in any spot with appropriate habitat. Thus they rarely get specifically mentioned in the text.

What This Book Tells You

Mileposts and Exit Numbers provide a convenient way of locating roads, rest stops and roadside birding spots–even if you can't stop. I-5 itself in California does not have mileposts (although some state and county roads have them) but does have mile-marked freeway exits. All three states number their I-5 exits from south to north based on miles from the starting point, which is the southernmost border of each state. Washington State has markers along I-5 at every mile. Some other Washington roads do not have markers.

If the birder needs to leave the highway to bird, I use "exit" and give the exit number. When there is something of note at a particular area along the highway with no actual need to leave the roadway, I use "mile."

County lines are not always signed along the highway, but I call them out because some serious listers keep county life lists.

Driving time or distance for locations not immediately along the road. Time can vary radically depending on how often you pull off to check that bird on the wire. In most cases I have driven these exact routes myself and not allowed myself birding stops to get time estimates. Sometimes I have noted stated online driving time estimates to be as much as 50% off the time I clocked on a certain route. In larger cities and congested areas at major resorts traffic can be occasionally or often slow. The four large urban areas in this guide all can have very slow commute time tie-ups. Those are Portland, Sacramento, San Francisco Bay Area, Seattle-Tacoma.

Information about facilities such as toilets, picnic areas, trails, campsites, boating, and RV facilities, etc., near birding locations, and whether fees or tolls are required.

Significant wildlife or nature centers along the route.

A bit about the habitat you pass through. We all know how important habitat is to birds, both resident and migratory. If you are familiar with this part of the United States you will know what birds to expect in oak savannah. If you're unfamiliar with the Interstate 5 corridor you will find I often re-list the same birds for each similar piece of habitat.

Seasonality of birds to be seen or heard. I've included an appendix on the specialty species that can be found in this region but that have limited ranges. Some long-distance migrants are only seasonal in this area.

Weather

If you are from east of the Sierra Nevada Mountains you may not know that the Pacific Slope has a rainy season and a dry season. Roughly, you can expect rain anytime from October through April. Normally you wouldn't expect rain May through September. Light rain becomes more likely as you move northward even in the "dry season." Portland and Seattle are known for their frequent heavy fog which looks like light rain if you're from somewhere else. In most of this area the daytime temperatures vary depending on the proximity to the Pacific Ocean, season and elevation. In warm months the nights will seem cooler to a visitor from the eastern United States, where summer nights are generally warm. Here, in August, a 100-degree day can be followed by a 60-degree night and even lower night temperatures in the mountains. As you change elevation expect about a 4-degree drop in temperature for each 1000 feet in elevation you rise.

This book covers areas with dry summers, foggy summers, snowy winters or year-round mild temperatures. Redding can be as hot as Phoenix in summer, yet it gets heavy rain in winter and even occasional snow. Portland, Seattle and San Francisco have moderate maritime climates. The Siskiyou Pass, over 4,000 feet elevation, gets heavy winter snowfall. Between November and April, it's wise to check local weather reports for possible snow or heavy rain. Heavy winter ground fog is possible in both the Sacramento and Willamette Valleys. This can produce very dangerous driving conditions.

In the summer and early fall much of the area south of Eugene, OR, has low humidity. If you are from the humid eastern United States, be especially careful about dehydration, even on windless days. Even the cool-feeling mountains can be dehydrating on sunny days.

Pests

The dry western summer means that insect populations are generally lower than in the East, hence fewer warblers and vireos than in many eastern locations. There are no chiggers, deer flies, copperheads or water moccasins. There are abundant ticks in brush land, rattlesnakes in rocky habitat and mosquitoes in marshy areas. West Nile Virus and Lyme's Disease are both found in the region. There are few scorpions, but black widow and brown recluse spiders are present in their usual haunts.

You won't find poison ivy or sumac here, but there is poison oak, which often affects the same sensitive victims. Many birds eat the pale poison oak berries and thus spread the plant. Nettles abound and irritate your skin with the slightest touch.

Some Practical Advice

All three states included in this guide charge admission to state properties. Some counties do as well. Most city parks are free, but not all. Rules about dogs, alcohol, bikes, boats and horses vary widely. Some parks are "closed" certain days or in certain seasons. Some parks may be closed altogether by state budget issues. Many parks and wildlife areas are Day Use only. Many visitors centers are not open every day of the week. It is best to confirm online or by phone the hours and operation of any park where you may want to stop. National Wildlife Refuges and some state properties have hunting seasons. Note: If you want to use a photo blind, you will need to reserve in advance at most refuges where they exist.

In Washington State the price of an annual Discover Pass equals the cost of three single admissions, and all state-operated properties charge admission. If you're doing much birding in Washington, it's cheapest to get a Discover Pass that can be ordered online or purchased from licensed dealers in the state. California State Parks offer a blizzard of passes of various kinds, including those for over-sized vehicles like a large RV. Oregon Parks and Recreation Department offers both one- and two-year passes good with any vehicle you drive. These can be ordered by phone or purchased from local vendors.

In Oregon it is illegal to pump your own vehicle fuel except on federal lands like Crater Lake National Park. Oregon has no sales tax and gasoline tends to be cheaper there than in California.

If you are going south on Interstate 5 into California you'll have to stop at an inspection station where all vehicles are checked for homegrown produce and farm products. You can find information online by checking "California Border Protection Station." Most store-bought fruit is OK but check online if you are unfamiliar with these rules.

All three states are within the Pacific Time Zone.

Sacramento, Portland and Seattle-Tacoma have major airports. There are three commercial airports in the San Francisco-Oakland-San Jose metroplex. Three of the smaller cities along the way also have commercial airplane service: Redding, Medford and Eugene.

Amtrak serves most of the major cities and towns along I-5 north of Sacramento except those between Dunsmuir, CA, and Eugene, OR. There is regular train service between Oakland and Davis and Sacramento. The Eugene-to-Portland Amtrak service runs several times daily as well.

For hikers, the Pacific Crest Trail (PCT) parallels this route, first in the Sierra Nevada east of Sacramento. Then near the California-Oregon border it twists through the Siskiyou Mountains and joins the Cascades for the rest of its route north to Canada. There is copious information on the PCT online. For boaters—from kayak or canoe to motorboat—many of the lakes, reservoirs and rivers along this route will be inviting. Most will tend to have lower water levels in late summer and early autumn.

A Word on Maps and a Word of Caution

The publishers and author have worked very hard to make sure the maps in this book are correct and useful. Jill Livingston of Living Gold Press has far exceeded the author's expectations in producing useful maps that can be followed in the field. In researching this book the author drove thousands of miles, used Internet sites and printed maps. Here a word of caution about online sources: Bing maps, Mapquest and Google Maps all proved to be imperfect. At one or more times each of these widely used map sites were: 1) confusing, 2) incomplete, 3) wrong. Sometimes an online source was all three at once.

Printed maps were slightly more dependable but often out-dated by recent road changes or natural events. My advice: never enter a rural, sparsely populated birding area without both a good map and local advice and confirmation. In-car GPS systems are also less than dependable, especially in rugged, rural areas.

My word of caution: if you are visiting from a warm or flat part of the United States, please take our mountains seriously. From Redding to Eugene and anywhere in the Cascade Range, be careful in winter.

I was a work associate and friend of James Kim of San Francisco. In late November 2006, James, his wife and two young children were on a vacation trip. They were headed along I-5 and stopped one evening to have dinner in Roseburg. They were using a printed map widely distributed by the State of Oregon. After dinner the family was headed to the Oregon Coast to stay overnight. The map clearly showed a small road going through the Coastal Range near Grants Pass. It was raining as they neared the turn-off but they believed the map. What they didn't know was the road was a seasonal Forest Service road not plowed in winter and supposedly closed. The gate had been opened so the Kims proceeded uphill into tragedy and death. They became stranded in heavy snow. There was no cell phone service. My friend, James, died trying to reach help for his family. His wife and children were finally found after more than a week by a rescue helicopter.

Please do not stray from paved highways in the mountainous areas in winter. The temperature drops 4 degrees every thousand feet of increased elevation. What may be drizzle at 1500 feet can become a blizzard at 4000. If you have any doubts about conditions, check locally.

Nomenclature and Terms Used

Names of Birds. Throughout this book, I have used the common names of bird species as set forth in the American Ornithological Union checklist, but I have frequently shortened longer names. When I write "Scrub-Jay" it is the Western Scrub-Jay, the only Scrub-Jay species in the area. "Raven" refers to the Common Raven, "Crow" to the American Crow. "Flicker" is the Northern Flicker, "Robin" is the American Robin, "Pintail" is the Northern Pintail, "Downy" is the Downy Woodpecker, "Junco" is the Dark-eyed Junco, and so forth. In general I have not tried to sort through the complexities of subspecies with many migrant or nomadic forms, such as Fox

Sparrow, Junco, Red Crossbill and Song Sparrow. It is true that in winter, many locations described in this book will have more than one subspecies of Song or Fox Sparrow in residence, but I don't distinguish beyond the common name.

Terms Denoting Frequency. In using terms denoting frequency, I have hewed to definitions often found on checklists. "Abundant" means you should see this species nearly every time you visit the right habitat in a given location. "Common" means you should see the species more than half the times you visit. "Uncommon" means you will not usually see the species. "Rare" means you will be lucky to see this species.

Names of Trees. Oregon white oak and Garry oak are the same species. In Washington State the tree is usually referred to as Garry Oak. Similarly, the California bay laurel is called the Oregon myrtle north of the California-Oregon border.

Names of Highways. In titles and upon first usage in a section of text where the roadway is not specified in the title, terms such as Interstate 80 and California State Highway 128 are spelled out. However, in text where the meaning is clear, abbreviations such as I-80 and CA 128 are used.

Important Birding Area, abbreviated IBA, is a specific designation for an area recognized as being globally important habitat for the conservation of bird populations. IBAs are determined by an internationally agreed set of criteria. Currently there are about 10,000 IBAs worldwide. In the United States the program is administered by the National Audubon Society.

NWR. The full-length term National Wildlife Refuge is pretty universally known in its abbreviated form: NWR. You'll find both terms used freely in this book.

Chapter 1
San Francisco

San Francisco is geographically small, less than fifty square miles of land and lake. Yet it's surely one of the richest American cities for birdlife. Surrounded on three sides by saltwater, graced with large urban parks, San Francisco can be a good place for birding any day of the year. Its attributes include a mild climate and mix of habitat, from native oak forests to restored salt marshes, from freshwater streams to coastal sand dunes. The groves of Monterey cypress, eucalyptus and Monterey pine were all planted but still draw crowds of birds. Located on the Pacific Flyway, San Francisco has several well-known migrant traps, from Land's End to Golden Gate Park's Chain-of-Lakes to Mt. Davidson. A determined birder with plenty of time and energy can compile an annual list of over 270 species just within the city limits. A pelagic trip in late summer or early fall could easily add another dozen or more species.

A few vagrants I've been lucky enough to see in San Francisco include Yellow-throated and Philadelphia Vireo; Prothonotary, Hooded, Blackburnian, and Lucy's Warbler; Northern Waterthrush; Lapland Longspur; and Tufted Duck. Green-tailed Towhee, Townsend's Warbler, Townsend's Solitaire, Nuttall's Woodpecker, Lawrence's Goldfinch, Red Crossbill, Lark Bunting and Tricolored Blackbird are inland species that occasionally show up in San Francisco as autumn or winter vagrants. There are numerous active birders in San Francisco, and they find interesting vagrants every year. Each spring these birders do a rare bird round-up to look for spring rarities.

If you leaf through a Western Field Guide you'll notice an interesting mix of birds that are normally limited to the foggy coastal littoral of California, some ranging north into Oregon or south to Mexico. Some of these birds are sedentary; most are rarely or never seen east of the Sierra. Most are easy to find within San Francisco in the right season: Sooty Shearwater (offshore), Western and Heermann's Gulls, Black Oystercatcher, Brandt's Cormorant, Anna's and Allen's Hummingbird, Chestnut-backed Chickadee, California Towhee, Hooded Oriole (look for nesting birds in fan palms). Here the Pygmy Nuthatch nests at sea level. In winter every flock of Yellow-rumped Warblers will include a Townsend's Warbler or two.

A thorough explanation of San Francisco birding spots and those near the city would require an entire additional book, but I will touch on some. The Golden Gate National Recreation Area (GGNRA) was the first one created in the U.S. It has numerous parcels in San Francisco and Marin County just north across the Golden Gate Bridge. Much of the GGNRA land was once in various military bases so it includes habitat that has never been heavily developed nor farmed. Altogether GGNRA controls over 80,000 acres in three counties. In San Francisco GGNRA manages the Presidio, the city's largest public park, along with Land's End, Fort Funston, Fort Mason, Ocean Beach and Sutro Heights.

Following are just a few of my favorite San Francisco birding spots, briefly described.

Fort Funston. Part of the Golden Gate National Recreation Area (GGNRA), this is a fine spot for scoping loons and sea-going ducks as well as dolphins, harbor porpoise and Gray Whales on migration. There's a great place for a sea watch at the overlook next to the parking lot and hang-glider launch. At the north end of the park are woods where warblers and other migrants collect annually.

Golden Gate Park. Covering over a thousand acres, Golden Gate Park includes cultivated forest, natural but reshaped lakes, and grassy meadows. The west end of the park is a good migrant trap in autumn. Great Horned Owls are easily seen spring breeders here as are Red-shouldered Hawks. Wintering ducks gather in the park's ponds. Stow Lake has a small Great Blue Heron nesting colony.

Heron's Head Park. A reclaimed industrial dock area, Heron's Head Park is now home to birds that favor the quiet, protected waters of San Francisco Bay. This is the best spot in the city for Avocet or Stilt, Western Meadowlark and other birds unlikely in an urban setting.

Lake Merced. This large freshwater lake is separated from the nearby Pacific by a natural, narrow sand dam. It's home to many marsh dwellers and waterbirds, including a breeding population of Clark's Grebe. Trees along the margins of the lake are wonderful migrant traps in fall for unusual warblers and eastern vireos. Some winters a Tropical Kingbird will settle near the lake. In winter the southeast corner of the lake is an excellent spot to study gull species, and try to pick out the Thayer's.

Land's End and Sutro Heights. Both areas are part of the Golden Gate National Recreation Area. Land's End and Cliff House have toilets. Brandt's Cormorant, Black Oystercatcher and Western Gull often nest on offshore rocks at this western outpost of San Francisco. Pigeon Guillemot prefer cliff-face nests. In winter, this is a good spot for rock-loving shorebirds like Black Turnstone and Surfbird. Wandering Tattler stop on their annual migrations. The Sutro Baths used to be an attraction at Land's End, and the old swimming pools collect Red-necked Phalarope every fall. The overlook at Land's End and the decks on the Cliff House are great for scoping alcids, loons, ducks and possible Parasitic Jaegers. Some goodies I've seen here include Marbled Murrelet, Cassin's Auklet and Tufted Puffin. Merlin hunt the area in winter. During migration, Gray Whales may surface just a few yards offshore. Hooded Oriole, Black Phoebe and Pygmy Nuthatch nest in Sutro Heights annually.

Mount Davidson. Sticking its tree-covered peak above the surrounding houses, this hill attracts migrating birds seeking a shady, quiet place to rest. During migration, this small park can abound in flycatchers, warblers, sparrows, hummingbirds, even a Townsend's Solitaire or Blue-gray Gnatcatcher on occasion. May be the best spot in San Francisco for vagrant hummingbirds.

Ocean Beach. Ocean Beach is a sandy strand that covers several miles, all part of the Golden Gate National Recreation Area (GGNRA). It's a good place to find birds that like a beach, from Sanderling to Marbled Godwit. A small group of scarce Snowy Plover always overwinters here. It's a good place for scoping the open ocean, as well. Watch for flocks of Sooty Shearwater in summer; they can number in the thousands. At the south end, the bluffs house the only Bank Swallow colony for fifty miles in any direction. Don't let the Ravens pilfer your backpack. They'll be watching your every move.

Presidio. A large former military base, now the heart of the GGNRA, the Presidio is the largest parcel of open space in San Francisco. At Crissy Field there's a restored saltwater marsh that attracts migrant shorebirds. I once saw a Wilson's Phalarope here. Around El Polin Spring, the restored brush habitat and the water attract many interesting birds in summer and fall when the climate is dry. Olive-sided Flycatcher and Hooded Oriole usually nest near the intersection of Kobbe and Upton. In fall, at Battery Godfrey just south of the Golden Gate Bridge, you can scope the open skies for raptors making their scary flight from Marin across the Golden Gate to solid land.

Beyond San Francisco. To the south, along the coast and reached via CA 1 are Princeton Harbor, Half Moon Bay, Pescadero Lagoon and Marsh, Santa Cruz, Moss Landing, Elkhorn Slough and the incredibly rich habitat of Monterey and its bay. The lagoons at Foster City and the Palo Alto Baylands always yield plentiful water-loving birds. These can be reached via US101, which is nearly always heavily trafficked as it connects San Francisco and Silicon Valley with its numerous high tech firms.

Southeast of San Francisco you can find good birding at Mount Hamilton and Mines Road. Also, the Sunol Regional Wilderness and Pacheco Valley are worth visiting.

North of San Francisco, in the Marin Headlands (see Chapter 2) is Hawk Hill, where raptor counts are conducted every fall. It's a high point, where migrating hawks ride the thermals to get high enough to coast across the isthmus. Further north are Bolinas Lagoon, Point Reyes National Seashore, Tomales Bay and Bodega Bay.

It's no wonder that the San Francisco area has many fine and active birders with active internet email lists and websites to share sightings.

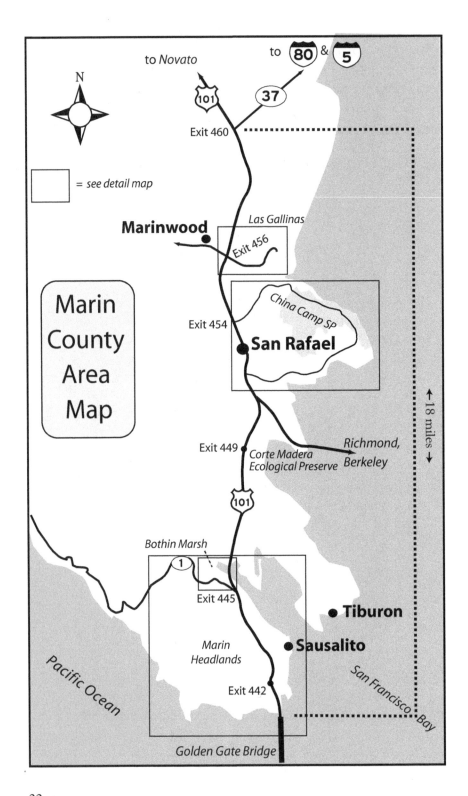

N

= see detail map

to *Novato*

to 80 & 5

101

37

Exit 460

Marinwood

Las Gallinas

Exit 456

Marin
County
Area
Map

China Camp SP

Exit 454

San Rafael

Richmond,
Berkeley

Exit 449

*Corte Madera
Ecological Preserve*

101

← 18 miles →

Bothin Marsh

1

Exit 445

Tiburon

*Marin
Headlands*

Sausalito

Pacific Ocean

San Francisco Bay

Exit 442

Golden Gate Bridge

Oak Titmouse

Chapter 2
North Bay Area

US101 and CA 37
Marin, Sonoma and Solano Counties

If you're heading north from western San Francisco or from the San Francisco Peninsula you can take what I consider to be the best route. I'll start this at the north end of the **Golden Gate Bridge**, US101. Only southbound traffic pays the bridge toll.

Crossing the bridge, you see soaring gulls or Brown Pelicans, often through fog (May-December). On a clear day you can watch for Peregrines who sometimes hunt from the bridge towers. If you stop at either end of the bridge and walk out onto the span you may see Western and Clark's Grebes, Surf Scoters, and Brandt's and Pelagic Cormorants in the swift current below. Gulls could be Western (all year) and any of a slew of wintering gulls: Glaucous-winged, California, Herring and Mew. Heermann's Gulls–who breed further south– are around summer and fall, as are Elegant Terns. Caspian and Forster's Terns are possible in the summer. There are nesting colonies of Brandt's Cormorants, Pelagic Cormorants, and Pigeon Guillemots on Alcatraz Island, and they often fly through the Golden Gate to the open ocean. Brown Pelicans may soar between the bridge towers in graceful lines, with wings fixed, floating more than they flap. They seem to have invented hang gliding and may have originated the chorus line.

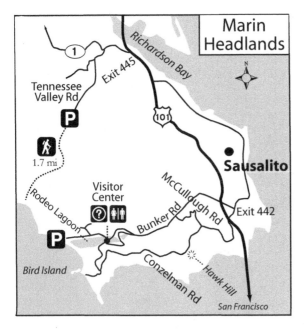

US101 Exit 442. At the north end of the Golden Gate Bridge, you can exit at Alexander Avenue and follow signs to the **Marin Headlands,** which will take you under the freeway then up onto the hills west of US101. This area was once a military base, thus saved from development, and now the spectacular views belong to all of us. This is a unit of the Golden Gate National Recreation Area. What you'll find: Rodeo Lagoon has a visitors center overlooking the lagoon, toilets, trails and picnic tables. You will recognize all the buildings as former barracks or other military structures.

The Marin Headlands is an area that's heavily birded by local birders, and it has an annual raptor count on Hawk Hill. EBird lists over 265 species for the area. On these brushy slopes live Anna's Hummingbird, Spotted and California Towhee, White-crowned Sparrow, Wrentit. Orange-crowned and Wilson's Warbler and Black-headed Grosbeak are here in spring and summer. Allen's Hummingbird are present February through July. In fall the similar Rufous Hummingbird migrates through, as well as numerous Lincoln's Sparrows.

In fall, Hawk Hill is one of Northern California's best hawk-watching spots. It's on Conzelman Road about 1.8 miles west of the freeway. You will note the small cluster of Monterey Cypresses along the west slope of the hill. On top are old military gun emplacements that make nice, flat viewing stations for the hawk counters. The seasonal activity here is managed by the Golden Gate Raptor Observatory (GGRO). It runs from August 16 to December 5. They welcome visiting birders during their count season, rain, shine or fog. Expect wind regardless of overall weather conditions.

Recent counts have found 19 raptor species. Peak numbers are usually in late September and early October. Most common species passing here are (1) Red-tailed Hawk, (2) Turkey Vulture, (3) Sharp-shinned Hawk, (4) Cooper's Hawk. They also get a dozen or more of the less abundant species: Broad-winged, Swainson's, Ferruginous, White-tailed Kite, Osprey and Merlin. Peregrine and Harrier often number over 200 in a single season.

Returning back east to US101, Conzelman Road intersects with McCullough Road between Hawk Hill and US101. McCullough takes you north over the ridge and down into Gerbode Valley that drains into Rodeo Lake which feeds a creek flowing into brackish Rodeo Lagoon. At the bottom of McCullough Road turn left (west) on Bunker Road toward the ocean. The creek here flows through a sand dune into the Pacific Ocean. This area can be rich in warblers in spring and summer. In spring listen for the high-pitched upward swirl of the Swainson's Thrush's song. Both Lesser and American Goldfinch abound in summer. Violet-green and Northern Rough-winged are among the breeding swallows in spring and summer. California Quail, Hutton's Vireo, Anna's Hummingbird, Bushtit, Chestnut-backed Chickadee, Wrentit, Bewick's and Marsh Wren, and Western Bluebird are here year-round. Look for Black Phoebe insect-hawking along the shoreline. Look for Hutton's Vireo in willows or oaks. Allen's Hummingbird is around from February through July. Ducks, gulls, geese, loons, grebes and Brown Pelicans (summer and fall) are often abundant here. In winter Fox and Golden-crowned Sparrows will find refuge in the dense brush. You can scope the Pacific Ocean from Rodeo Beach. Offshore you should find Red-throated and Pacific Loons from November to May. The later sometimes pass northward in flocks of thousands. Surf Scoter will be abundant year-round, check for less common White-winged in cold months as well. Cormorants and Common Murre may feed close to shore if there's a school of fish about.

South of the beach are some offshore rocks called Bird Island. Check for Black Oystercatcher all year. Look for these other rock lovers in fall and winter: both turnstones, Surfbird, and Wandering Tattler in September. Also likely are Pelagic and possibly Brandt's Cormorant. There is a trail that takes you up the hill overlooking the rocks. The hike is especially worthwhile in late spring. In autumn, scan the near shore for Parasitic Jaeger. They'll likely be chasing terns or gulls. The beach and lagoon can attract uncommon birds on migration, from Pectoral Sandpiper to Common Tern to Common Blackpoll.

EBird reports over 240 species for Rodeo Lagoon and the surrounding area. This includes possible breeding populations of Wood Duck and Cinnamon Teal. Also reported in winter: Brant and Black Scoter offshore, Cackling Geese, Blue-winged Teal, nine gull species including Mew, Heermann's and Thayer's. Heermann's heads back southward to breed in January. You may see all three locally nesting cormorant species: Brandt's, Pelagic and Double-crested.

To return to the freeway, you can retrace your route. Alternatively, you can go east from Rodeo Beach on Bunker Road to a stop light that controls access to a one-lane tunnel through the hills. At the east end of the tunnel, you turn right and make a short drive back to the US101 on-ramp.

US101 Exit 445. For some good marsh and woodland birding, leave US101, exiting onto California Highway 1 northbound. Just off the freeway on the east side of CA 1 you will see a large motel. Pull into the parking lot as far from the highway as possible. You'll be facing the marsh that borders Richardson Bay, a shallow finger of the greater San Francisco Bay. A trail for pedestrians and bikes follows an old rail bed through the marsh just north of the motel. Walk this trail (Mill Valley-Sausalito Path) across **Bothin Marsh Preserve**. The 106-acre marsh belongs to the Marin County Open Space District. You can get

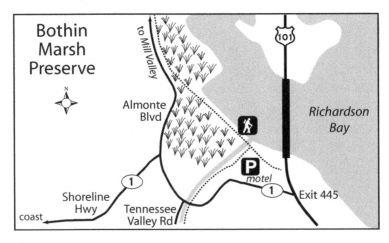

to and from Bothin Marsh in about four minutes driving time from either direction on US101.

Numerous shorebirds are here from September through April: Willet, Marbled Godwit, Long-billed Curlew, Western and Least Sandpipers possible, Black-bellied and Semipalmated Plovers. Several gull species may be seen here in winter, including Mew and Glaucous-winged. Caspian and Forster's Terns fish in the Bay in warm months. Wintering ducks include Bufflehead, Lesser Scaup, Northern Pintail and Red-breasted Merganser. Common Loons are occasional as well. Year-round there are Great Blue Heron, Great Egret and Snowy Egret. Best of all: during very high tides scan the exposed pickleweed for the endangered Clapper Rail. The bird may stand with just its head sticking above the plants. Also present is endangered Salt-marsh Harvest Mouse.

To reach the **Tennessee Valley** unit of the Golden Gate National Recreation Area, it's another ten minutes' drive from Bothin Marsh. Continue past the motel parking lot a little further north on CA 1 to Tennessee Valley Road, about 0.4 mile from US101, and turn left. Along the creek, as you leave the residential edge of Tamalpais Junction, there are Western Scrub-Jay, Black-headed Grosbeak (spring and summer), Bushtit, Wrentit, and Spotted and California Towhee (year-round).

The Tennessee Valley Trail winds 1.7 miles from the parking lot westward to the Pacific Ocean. There are a lush riparian strip, grassy hillsides and a freshwater pond along this trail. Species to be found here include Pacific-slope Flycatcher, Orange-crowned and Wilson's Warbler, Swainson's Thrush, Black-headed Grosbeak, and swallows in spring and summer. Look for Golden-crowned Sparrows and Say's Phoebe in winter. Great Horned Owl, Spotted and California Towhee, Wrentit, White-crowned Sparrow, Anna's Hummingbird, Chestnut-backed Chickadee, Bushtit, California Quail, Black Phoebe, Bewick's Wren and Pygmy Nuthatch are here year-round. At the pond check for dabbling ducks like Shoveler and Wigeon, Pied-billed Grebe, Green Heron, Virginia Rail, Sora, Common Yellowthroat and Marsh Wren. Many western specialty species pass through on migration. EBird lists over 115 species for Tennessee Valley and the ocean offshore.

To return to US101, retrace your route to the CA 1 interchange, US101 Exit 445.

US101 Exit 447. Take this exit to Tiburon, traveling east on Tiburon Boulevard (CA 131) to the **Richardson Bay Audubon Center.** It's about half a mile east from US101. This center overlooks and monitors the Richardson Bay Audubon Sanctuary. This shallow bay is home to thousands of wintering waterbirds each fall and winter, including Western and Clark's Grebe, Greater Scaup, Bufflehead, Double-crested Cormorant and American Coot. Egrets and Great Blue Herons hunt in the shallows. In summer Forster's and Caspian Terns may fish here. Several gull species regularly visit as well.

EBird shows over 100 species reported for Richardson Bay, including Brown Pelican, Marbled Godwit, Black Turnstone, Least Sandpiper, Elegant Tern in summer and fall, Nuttall's Woodpecker, Black Phoebe, Chestnut-backed Chickadee, Oak Titmouse, Bushtit, California Towhee, Spotted Towhee, and Golden-crowned Sparrow (winter).

US101 Exit 449. Watch for the Paradise Drive exit a few miles north of the Richardson Bay Bridge and south of Sir Francis Drake Boulevard. Take that exit and look for Redwood Highway on the east side of the freeway. Turn north. If you are southbound on US101 you will have to cross over the freeway.

You will notice a saltwater channel along the roadside. The open space on your right is **Corte Madera Ecological Preserve.** Just 100 yards north of the large shopping center, you'll see a four-car parking lot and bench next to the marsh. Park here and check out the birds. To return to US101 southbound, retrace your route. If you are northbound, turn north on Redwood Road and watch for signs taking you back onto US101.

At this preserve, you can often get thirty species in fifteen minutes just walking a few feet from your car. Year-round birds include Gadwall, White-tailed Kite, Great Blue Heron, Great Egret, Snowy Egret, Black-necked Stilt, American Avocet and Killdeer. White Pelicans are frequently seen in this small lagoon, like huge sailboats in a bathtub. In warm months Forster's Terns may come here to fish. A variety of smaller gulls may be loafing on the mudflats: Mew (winter), California, Ring-billed. Over a dozen migratory shorebirds and twenty species of waterfowl can be found here. In winter five species of grebe are possible: Eared, Horned, Pied-billed, Clark's and Western. Black Skimmers from the colony about 50 miles south have been seen here, as well as the usual wintering gulls and summering terns. Expect Common Yellowthroat in spring. Song Sparrows abound.

EBird shows over 150 species for this site and the Corte Madera Marsh that lies between US101 and San Francisco Bay.

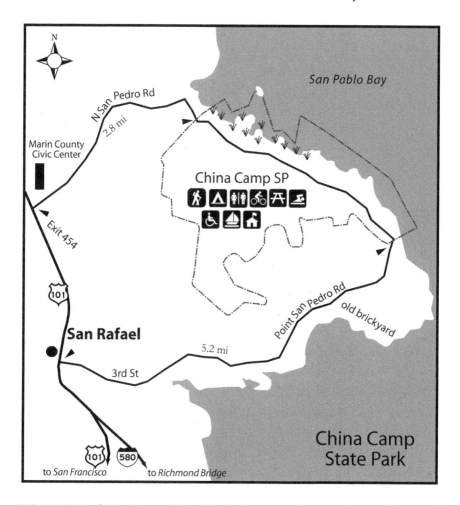

US101 Exit 452. Central San Rafael, go east here to San Pablo Road. The only known Vaux's Swift roost in the Bay Area was discovered a few years ago by birder Rusty Scalf. They roost in the long-unused chimneys of the old brickyard, 4 miles east along Point San Pedro

Road. From late August to early October you'll find south-bound Vaux's Swifts (get there before 6 p.m.)

US101 Exit 454. Take the exit onto North San Pedro Road and go east for **China Camp State Park.** On your left you will pass the Marin County Civic Center, designed by Frank Lloyd Wright. Three miles from I-5, you will enter China Camp State Park. Here are over 1,500 acres of open space and salt marsh on the margin of San Francisco Bay. What you'll find: toilets, picnic areas, swimming, boating, wind surf-ing, campsites and horseback riding. Dogs are allowed on leash. There are 15 miles of hiking trails along the bay and into the oak woodlands and brush on the upper slopes.

Over 100 species have been reported to eBird from here, includ-ing Loggerhead Shrike and the elusive Clapper Rail and Black Rail in spring. Some resident birds here are Anna's Hummingbird, Hutton's Vireo, Bushtit, Oak Titmouse, Chestnut-backed Chickadee, Bewick's Wren, and Spotted and California Towhee. There are reports of Cali-fornia Thrasher as well. The Thrasher can be difficult to find but he's a great songster in spring.

US101 Exit 456. Turn onto Smith Ranch Road going eastward to reach **Las Gallinas Ponds.** About 0.7 mile from US101 you will see the entrance to **John F. McInnis Park.** On your left, just across the railroad tracks and before you enter the park, there's a narrow paved road to your left (north). This is Smith Ranch Road; take it. It passes sports fields, then curves around an oak-covered hill and heads to a sewage treatment plant about 0.6 mile further on. Take the left-hand fork there; the road curves around the perimeter fence of the sewer plant. After 0.2 mile from sewer plant entrance you come to small dirt parking lot. There are toilets, and you can park here. Just across the bridge are trails that circle the Las Gallinas sewer ponds, now restored as wetlands. This area is administered by the Las Gallinas Sewer Dis-trict. There are 3.5 miles of hiking and birding trails here. There are islands in the ponds, which usually contain some water even in the dry mid-summer.

This is a heavenly spot for waterfowl, shorebirds, raptors and summering swallows. I got my lifer Pectoral Sandpiper here, as it's

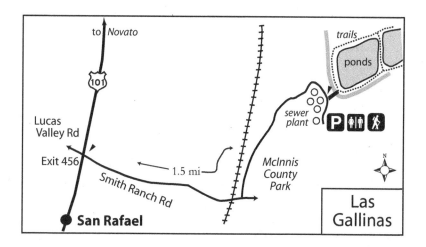

a hotspot during fall migration. And in summer I've seen three hundred Cliff Swallows swirling over the canal next to the parking lot. Year-round birds include Cinnamon Teal, Gadwall, American Avocet, Black-necked Stilt, California Quail, Great Blue Heron, Great Egret, Snowy Egret, Green Heron, Black-crowned Night-Heron, Osprey, White-tailed Kite, Northern Harrier, Black Phoebe, Marsh Wren and California Towhee. Breeding season birds include Cliff, Barn, Tree and Violet-green Swallows. The Tree and Violet-green are hardy enough to be seen even in winter. Wintering birds include possible Cackling Goose; most dabbling ducks of the western United States; Bufflehead; Hooded and Common Mergansers; and Horned, Eared and Western Grebes. Among wintering shorebirds you may find Long-billed Curlew, Marbled Godwit, both dowitchers, Dunlin and Wilson's Snipe. Merlin and Prairie Falcon join Peregrine and Kestrel for the winter hunting season in this flat and open marshland. White Pelicans are possible any month, as some no longer migrate out of the Bay Area for breeding season. EBird reports over 200 species have been identified at this frequently birded location. That includes more than thirty species of waterfowl.

US101 Exit 460A. Exit US101 here for California Highway 37. If you are heading east or north, turn your trip odometer to 00 here. If you have come across CA 37 from the east, cross to the other side of US101 and head south toward San Francisco and the Golden Gate Bridge. Southbound traffic pays a toll.

For the next 17 miles CA 37 crosses farmland that was once salt-water marsh. Some has been restored. Birdlife can be abundant during migration. Many shorebirds and waterfowl winter here. You may spot Beechey's (California) Ground Squirrel on fence posts, alert for Red-tailed Hawks or just watching the traffic. In many places the highway shoulder is narrow and not safe for stopping. Fortunately there are some well-placed pullouts and overlooks.

Expect Western Meadowlark, Starling, Red-winged Blackbird, American Goldfinch in summer, Barn and Cliff Swallow in warm months, Brewer's Blackbird and White-crowned Sparrow. Great Blue Heron, Great Egret and Snowy Egret may work the fields amidst flocks of Canada Geese. Jackrabbits bound, and abound here.

CA 37 Mile 3. Intersection with Atherton Avenue. If you leave CA 37 here and turn west on Atherton (toward Novato), you can find a remnant of typical oak savannah. After 0.4 mile, turn left on Olive. Head south for another 0.4 mile, then left onto Deer Island Road for 0.2 mile to the small dirt parking lot at the trailhead for **Deer Island Open Space Preserve.** Oak forest lovers include Nuttall's Woodpecker, Oak Titmouse, White-breasted Nuthatch, Western Scrub-Jay and Western Bluebird. The hillock overlooks marsh on all sides, including Simmons Slough.

CA 37 Mile 4. Petaluma River Bridge. If you are eastbound, you've entered Sonoma County. Westbound, you are crossing into Marin County. I rarely see birds along this stretch of the Petaluma River, which empties into the San Pablo Bay arm of San Francisco Bay just to the south. You may spot an egret or a fishing Forster's Tern above the river. Just east of the bridge you can turn onto Railroad Avenue and take it to **Port Sonoma.** The port and the marsh to the south are good for waterfowl and shorebirds in fall and winter. There are over 5 miles of hiking trails into the saltwater marsh where the Petaluma Estuary opens into San Pablo Bay. Among the birds you can find here are Long-billed Curlew, Whimbrel on migration, Dunlin, American Avocet and Black-necked Stilt. Gulls in winter include Mew and California. Western Gull is year-round. Caspian and Forster's Tern may be seen here in warm months.

CA 37 Mile 6. Turn north on Lakeville Highway for **Tolay Regional Park**, run by Sonoma County Park Department. You go about 6 miles north on Lakeville Highway, then turn right onto Cannon Lane and go 1.2 miles to the park. What you'll find: picnic areas, toilets, and numerous historic displays, including a reconstructed Native American village. There's an historic farm, grasslands, ridges, a freshwater lake, wetlands, and many other natural resources. There is an entry fee, and you must go through an orientation to get an access permit, so this isn't appropriate for casual passers-by.

Tolay Regional Park is between the Petaluma River and Sonoma Valley and covers nearly 1,800 acres. It provides habitat for several species of special status including the Burrowing Owl, Golden Eagle, White-tailed Kite, Horned Lark and Northern Harrier. Other interesting species here are the California red-legged frog and the northwestern pond turtle. EBird has 160 species recorded for this park including more than 20 waterfowl. Birds you can find here include California Quail, Red-shouldered Hawk, Peregrine, Common Gallinule, Barn and Great Horned Owls, Anna's Hummingbird, Nuttall's and Acorn Woodpeckers, Black Phoebe, Hutton's Vireo, and Marsh and Bewick's Wrens.

In the breeding season, expect Allen's Hummingbird, Pacific-slope and Ash-throated Flycatcher, Violet-green Swallow and Bullock's Oriole. Wintering birds include occasional Ferruginous and Rough-legged Hawks, Merlin, Prairie Falcon, Long-billed Curlew, Wilson's Snipe, California and Glaucous-winged Gulls, Red-breasted Sapsucker, Say's Phoebe, American Pipit, and Lincoln's and Golden-crowned among the sparrows.

Despite the claim of one park district web page, there are no reports on eBird of Tricolored Blackbird at Tolay Park.

The headquarters of the **San Pablo Bay Wildlife Refuge** is at 7715 Lakeville Road. That is about two miles north of CA 37. During weekday business hours there are toilets and drinking water available but no formal visitors center at the headquarters.

CA 37 Mile 8. Just past the intersection with CA 121 at Sears Point Raceway you will see a parking lot on the right, south of the highway next to an impoundment. This is the **Tubb's Island** section of **San**

Highway 37 Area Map

west

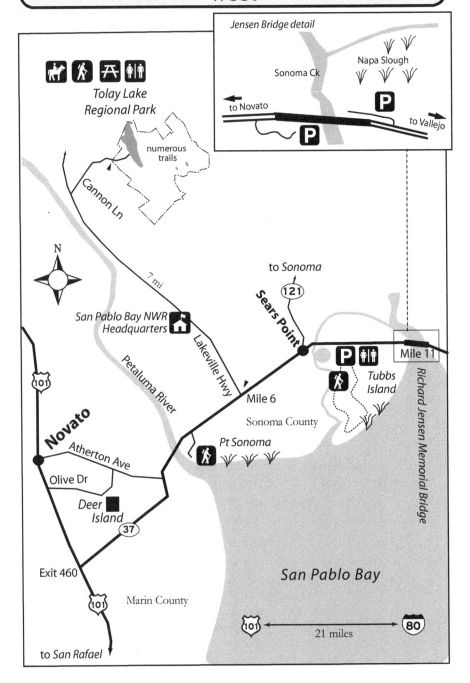

Jensen Bridge detail

Sonoma Ck

Napa Slough

to Novato

to Vallejo

🅿

🅿

Tolay Lake
Regional Park

numerous
trails

Cannon Ln

N

7 mi

to *Sonoma*

121

Sears Point

San Pablo Bay NWR
Headquarters

Lakeville Hwy

🅿 🚹

Mile 11

Richard Jensen Memorial Bridge

Petaluma River

Mile 6

Tubbs
Island

Sonoma County

Novato

Atherton Ave

Pt Sonoma

Olive Dr

Deer ◼
Island

37

Exit 460

101

Marin County

San Pablo Bay

101

80

21 miles

to *San Rafael*

Highway 37 Area Map
east

White Slough detail

Exit 19

37

Palm Dr

Sonoma Blvd

Yolano Dr

Sacramento St

trail

Exit 18

N

Napa County

see detail

Skaggs Island Rd

Napa-Sonoma Marshes

trail

Napa River

see detail

Exit 19

37

Exit 33

Richard Jensen Memorial Bridge

P

MP14

Solano County

P

Sonoma Blvd

Vallejo

80

San Pablo Bay

Mare
Island

Exit
30

780

101 ←——— 21 miles ———→ 80

Carquinez Bridge

to *San Francisco*

Pablo Bay National Wildlife Refuge (NWR). What you'll find: toilet, trail, a lagoon adjacent to the parking lot, and a trail south into the marshland. The Lower Tubbs Island Trail runs over 8 miles round trip through the marsh, along Tolay Creek and out to San Pablo Bay. It's a level walk just above sea level. Shorebirds and ducks are around in winter. One summer Blue Grosbeak unexpectedly nested here. Horned Lark may show up in winter and spring on the trail that runs along the top of the old dikes. EBird shows over 130 species for this part of the San Pablo NWR.

Anywhere along CA 37 you may expect Harrier, White-tailed Kite, Red-tailed Hawk, summering and migrating swallows, and even an occasional Vaux's Swift on passage. Numerous shorebirds are here in fall and winter. Black-necked Stilt and American Avocet are resident in the area year-round. Concentrations of shorebirds and ducks may attract hunting Peregrine in fall and winter. Great Egret, Snowy Egret and Great Blue-Heron are common. Check for Black-crowned Night-Heron at dusk. Wintering waterfowl include Canvasback, Bufflehead, both scaup, and Common Goldeneye. There are occasional Black Rail reports here as well. The Canvasback gathering here each winter is believed to be the largest on the Pacific Coast. Check the flocks for possible Redheads or even an occasional Tufted Duck or Common Pochard from far afield. Gadwall nest here, as do Black-necked Stilt and American Kestrel. Clapper Rail may be seen during highest tides, especially in winter. Virginia Rail are present. Caspian Tern fish here in the warm months. Migratory shorebirds can include Marbled Godwit, Long-billed Curlew and Least Sandpiper. There are no sandy beaches but there are miles of mudflats.

CA 37 Mile 11. The **Richard "Fresh Air" Jensen Memorial Bridge** has wildlife-viewing points in each direction. Each has a small parking lot but no other facilities. West of the bridge you're in Sonoma County, east of it you're in Solano County. The stream is Sonoma Creek. Birds you might see include summering swallows, White-tailed Kite, Harrier, Red-tailed Hawk, Red-winged Blackbirds, Black-necked Stilt and Killdeer. House Finch, American Goldfinch, Song Sparrow and Black Phoebe nest here. On the north side of the road, the edge of the lagoon attracts shorebirds including Marbled Godwit, Long-billed Curlew, Willet and Western Sandpiper in fall and winter.

CA 37 Mile 12. Turn north here onto **Skaggs Island Road**. The road is most safely accessed from the westbound lanes. There is a break in the traffic barrier, so you can turn onto Skaggs Island Road even if you're eastbound. This is the entrance to a former United States Navy installation, which became a 3,300-acre unit of the **San Pablo Bay National Wildlife Refuge (NWR)** in early 2011. The refuge and surrounding wetlands are ranked as an Important Bird Area (IBA) under the Audubon Society program. Driving up the road there's an arched bridge that gives you a fine vantage point over the surrounding marshes. The lagoons often have White Pelican, American Avocet, Black-necked Stilt, and in winter a variety of shorebirds and waterfowl. Long-billed Curlew sometimes stage here in fall before they disperse for the winter. Large flocks of Dunlin, Western Sandpiper and Marbled Godwit may occur in fall or spring migration. Wintering birds include Shoveler, American Wigeon and an occasional Eurasian Wigeon, American Coot, Pied-billed Grebe, and Golden-crowned Sparrows in the brush and fennel thickets. On winter evenings these flat, damp marshes are a good place to spot a hunting Short-eared Owl. Forster's Tern may be seen fishing here in summer.

CA 37 Mile 14. Accessible only from westbound lanes is a pullout and small parking lot with an entrance to a trail heading north from CA 37 into the marshes. On your left is a large impoundment, part of Island #1. On your right is Cullinan Ranch Unit. Both are part of the **San Pablo Bay NWR**. The trail is level and affords good views over the lagoons and marshland. All the birds seen at Skaggs Island may occur here, as well as Northern Harrier, White-tailed Kite and Red-tailed Hawk.

CA 37 Mile 18. Just west of the Napa River Bridge, you can exit to go onto **Mare Island**. Mare Island is a former Navy submarine base. Some of the buildings are in use, many are moldering. Empty lots and former ball fields may have grassland species. Westbound, north of the bridge, you can pull off CA 37 for an overlook with views northward along the **Napa River** and bordering marshes. Peregrines usually nest under the Napa River Bridge. It is also used by White-throated Swifts. Shorebirds and ducks use the wetlands on both sides of the river and northward from the bridge. The Napa River empties into San Pablo Bay to the south.

As you leave the bridge eastbound and enter Vallejo, CA 37 veers north and passes **South White Slough** and its marshland. The open lagoon on the right often has dense gatherings of shorebirds, White Pelicans, a handful of Caspian Terns, waterfowl, herons and egrets. You have to exit CA 37 to get a good look (see *Highway 37 Area Map, East*).

CA 37 Mile 19. Exit onto Sonoma Boulevard, then head west on Yolano Street and follow the map. You can park at the south end of Palm Drive. The trail that parallels the loud highway on the western edge of South White Slough offers good viewing of the birds in and around the water. Best viewing will be in fall and winter, but Caspian Terns may show up in summer. Herons and egrets are here year-round. Stilts and Avocets are also possible any time of year.

CA 37 Mile 21 / I-80 Exit 33. Here CA 37 intersects with Interstate 80. From this point, Sacramento is east on I-80, Berkeley and San Francisco via the Bay Bridge are west on I-80, and Marin County or San Francisco via the Golden Gate Bridge are west on CA 37.

If you're in this area in winter, check local rare bird alerts and regional email lists for possible rarities. I saw my first-ever Glaucous Gull and Mountain Plover wintering in Solano and Yolo Counties in otherwise unremarkable pasturelands.

I-80 South of CA 37 Interchange (I-80 Exit 33). For this short section of I-80 in Solano County that lies south of the above-mentioned interchange and north of the Contra Costa County line at Carquinez Strait, see Chapter 3.

Wrentit

This shy, hard-to-spot skulker is America's only member of the Old World's babbler family. There are 272 other babbler species in the forests of Asia and Africa. The bird's Latin name, *Chamaea fasciata,* reminds us of the long-standing taxonomic confusion over this small bird that was not quite a wren and not quite a tit. (Birds in the chickadee family are known as "tits" in England: Blue Tit, Great Tit, and so on.) The bird was first found in California by Dr. William Gambel, who called it a "wrentit," but the first scientific description was written by John Cassin, using Gambel's observations and specimens. Cassin called the bird a "ground wren." The Wrentit was long considered a close cousin of wrens, and not until modern genetics was the taxonomy clear: this bird is the one and only American babbler.

Wrentits stick to dense brush, preferring fairly low elevations, often near water. Rarely is a Wrentit seen more than a few feet above the ground. The mated pair stays together, on their territory, year round. They are among the most sedentary of North American birds. They don't wander nor do they disperse far in late summer. Migration is out of the question. It's amazing to imagine their ancestors actually spreading across the old Siberian Land Bridge, down the Pacific Coast, and then getting isolated here from all their kind.

Today's Wrentits show no inclination to much movement. There is, however, some evidence that the population may be expanding northward. Lewis and Clark did not report seeing the bird, but specimens were collected 90 years later in the Astoria area, so perhaps the Wrentit was newly arrived there, having slowly moved up the coast.

Wrentits are found only in coastal parts of Oregon, California and Baja California. The only claim of a sighting in Washington State was in 1937, and the species is not on the Washington Ornithological Society's state checklist.

The Wrentit is generally about 6.5 inches long, with dark brown plumage, a whitish eye and a long, narrow tail. Its most common call is like a bouncing ball. Its diet consists mainly of insects, with some berries. Though monogamous, Wrentits will nest cooperatively. This is a useful tactic for a species that prefers to stay in one place. When in motion, the Wrentit hops more than it flies. It will often share habitat with Song Sparrow and Bewick's Wren. The Wrentit, however, is less responsive to pishing.

East BayArea Map

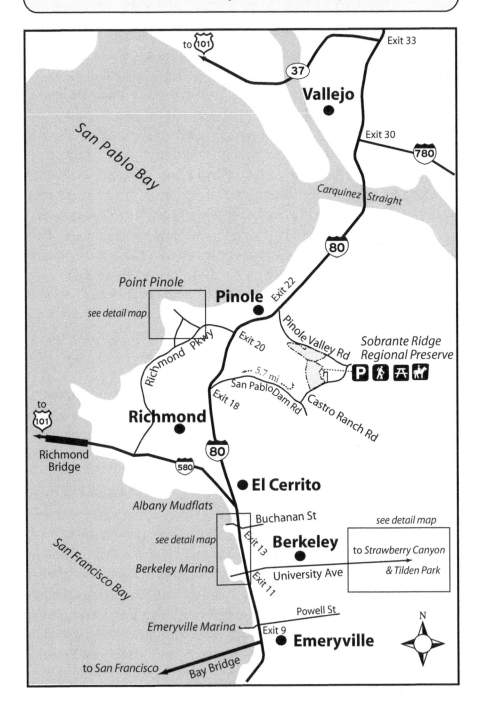

Chestnut-backed Chickadee

Chapter 3

East Bay Area

Interstate 80, Oakland to Vallejo
Alameda, Contra Costa and Solano Counties

Crossing the **San Francisco-Oakland Bay Bridge** to Interstate 80, watch for Avocet, Stilt and wintering ducks when you come off the eastern end of the Bay Bridge. While on the bridge you may notice Peregrine Falcon and Caspian Tern in summer, and Western Gull any time of year. Brown Pelicans frequent San Francisco Bay and are most abundant from May through December.

I-80 Exit 9. Emeryville Marina. Exit here onto Powell Street and go west of I-80 for the **Emeryville Marina.** On the eastern shore of the Bay where winds are normally from the west, this marina can pick up some interesting wintering birds: King Eider (once); White-winged Scoter; Long-tailed Duck; Clark's, Eared and Horned Grebe; Elegant Tern; and Heermann's Gull. Black Oystercatchers show up on the rocks after breeding season. In fall, a full panoply of common migrants move through the trees and shrubs around the marina. Nearly 90 species have been reported to eBird from this site.

I-80 Exit 11. Berkeley. Exit here onto University Avenue and head to the west side of I-80 to bird the bayside sections of Berkeley. Here you can find **Aquatic Park, Shorebird Park,** the **Berkeley Marina** and the **Berkeley Pier** (see *East Bay Waterfront* map).

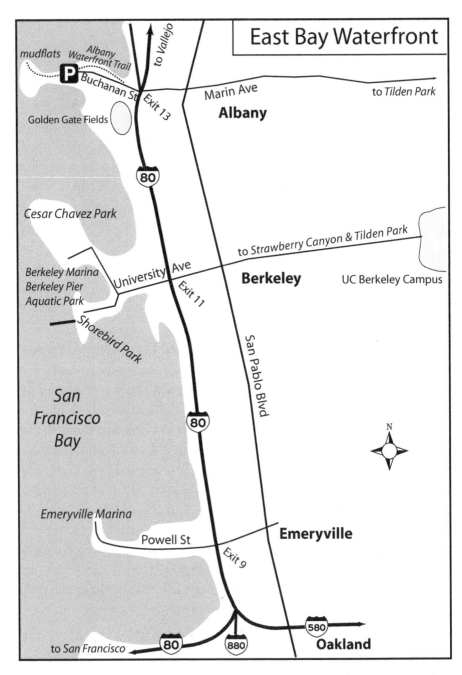

East Bay Waterfront

mudflats
Albany Waterfront Trail
P
Buchanan St
to Vallejo
Exit 13
Marin Ave
to *Tilden Park*
Albany

Golden Gate Fields

80

Cesar Chavez Park

to *Strawberry Canyon & Tilden Park*

Berkeley Marina
Berkeley Pier
Aquatic Park
University Ave
Exit 11
Berkeley
UC Berkeley Campus

Shorebird Park

San Pablo Blvd

San Francisco Bay

80

N

Emeryville Marina
Powell St
Exit 9
Emeryville

580

80
880
Oakland

to *San Francisco*

Despite heavy urban use, this area just north of the Bay Bridge offers great birding in fall and winter for waterfowl and shorebirds. EBird tells us 170 species have been reported here. The area is intensively birded, so rarities are usually spotted and reported. Some of the less common waterfowl have included Ross's and Cackling Goose, Brant, Tufted Duck, and White-winged and Black Scoter (in addition to the abundant Surf Scoter), Long-tailed Duck, Barrow's Goldeneye and all three mergansers. In addition to the Common Loon, the Pacific, Red-throated and even Yellow-billed Loon have been reported. Red-necked Grebe and occasionally Pelagic and Brandt's Cormorant may be blown in from the Pacific.

Berkeley is directly opposite the Golden Gate so it can get the benefit of big winter storms that push usually pelagic species into the Bay. It can also be windy, even on a "warm" summer day. Some ocean birds that have blown in during autumn include Pomarine Jaeger and Parasitic Jaeger, Common Murre and Pigeon Guillemot. Over two dozen shorebirds have been recorded including Red Knot and Red Phalarope, the latter probably driven into land by a strong wind. This bird usually winters far off the Pacific Coast in open ocean. Also on record here: nine species of gull and five terns, including Common and Least (an endangered western subspecies that breeds a few miles to the south on Alameda Island). Year-round land birds include Anna's Hummingbird, Black Phoebe, Chestnut-backed Chickadee, Bushtit, California Towhee and Brewer's Blackbird.

For a relaxing mix of flora, birding and a soupçon of intellectual stimulus, you can head east on University Avenue to the **University of California's Berkeley** campus. See *Berkeley* map. Still further east, beyond the football stadium, you will find the university's botanical garden in **Strawberry Canyon**. There is a charge for parking as well as an admission fee to enter the 34-acre botanical garden. Once inside, you'll find picnic tables, trails, toilets, extensive gardens, huge greenhouses and a shop. There is a free shuttle from the main campus on weekdays. The U.C. Berkeley campus offers a rich mix of land birds like Hutton's Vireo and Chestnut-backed Chickadee. EBird shows over 80 species here, including Anna's Hummingbird, Nuttall's Woodpecker, Black Phoebe, Steller's Jay, Bushtit, Wrentit, Brown Creeper and Townsend's Warbler(winter). Two spring birds to look for: Wilson's Warbler and, around fan palms, Hooded Oriole.

I-80 Exit 11 will also be your exit for **Tilden Park** in the Berkeley Hills above the campus. Go east on University Avenue. After a mile turn left on Oxford Street, right on Rose Street, left on Spruce Street.

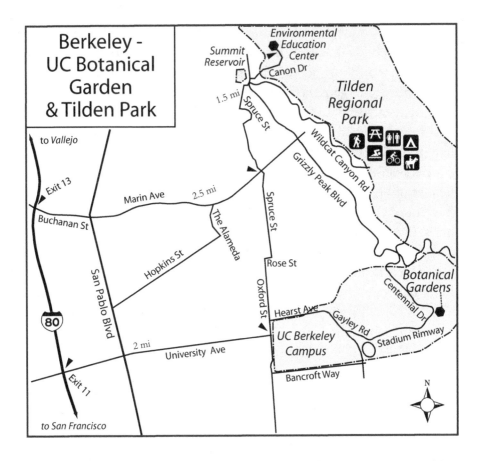

Berkeley -
UC Botanical
Garden
& Tilden Park

to *Vallejo*

Exit 13

Buchanan St

Marin Ave   2.5 mi

San Pablo Blvd

Hopkins St

The Alameda

80

2 mi   University Ave

Exit 11

to *San Francisco*

Summit
Reservoir

1.5 mi

Spruce St

*Environmental
Education
Center*

Canon Dr

*Tilden
Regional
Park*

Wildcat Canyon Rd

Grizzly Peak Blvd

Spruce St

Rose St

Oxford St

Hearst Ave

Gayley Rd

Stadium Rimway

*UC Berkeley
Campus*

Bancroft Way

*Botanical
Gardens*

Centennial Dr

N

Proceed winding around to the intersection of Spruce Street, Wildcat Canyon Road, and Grizzly Peak Boulevard. Turn right on Wildcat, then an immediate left onto Canon Drive and follow it into the park (see above map). Inside Tilden Park there's a newt crossing on South Park Drive, so that road is closed in winter (for the newts).

What you'll find: In addition to forest, creeks, a botanical garden, plenty of picnic areas, toilets, recreation grounds, a golf course and hiking trails, there is Lake Anza for swimming. There's also a small farm, steam train and an environmental education center. The park, run by a regional park district, consists of almost 2,100 acres of open space. While birding you may see the resident mule deer or aptly named banana slugs. You are unlikely to see the mountain lions that are known to hunt here.

Tilden is good for both resident and migrating species: Anna's Hummingbird, Black Phoebe, Spotted Towhee, Chestnut-backed

Chickadee, California Towhee, California Thrasher, California Quail, and Wrentit. Summer birds here include Pacific-slope Flycatcher, Swainson's Thrush, Warbling Vireo, Lazuli Bunting and Wilson's Warbler. Winter birds will include Golden-crowned Sparrow, Townsend's Warbler and Red-breasted Sapsucker. Rarities have been found as well: Broad-winged Hawk, Northern Saw-whet Owl, Black-chinned Hummingbird, Red-eyed Vireo, Phainopepla, Worm-eating Warbler, Chestnut-sided Warbler, Black-and-white Warbler, Hooded Warbler, American Redstart, Red-naped Sapsucker. Some of the best birding is in the nature area and the botanical garden.

I-80 Exit 13. Albany Mudflats. After exiting, take Buchanan Street west from I-5 to the parking area. The Albany Mudflats are one part of **Eastshore State Park.** This park consists of 1,817 acres, spanning the shorelines of Albany, Richmond, El Cerrito and Emeryville. It runs 8.5 miles along the eastern shore of San Francisco Bay west of I-80. Caesar E. Chavez Park and Point Isabel Regional Shoreline are adjacent areas of open space. The two current access points to the publicly owned shoreline are (1) from Marina Boulevard in west Berkeley and (2) from the parking area at the west end of Buchanan Street in Albany. Eventually there will be a trail along the Bay shoreline from Point Isabel south to Berkeley's Shorebird Park (see *Eastbay Waterfront* map).

Overall, eBird shows over 130 species for Eastshore State Park. More than 105 species have been seen on the Albany Mudflats alone. That includes 19 species of waterfowl, five grebes and a score of shorebirds including Red Knot, Marbled Godwit and Black-bellied Plover. Marbled Godwit and Long-billed Curlew can usually be found here year-round. Among the land birds may be Anna's Hummingbird, Black Phoebe, Bushtit, White-crowned Sparrow and California Towhee.

North Basin and Berkeley Meadow are also rewarding areas to bird. Brown Pelicans will regularly fish this area in late summer and fall. Ducks, shorebirds, gulls and terns are especially abundant along Eastshore Park.

You can also take Exit 13 for **Tilden Park** (see Page 43). Head east on Buchanan, then go eastward on Marin Avenue, uphill to its end (see *Berkeley* map).

I-80 Exit 18. Exit here onto eastbound San Pablo Dam Road for **Sobrante Ridge Regional Preserve.** This is a good place to find many of the woodland specialty species of Central California. There are over 275 acres of oak and madrone woodland. Shrubs include the endangered Pallid Manzanita which grows only here in the East Bay. What you'll find: picnic tables along the trail, and a drinking fountain. Horses are allowed; dogs on leash are OK.

Species you can find here include California Quail, Red-shouldered Hawk, Band-tailed Pigeon, Anna's Hummingbird, Nuttall's Woodpecker, Black Phoebe, Hutton's Vireo, Steller's Jay, Scrub-Jay, Oak Titmouse, Bushtit, Wrentit, Wilson's Warbler, California and Spotted Towhee. The only migrant on this list is the Wilson's Warbler.

I-80 Exit 20. Exit onto Richmond Parkway southbound for the **Point Pinole Regional Shoreline.** What you'll find: fishing, picnic areas, bike paths, toilets; dogs are allowed. Fees are charged for vehicles and dogs. There's a shuttle bus to near the top of Point Pinole, which is over 1.5 miles from the parking lot. The park has over 2,300 acres of eucalyptus woodland and grassland bordering on San Francisco Bay, west of I-5. On the south edge of the park, bordering the Bay, is Parchester Marsh. There are 12 miles of fine trails and ponds as well. There's a fishing pier that extends into the Bay. Some of this parkland was once used for dynamite manufacture. Geologic markers delineate the line of the Hayward Earthquake Fault, which runs beneath the park. See *Point Pinole Regional Seashore* map.

Here you may find wintering shorebirds and ducks. Fall migration can be a busy time as Point Pinole is on the Pacific Flyway. EBird reports over 150 species here: Pintail; Canvasback; both scaup; White-winged Scoter; Red-breasted Merganser; Eared, Horned, Western and Clark's Grebes; White and Brown Pelican; Red-shouldered Hawk; White-tailed Kite; wintering Merlin; and over a score of shorebirds. Seven species of gull have been reported including Mew and Thayer's. Forster's and Caspian Terns are regular in warm months, and in fall an Elegant Tern may turn up. Land birds here include Black Phoebe, Nuttall's Woodpecker, Hutton's Vireo, Chestnut-backed Chickadee, Wrentit, Oak Titmouse, Bushtit, Spotted and California Towhee,

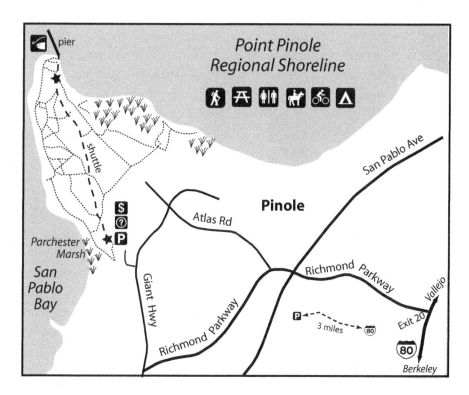

Lesser Goldfinch. Golden-crowned Sparrows are common wintering birds.

I-80 Mile 27. Carquinez Brtidge and Strait. This is the Solano County line.

I-80 Exit 30. Benicia State Recreation Area. Exit here onto I-780 eastbound and continue to the State Park Road exit. Take this road south and follow signs for **Benicia State Recreation Area (SRA)**, a marsh on the shore of Southhampton Bay. It's about 3 miles from Exit 30. What you'll find: picnic areas, restrooms, 2.5 miles of trail including bike trails, parking, RV camping, fishing, fee. The park has over 700 acres of hillsides, grassland, beaches and marsh. Dogs must be leashed, and the park closes at sunset. There are 2 miles of road and hiking trails. Benicia SRA is part of Suisun Marsh, which has been designated an Important Bird Area (IBA). Here live endangered California Clapper Rails (*Rallus longirostris obsoletus*) and Black Rails (*Laterallus jamaicensis*).

Among the other grassland and marsh birds found here are Lesser and American Goldfinch, Western Kingbird in summer, Marsh Wren, Anna's Hummingbird and Allen's Hummingbird (from February through July). Wintering birds include Greater White-fronted Goose; Cackling Goose; both scaup; Surf Scoter; both goldeneyes; Pelagic Cormorant; Least Sandpiper; Glaucous-winged Gull; and Lincoln's, White-crowned and Golden-crowned Sparrow. Western Gull are always present along the Bay. White-tailed Kite and Red-shouldered Hawk are year-round raptors. Among more than 170 species reported here on eBird are Nuttall's Woodpecker, Black Phoebe, Chestnut-backed Chickadee, Marsh Wren and California Towhee.

I-80 Exit 33. I-80/CA37 Junction. Turn west here for North Bay Area/Marin County (Chapter 2) or continue north on I-80 for more Solano County and Yolo County (Chapter 4).

Yellow-billed Magpie

The Yellow-billed Magpie (*Pica nuttalli*) is one of only two California endemics. The other is the Island Scrub-Jay, found only on Santa Cruz Island off the Ventura County Coast in Southern California. The Yellow-billed Magpie is found along I-5 in California between Vallejo and Redding. There may be less than a half million of these birds alive. West Nile Virus has been hard on this species, as well as many other Corvids (jays and crows).

The Yellow-billed Magpie likes farmland, gardens, oak savannah and a little running water in the summer. An irrigation canal full of dirty water is just fine. Big trees for nesting are required. Any magpie you spot north of Mount Shasta will be a Black-billed Magpie (*Pica hudsonia*), which is widespread in arid portions of the western two-thirds of North America.

According to Birds of North America (online), the Yellow-billed Magpie often nests in loose colonies of 3 to 30 pairs. Mated pairs tend to stay together as long as both live. They nest only once per year, usually beginning in late winter, when water and food are plentiful. The species is non-migratory, but moves around to forage.

In general, the Yellow-billed Magpie is smaller than its black-billed cousin. Usually less than 17 inches long, mature individuals' average weight is around 5 ounces, with males usually visibly bigger than females. In flight the long, tapered tail and black-white wing patterns are distinctive within its limited range. These gregarious birds are often quite voluble. They seem to like to live in towns and around farms, so can be unintended victims of poisons, especially those meant for ground squirrels.

This magpie's wide range of foods is typical of corvids: ground-dwelling invertebrates, small mammals, carrion, fruit, grain, acorns. They will cache some foods, like acorns. I once counted more than two dozen of these birds on the ground beneath a small grove of walnut trees.

This magpie's Latin species name, *nuttalli*, commemorates Thomas Nuttall (1786-1859). He was one of America's greatest naturalists in the first half of the 19th century. His scientific discoveries include a score of birds and hundreds of plants. He wrote the first field guide to birds of the United States, published in 1831-1832. In the 1830s he came west with his protégé, John Townsend. Townsend stayed mostly in the Astoria, Oregon area. From 1834 to 1836, Nuttall explored the Oregon Territory, Hawaii and California when it was still part of Mexico. He first discovered the Yellow-billed Magpie for science near the "village" of Santa Barbara.

I-80 Area Map

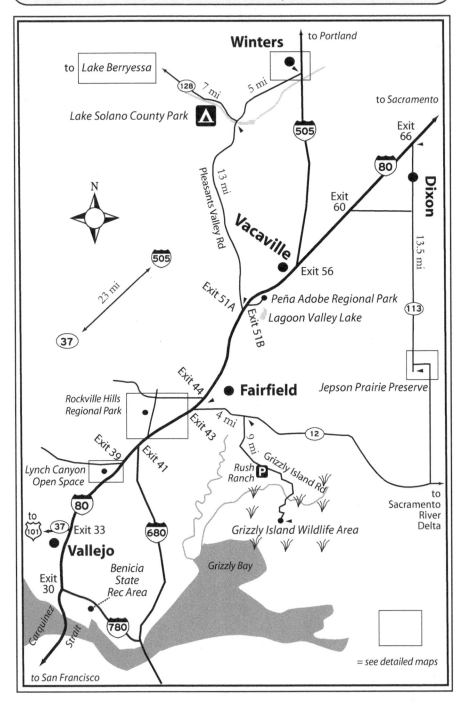

Winters

to Portland

to Lake Berryessa

128 7 mi   5 mi

505

Lake Solano County Park

to Sacramento

Exit 66

80

Dixon

Exit 60

13.5 mi

13 mi

Pleasants Valley Rd

Vacaville

505

23 mi

37

Exit 56

Exit 51A

Peña Adobe Regional Park

Exit 51B

Lagoon Valley Lake

113

Jepson Prairie Preserve

Exit 44

Fairfield

Rockville Hills
Regional Park

Exit 43

4 mi

12

Exit 39

Exit 41

9 mi

Grizzly Island Rd

Lynch Canyon
Open Space

Rush
Ranch

P

80

to
101

37

Exit 33

Grizzly Island Wildlife Area

to
Sacramento
River
Delta

Vallejo

680

Benicia
State
Rec Area

Grizzly Bay

Exit
30

Carquinez

Strait

780

= see detailed maps

to San Francisco

Chapter 4
Bay to Valley Connector

I- 80 to I-505 Cutoff
Solano and Yolo Counties

We are continuing east from I-80 Exit 33 toward Sacramento, having already crossed over Carquinez Strait and passed Vallejo and the I-80 intersection with CA 37.

I-80 Exit 39. Exit here to the east and then head south on McGary Road to Lynch Road, which goes north from McGary under I-80 to **Lynch Canyon.** What you'll find: There will be a parking area on your

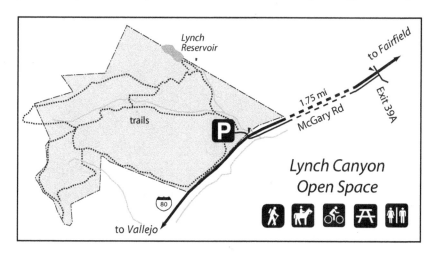

left and a parking fee is charged. There are toilets and picnic tables, as well. Lynch Canyon is controlled by the Solano Land Trust. It is over a thousand acres of rolling hills, with oak savannah, steep grassland, and a riparian strip with wetland meadow. It is home to California Quail, Golden Eagle, White-tailed Kite, Anna's Hummingbird, Acorn and Nuttall's Woodpecker, Black Phoebe, Say's Phoebe in winter, Western Bluebird and Western Meadowlark.

I-80 Exit 41. Exit here onto Suisun Valley Road northbound. Then turn west on Rockville Road and go 0.75 mile to the entrance of **Rockville Hills Regional Park.** What you'll find: picnic areas, toilets, trails, bicycling, dogs allowed on leash. You'll need to pay a day-use fee, or you can buy a six-month pass; in addition, a separate use fee is charged for each dog. The park covers over 630 acres, mostly rolling hills, with open oak woodland, chaparral and a small lake. The park features steep trails that take you to the top of rock bluffs with views eastward across the lowlands. In the oaks is a cement water tank that attracts wildlife for a much-needed drink on hot summer days. That may include Red-breasted Sapsucker, Oak Titmouse and resident rodents. Birds you are likely to find here include Nuttall's Woodpecker, Spotted and California Towhee, Black Phoebe, Oak Titmouse and Western Scrub-Jay.

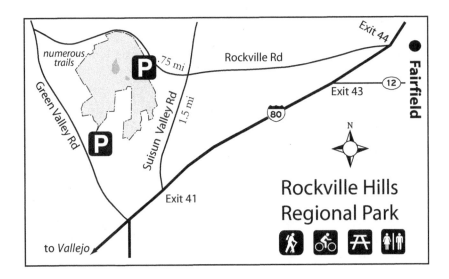

I-80 Exit 43. Exit onto CA 12. To reach **Grizzly Island Wildlife Area,** take CA 12 east for about 4 miles, then turn south onto Grizzly Island Road toward Grizzly Island Wildlife Area (GIWA), administered by California Department of Fish and Wildlife. The headquarters for Grizzly Island is 9 miles south of CA 12. There are multiple units of the wildlife area along this road. The GIWA covers 8,600 acres and is located in the heart of the 84,000-acre Suisun Marsh. The Suisun Marsh is the largest contiguous estuarine marsh in the United States. See *I-80 Area Map.*

About halfway to the end of Grizzly Island Road you will pass through Rush Ranch, administered by Solano Land Trust. It includes a swath of former ranchland, now in grass, and a trail that skirts the edge of the wetlands west of the ranch building. One trail provides hilltop views of surrounding marshlands. Open year round (no hunting allowed): picnic tables, running water, trails, indoor restrooms.

What you'll find at the Wildlife Area: access roads, parking areas, toilets, a public phone, information, disabled access for nature viewing. No camping is allowed. Fishing is allowed, and in season, hunting of waterfowl, dove, pheasant, tule elk, and rabbit is permitted. During elk hunting season the Grizzly Island trails are closed so birding is only possible from entrance road. There is a seven-mile auto route with several parking areas for viewing the marshland. Trails are level, but much of the area may flood during wet winters. There is a large herd of elk. Jackrabbits bound, and abound. River otter and wild pigs are also found here.

Birds include breeding Black Rail, American Bittern, Northern Harrier and Short-eared Owl, White-tailed Kite, Western Meadowlark and Mockingbird. Rough-legged Hawk may winter here. Over two dozen waterfowl species have been reported in fall and winter. Among them: Eurasian Wigeon, Tundra Swan, both scaup, Redhead and Barrow's Goldeneye. Five grebe species, 16 species of raptors and 20 species of shorebirds have been seen. It is a very good spot for Loggerhead Shrike. Among the eight species of Icterids reported are Tricolored Blackbird and Great-tailed Grackle in winter. The latter species is steadily expanding its range northward. EBird shows over 175 species for this area.

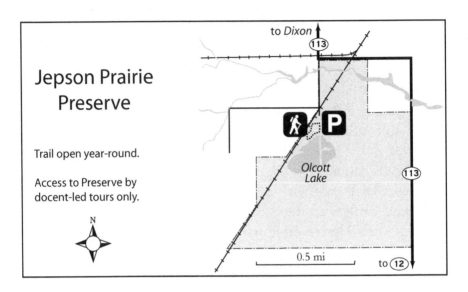

Jepson Prairie Preserve. If you continue east on CA 12 you'll be able to reach one of the few remaining tracts of native California prairie. Located 10 miles south of Dixon, **Jepson Prairie Preserve** is the premier native bunchgrass prairie in California. It is a designated IBA, and is administered by the Solano Land Trust.

To reach Jepson Prairie if you are eastbound on I-80, from Exit 43 take CA 12 East about 17 miles. Turn left onto CA 113 North and travel about 8 miles. Continue on CA 113 as it takes a 90-degree turn to the west, then in about 1 mile when it takes a 90-degree turn north. Turn left here onto Cook Lane. Now go 0.7 miles over the creek and railroad tracks until you see the eucalyptus grove and interpretive sign. Pull into one of the designated parking areas.

Alternately, if you're westbound from Sacramento on I-80 take Exit 66 to CA 113 South at Dixon. Travel about 12 miles. When CA 113 makes a 90-degree turn to the east, continue straight onto Cook Lane, do not turn.

What you'll find: designated parking areas, a pit toilet, a self-guided trail area. Access to other parts of the preserve is only through docent-led tours. Pets are not allowed and no water is available. The preserve covers over 1,500 acres, centered around Olcutt Lake. It is closed during late spring and summer. The grasslands are dotted with rare vernal pools. Hundreds of acres of private ranch land surround the preserve.

Along nearby Robinson Road there is often a wintering flock of Mountain Plover, a scarce bird along the Pacific Coast. The prairie also is home to Harrier, Western Meadowlark, diminished populations of both Burrowing Owl and Loggerhead Shrike. In winter the pools often shelter ducks and shorebirds. Olcutt Lake can be as large as 93 acres at its springtime peak, but by summer it's usually dried up. It's rarely more than 3 feet deep at any point. The lake is home to some endangered animals as well as a haven for herons, egrets, American Avocets and wintering waterfowl. EBird lists over 125 birds for Jepson Prairie and Robinson Road. Wintering birds can include Tundra Swan; over a dozen species of ducks; Glaucous Gull; Merlin; Prairie Falcon; Rough-legged and Ferruginous Hawk; several shorebirds, with Avocet and Stilt being local residents; Say's Phoebe; and Golden-crowned and White-crowned Sparrow. Black Phoebe, Loggerhead Shrike, Horned Lark and the California endemic, Yellow-billed Magpie, are all resident.

I-80 Mile 45. Fairfield and Surrounding Areas. Fairfield has a Mediterranean climate. Here are some average maximum temperatures: January, 54; April, 71; July, 88; October, 78. Nightime freezing temperatures are rare. The rainy season runs from October through April, with annual rainfall totaling about 19 inches. Some of oak savannah on the hills in the rural areas here are much like they would have looked in pre-Colonial times.

I-80 Exit 51B. Peña Adobe Regional Park and Lagoon Valley Lake. Exit here for Peña Adobe Road. Follow the signs on the 0.4 mile drive to **Peña Adobe Regional Park,** southeast of the freeway. What you'll find: plenty of parking, toilets, drinking water and picnic areas. Dogs are allowed on leash. Adjacent to the park is **Lagoon Valley Lake.** There is an entry fee for cars at Lagoon Valley Lake, but many people park at the entrance and walk in. The drive from I-80 is only 3 minutes.

EBird lists over 115 species for this location, including eight warbler species during fall migration. Among summer birds are Bullock's Oriole, five species of swallow, Mockingbird, Bewick's Wren, Marsh Wren, Blue-gray Gnatcatcher, Nuttall's Woodpecker, Oak Titmouse and Hutton's Vireo. The lake attracts over fifteen species of waterfowl.

Accessed from Exit 51A on the opposite (northwest) side of I-80, are **Pleasants Valley Road** and **Lake Solano County Park.** Pleasants Valley Road runs north all the way to CA 128, bypassing Vacaville and the I-80/I-505 intersection. This route basically parallels I-505 several miles to the west, so instead of taking busy I-80 and then I-505 northward, you could: Take Pleasants Valley Road to CA 128, thence west on CA 128 to I-505 at Exit 11 as an alternate route, and do a little birding along the way (see *I-80 Area Map*).

This route will first take you by Lake Solano County Park (8685 Pleasants Valley Road) on Putah Creek. What you'll find: picnic areas, campsites, parking, toilets, a public telephone and a boat launch for non-powered vessels. The day-use area of the park closes in later afternoon and is closed all night. Lake Solano County Park has Acorn and Nuttall's Woodpecker, Bushtit, Spotted and California Towhee, California Quail and many seasonal riparian species.

After you leave the park, continue on Pleasants Valley Road north to CA 128, then turn east to rejoin I-505 (Exit 11) east of Winters (good birding here, see Chapter 5).

Alternatively, on reaching CA 128, turn east to go to Lake Berryessa. See Chapter 5 for details.

I-80 Exit 56. Intersection of I-80 and I-505. I-505 is a shortcut between the San Francisco Bay Area and Interstate 5 northbound. If you're headed north, take I-505. If you're headed east to Sacramento or west toward San Francisco, stay on I-80.

Calliope Hummingbird

The smallest bird in North America, the Calliope is a resident of mountain slopes in California, Oregon and Washington, as well as other western regions of the United States and Canada. The best place to look for this tiny beauty along Interstate 5 is Jackson County, Oregon. In late spring it seeks mid-elevation slopes where manzanita is blooming. Later the Calliope may move upslope, following the blooming season.

The male Calliope is notable for the bright carmine and white striped gorget on his throat. The Calliope weighs just 2.3 to 3 grams, depending on season and migratory status. The Calliope's mass is just about half of a Bushtit's. The Bushtit itself is the smallest songbird found in the area covered by this book. The Calliope is a nano to the Bushtit's mini. It takes 22 Calliopes to equal a tennis ball in weight. Ten could be mailed in the United States for the cost of a first-class stamp. It would take eighty Calliope Hummingbirds to weigh as much as a cup of coffee, without the weight of the cup.

Calliope Hummingbirds can be found in the Pacific states from April through August. Then they migrate south to the southern Mexican highlands. The Calliope is the smallest long-distance migrant bird on earth.

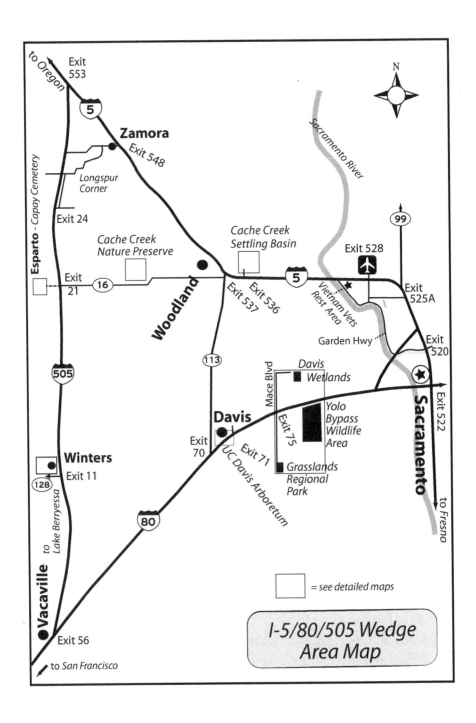

I-5/80/505 Wedge
Area Map

= see detailed maps

N

to Oregon

Exit 553

5

Zamora
Exit 548

Esparto - Capay Cemetery

Longspur
Corner

Exit 24

Cache Creek
Nature Preserve

Cache Creek
Settling Basin

Exit 528

Exit 525A

99

Woodland

Exit 21

16

Exit 537

Exit 536

5

Vietnam Vets
Rest Area

Sacramento River

Garden Hwy

Exit 520

505

113

Mace Blvd

Davis
Wetlands

Yolo
Bypass
Wildlife
Area

Exit 522

Sacramento

Davis

Exit 70

Exit 71

Exit 75

Grasslands
Regional
Park

Winters
Exit 11

128

UC Davis Arboretum

to Lake Berryessa

80

to Fresno

Vacaville

to San Francisco

Exit 56

Killdeer chick

Chapter 5

Lower Sacramento Valley "Wedge"

I-80 / I-505 / I-5
Solano, Yolo and Sacramento Counties

Look at the Area Map and you will notice that these three sections of interstate roughly form a pie wedge, with south-to-north I-505 forming the crust edge and Sacramento sitting at the tip of the pie. These freeway segments encompass parts of Solano, Yolo and Sacramento counties. We start with I-505 where it cuts north from I-80.

I-80 Exit 56. Intersection of I-80 and I-505. I-505 is a shortcut between the San Francisco Bay Area and Interstate 5 northbound. If you're headed north, take I-505. If you're headed east to Sacramento or west toward San Francisco, stay on I-80.

Interstate-505 North to Interstate 5.

I-505 Mile 1.5. This highway goes through an industrial park then out into grasslands and agricultural land. Anywhere along I-505, the length of which stretches the 32 miles between I-80 and I-5, you may encounter year-round residents such as Northern Harrier, Red-tailed Hawk, American Kestrel, as well as herons and egrets, Mourning Dove, American Crow, Common Raven, Yellow-billed Magpie (especially near farms), White-tailed Kite, Western Meadowlark and Brewer's Blackbird. In summer also look for Swainson's Hawk, Western Kingbird and Cliff Swallow. In fall, flocks of White-faced Ibis may swirl over flooded fields.

I-505 Exit 10. Putah Creek Road. I-505 crosses the county line at Exit 10 to Putah Creek Road: Yolo County lies to the north of Putah Creek, Solano County to the south. If you drive east on Putah Creek Road you are between mature walnut groves and Putah Creek. Warblers, vireos and flycatchers will stop here on spring migration. Expect Black Phoebe, Yellow Warbler and White-throated Swifts that nest here. The latter use the I-505 bridge for nesting.

Birding along Putah Creek, which flows through an area that is otherwise an arid grassland, can be productive any time of year. EBird shows over 175 species for the creek and its various bridges. Wood Duck, Great Egret, Red-shouldered and Red-tailed Hawk, Anna's Hummingbird, Belted Kingfisher, Nuttall's Woodpecker, Black Phoebe, Yellow-billed Magpie, Oak Titmouse, Bushtit, Bewick's and House Wren, Northern Mockingbird, Spotted and California Towhee and House Finch may be found along the stream in any season. Summer birds include Western Tanager, Wilson's Warbler, Black-headed Grosbeak and Bullock's Oriole.

You can easily access Winters and CA 128 to Lake Berryessa (see Exit 11 entry below) from this exit by turning north on Railroad Avenue and crossing the creek into Winters.

I-505 Exit 11. Winters and CA 128. Turn west towards the town of **Winters**, which sits on the north bank of Putah Creek, and you can arrive at the same locations mentioned above reachable from Exit 10 (see *Winters* map.) Drive west 0.4 mile to East Main Street. Turn left and follow East Main through a residential area for 0.6 mile. As you near Winters' historic business district, note the old band shell in the small city park. If you walk south through this small park past the modern community center, you will find Putah Creek and the 1906 railroad bridge, now a pedestrian bridge. It is high above the creek, affording you a chance for some canopy birding. Typical riparian species you could find here include Black Phoebe, Black-headed Grosbeak, Tree Swallow, White-breasted Nuthatch, Yellow Warbler, Wilson's Warbler, Western

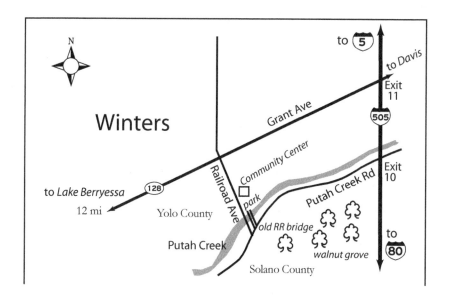

Scrub-Jay, Western Tanager, Green Heron and Belted Kingfisher.

If you cross the bridge, at the south end you will be on the edge of extensive walnut groves. Birding along the edge of the grove and the riparian forest can be especially good during spring migration.

If you continue west from I-5 Exit 11 beyond Winters, you will be on Grant Avenue/CA 128. This road roughly follows Putah Creek Valley along the north side of the creek up into the low hills along the boundary of Yolo and Napa Counties. Eventually you will reach Lake Berryessa.

Lake Berryessa. Continuing west past Winters on CA 128 from I-505 Exit 11, in about 12 miles, after passing Lake Solano, you will reach Monticello Dam and **Lake Berryessa.** It's right at the border of Napa (to the west) and Solano Counties.

Just before the lake, **Stebbins Cold Canyon Reserve,** part of the University of California Natural Reserve network, is located east of Monticello Dam off of CA128. It is bordered by **Putah Creek State Wildlife Refuge,** a designated IBA. Cold Canyon has a small entrance fee. A well-marked trail will take you up into Mountain Quail habitat. Watch for resident Golden Eagles.

What you'll find at Lake Berryessa: day use areas, houseboat rentals, boat ramps, picnic grounds and hiking trails. The lake is 16 miles

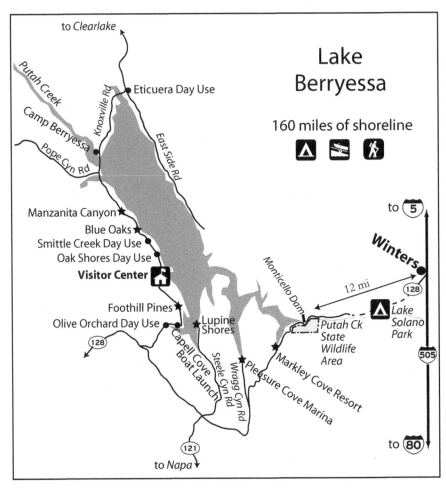

long with over 160 miles of shoreline. It's administered by the Bureau of Reclamation. The visitors center is on the west side of the lake.

EBird lists over 130 species for Lake Berryessa and the dam site, 180 if you include Lake Solano. Birds seen here include 20 species of waterfowl in winter including Tundra Swan and five species of grebe. Among the wintering ducks you can expect are Wood Duck, Barrow's Goldeneye and Hooded Merganser. Lewis's Woodpeckers and Red-breasted Sapsuckers show up in winter. There's an abundance and diversity of nesting raptors, including Osprey, Bald Eagle and Golden Eagle. Both Peregrine and Prairie Falcon breed in the rock outcrops of Blue Ridge, just east of Lake Berryessa. There are nesting White-throated Swift in summer. Birds of dry oak woodland are in the hills above the lake: Western Scrub-Jay, Western Bluebird, Oak Titmouse,

Nuttall's Woodpecker, Acorn Woodpecker, White-breasted Nuthatch and Bushtit. Look for Canyon Wren near the dam. Phainopepla are possible in riparian areas. Rufous-crowned Sparrows could be nesting on dry hillsides.

Grazing has been eliminated from the draw-down area on the eastern shore of the lake, which has allowed a lush grassland to develop, ideal for breeding Northern Harrier. Napa-Solano Audubon is currently monitoring the bird's progress. Other scarce open-country birds in the region are Burrowing Owl (winter only) and Loggerhead Shrike. Both lakes support small Great Blue Heron rookeries. Berryessa has had Purple Martins in the recent past.

I-505 Mile 16. Along the Yolo County stretch of I-505, you pass through no towns. The road parallels the range of hills to the west. While the hills on the western edge of the county average around 30 inches of rainfall a year, the valley floor through which you drive sees about half that much. The summers are hot and arid. Two hundred years ago this would have been oak savannah. Now it's largely farms, pastures, almond groves, and fields of annual crops. Irrigation is heavily used.

Driving through this area in the fall, you may see a flock of White-faced Ibis circling a flooded field. In spring and early summer Swainson's Hawks, Red-tails and Crows may follow a tractor across a field. Local breeding birds include Mourning Dove, Killdeer, Great Egret and Savannah Sparrow. You may spot a small flock of Cattle Egret in a pasture.

I-505 Mile 20. To the west of I-505 you'll see a remnant grove of the stately valley oaks that were once the dominant tree in this habitat.

I-505 Exit 21. Cache Creek Nature Preserve. Take this exit to get onto CA 16 and go east toward Woodland. Along the way you can also turn south on County Road 93 or 95 and drive around for some roadside birding. This area has Harrier, Yellow-billed Magpie, Western Meadowlark, Loggerhead Shrike, Burrowing Owl, and Tricolored Blackbird, especially around livestock. Look for Swainson's Hawk in summer, Ferruginous and Rough-legged Hawks, Merlin, and Prairie Falcon in winter. Mountain Plover is also possible in winter.

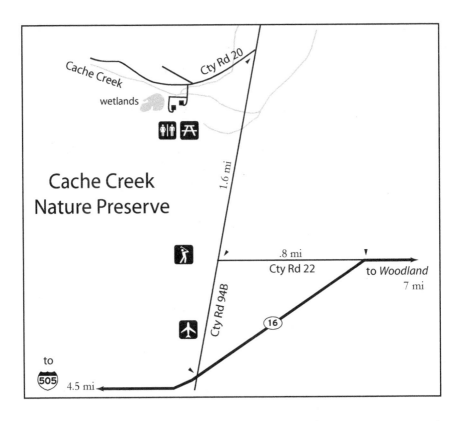

4.5 miles east of I-505, and before Woodland, you can turn north on County Road 94B to reach the Jan T. Lowrey **Cache Creek Nature Preserve (CCNP)**. What you'll find: toilets, trail, picnic areas, and a boardwalk. No fee is charged. Dogs are not allowed, nor boating. This 130-acre preserve is owned by Yolo County and maintained by the non-profit Cache Creek Conservancy. CCNP is open from 7 a.m. to 4 p.m., Monday through Friday. It is also open from 9 a.m. to 2 p.m. on the third Saturday of each month. Habitat here is wetlands, riparian forest and grasslands.

Here are raptors aplenty: Swainson's Hawk in spring and summer. Year round are Red-shouldered Hawk, Black-tailed Kite, Northern Harrier and Kestrel. Nuttall's Woodpecker is also a year-round resident. Other birds reported in this location include Lesser Nighthawk, Ash-throated Flycatcher, Say's Phoebe in winter, Black Phoebe all year, Loggerhead Shrike in summer, Yellow-billed Magpie, California Thrasher all year, Bushtit, Wrentit, Tricolored Blackbird, an occasional Great-tailed Grackle as this species expands its range northward, Lesser Goldfinch and California Towhee.

Among the mammals you might spot are Muskrat, Northern River Otter, American Beaver, Columbian Black-tailed Deer, Northern raccoon, jack rabbit, Bobcat, Coyote and Opossum. Evidence of these mammals can often be detected. Be on the lookout for tracks, scat, gnawed trees or even a musky scent.

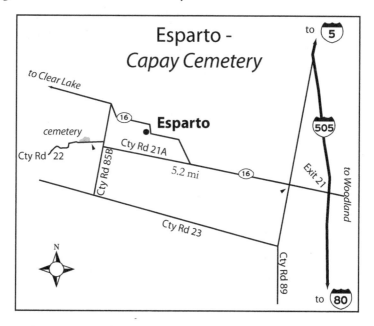

Capay Cemetery. If you go west on CA 16 from I-505 Exit 21, you will parallel Cache Creek and reach the town of Esparto. This area has Swainson's Hawk and Western Kingbird in summer, Bald Eagle and Yellow-billed Magpie year-round. To reach the **Capay Cemetery**, continue west past Esparto on CA 16, turn south on County Road 85B, then west to the cemetery on County Road 22. A plaque in the cemetery reads,

> *These grounds hold the graves of pioneer settlers in the Capay Valley and Lamb Valley and those of Esparto's early families. Established in 1876 by the trustees of Capay Lodge No. 230 Independent Order of Odd Fellows, it was the first public cemetery serving Capay Valley.*

The cemetery is still used. EBird data for the cemetery shows almost 100 species, including Swainson's Hawk (spring), Red-breasted Sapsucker (cold months), Phainopepla (fall), Black Phoebe, Yellow-billed Magpie, Oak Titmouse, Bushtit, and California and Spotted Towhee. There is even a report of a California Thrasher one autumn. Wintering sparrows can be abundant here.

I-505 Mile 22. Bridge over Cache Creek, which flows down from the hills to the west into the lowlands around the Yolo Bypass (a flood-control causeway). Most years Cache Creek never actually reaches the Sacramento River because so much of its water is diverted.

I-505 Exit 24. Longspur Corner. Take this exit onto County Road 19 on the east side of I-505. Take an immediate left to go north for about 2 miles on Road 90A paralleling the freeway to Road 16, then turn eastward. Proceed east about a half mile to a spot known locally as Longspur Corner, located at the intersection of County Road 16 and County Road 90B in the Dunnigan Hills. This is an excellent area in winter for raptors. Additionally, three species of longspur have been sighted here in recent winters. Burrowing Owls are resident. Be sure to check nearby plowed fields in winter for Mountain Plovers.

I-505 Exit 28. Exit here onto County Road E10, going east toward Zamora, where you can then get onto Interstate 5 at Exit 548 if you'd like. Wintering birds include Golden Eagle and Mountain Bluebird.

If there are cattle grazing in this vicinity, watch for possible flocks of Cattle Egret feeding alongside them. Without any apparent, direct human help, this species has spread from Africa to the New World and across the North American continent in a few decades. A view of white egrets, black Angus cattle and fresh green grass in spring can be memorable. Other likely birds here include Brewer's Blackbird, introduced Ring-necked Pheasant, summering Barn and Cliff Swallow, and Western Kingbird.

I-505 connects with Interstate 5 at I-5 Exit 552. Southbound I-5 goes to Sacramento, northbound heads to northern California, Oregon and Washington.

I-80 East from the I-505 Intersection to Sacramento.

I-80 Exit 71. University of California at Davis Arboretum. Take Exit 71 onto Old Davis Road and follow the map to the **U.C. Davis Arboretum.** What you'll find: 100 acres of gardens and many exotic plantings, toilets, drinking fountains, picnic areas, pathways, exhibits. Dogs are allowed on leash. Entrance is free but there is a fee for parking. The Arboretum is open every day. The office is open Monday through Friday, 8 a.m. to 5 p.m.

Over 110 bird species have been reported from the U.C. Davis campus and arboretum. This campus is one of the best places along I-80 to look for Yellow-billed Magpie. Nuttall's Woodpeckers are common in the woods, as are Bushtit and Anna's Hummingbird. Other common birds here are Northern Mockingbird, which is extending its Pacific Coast range northward, and Black Phoebe. Golden-

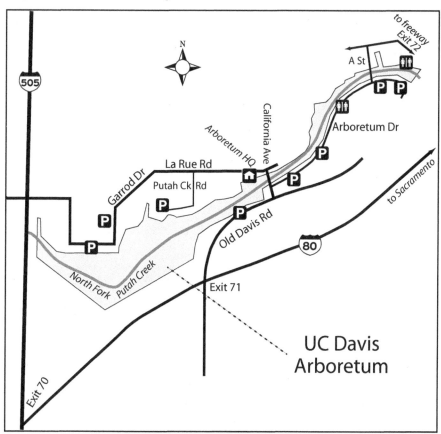

crowned Sparrows are abundant in fall and winter. Green Herons fish and nest along Putah Creek. Rarities seen here include Scissor-tailed Flycatcher, Dusky and Hammond's Flycatchers (both montane species) and Black-chinned Hummingbird.

Note: *You can reach Davis by regular Caltrain service from Emeryville or Sacramento.*

I-80 Exit 75. Davis Wetlands and **Grasslands Regional Park.** Take the Mace Boulevard exit and head north to get to the **Davis Wetlands,** about a 4-mile drive from I-80 (see *Davis Parks* map). This 400-acre municipal project provides great habitat for marsh and grassland birds. September 1 through February 15 the wetlands are open only on Mondays. The rest of the year they are open daily. Hours are 7 a.m. to 1 p.m., birders' hours.

EBird shows over 190 species reported for these wetlands. Some of the species recorded here are American Avocet; American Bittern; American White Pelican; Barn Owl; Belted Kingfisher; Black Phoebe; Black-necked Stilt; Cackling Goose; California Gull; Canvasback; Caspian Tern; Cattle Egret; Short-billed and Long-billed Dowitcher; Dunlin; Eared Grebe; Gadwall; Great Horned Owl; Greater Yellowlegs; Least Sandpiper; Loggerhead shrike; Long-billed Curlew; Common Gallinule; Northern Harrier; Northern Pintail; Northern Shoveler; Peregrine; Pied-billed Grebe; Redhead; Red-necked Phalarope in August and September; Red-shouldered Hawk; Ross's Goose; Ruddy Duck; Sharp-shinned Hawk; Snowy Egret; Swainson's Hawk; Green-winged, Cinnamon and Blue-winged Teal; Tree Swallow all year; Tricolored Blackbird; Western Grebe; Western Sandpiper; White-faced Ibis; and White-tailed Kite.

If you go south on Mace Boulevard from Exit 75 you can reach **Grasslands Regional Park.** It's at 30475 County Road 104 (Mace Boulevard), about 4 miles south of I-80. What you'll find: There is a day-use fee and off-leash dog area . The park accommodates a variety of recreational activities, including picnicing, model airplane soaring, archery, and horseshoes. The park has over 300 acres of grassland with vernal pools and oak forest. There is a specific area set aside

for Burrowing Owl nesting. By late summer this area is parched, dry grassland typical of unirrigated inland California.

Over 150 species have been reported to EBird from this park. Winter waterfowl have included Greater White-fronted and Cackling Goose, Blue-winged Teal and Lesser Scaup. American Bittern and White-faced Ibis may be seen here, along with more common herons and egrets. Fifteen species of raptor have been seen here, including Swainson's and Ferruginous Hawk, Prairie Falcon, Merlin and Peregrine. White-tailed Kite and Northern Harrier are here year-round. Long-eared Owl sometimes winter here. A dozen species of flycatcher have been reported including Gray, Least, Dusky and Olive-sided. Resident birds include Nuttall's Woodpecker, Black Phoebe, Yellow-billed Magpie, and Spotted and California Towhee. Eleven species of warbler have been found here, including Tennessee, Black-throated Gray, Townsend's, MacGillivray's and Hermit. Yellow, Wilson's and Orange-crowned are likely breeding warblers in this habitat. Other possible spring birds: Lazuli Bunting, Blue Grosbeak and the elusive Lawrence's Goldfinch.

I-80 Exit 78. The **Vic Fazio Wildlife Area,** a Globally Important Bird Area, is about 6 miles east of Davis. It is a refuge inside the much larger Yolo Bypass lowlands, which reverts to flood plain when the winters are wet or the Sacramento River overflows its banks.

From either direction on I-80 take Exit 78 for East Chiles Road, also designated as Road 32B. Once off the freeway, drive east toward the levee. The Fazio Wildlife Area includes land between the levee and the Sacramento River and Ship Channel to the east. The Fazio Wildlife Area—named for the local congressman who sponsored its creation—opened with 3,700 acres of lowlands. It was dedicated in 1997 after construction and restoration work by the Corps of Engineers. Since then it's been expanded to over 16,000 acres.

What you'll find: The Vic Fazio Wildlife Area is open dawn to sunset daily. Facilities are limited; portable toilets may be found. There are numerous hiking trails and a driving route when not flooded. The California Department of Fish and Wildlife administers the area in partnership with the Yolo Basin Foundation. The area contains both permanent and seasonal wetlands, riparian forest and open grasslands. Farming on the land aids in producing food and habitat for wildlife.

To find the eBird data for this area, search under hotspots for

"Yolo Bypass" and "Yolo Basin" records, not under "Fazio." Over 210 species are recorded on eBird for this site. Five species of geese include Greater White-fronted and Ross's. Tundra Swans, Wood Duck, Eurasian Wigeon, Blue-winged Teal, Cinnamon Teal, and a vagrant Long-tailed Duck have been reported, along with the regular wintering ducks of the California Central Valley. Both yellowlegs and Wilson's Snipe are present fall through spring.

Year-round birds include American Bittern, Black-crowned Night-Heron, Green Heron, White-faced Ibis, Virginia Rail, Sora, Common Moorhen (now Common Gallinule), Black Phoebe, Horned Lark, Pacific Marsh Wren, Yellow-headed Blackbird and Great-tailed Grackle (a recent colonizer of Central California). This is one of the northern-most areas where Tree Swallows are year-round as well. You might also see Muskrat.

Spring birds include American Avocets, hawks, Bullock's Orioles and Red-winged Blackbirds.

In summer, you can expect Yellow-headed Blackbird, Great Blue Heron, Great and Snowy Egret, finches, White-tailed Kite, Blue Grosbeak and Bullock's Oriole.

Autumn brings Snow Goose, shorebirds and Belted Kingfisher to the area.

Winter birds will include White Pelican, Tundra Swan, ducks, Bald Eagle, California Red-shouldered Hawk, Merlin and American Pipit.

I-80 Exit 82. Here you can exit onto US 50 eastbound for a straight shot into Sacramento. The climate here is warm and semi-arid. Along California's entire Central Valley, both north and south of Sacramento, most agriculture is dependent on irrigation. Sacramento has hot summers, with average highs over 90 in July and August. Temperatures over 100 have been recorded from May through October. Yet overnight lows tend to be below 60. December and January are the coldest months, with nightly lows around 38 and highs above 50. Snow is almost unheard of at this low elevation (25 feet above sea level), and total precipitation per year is less than 18 inches, most of it coming between November and March. Heavy ground fog, known locally as "tule fog"(pronounced too-lee), is common in cold months, and it can make driving hazardous.

I-80 Exit 86 and **I-5 Exit 522.** This is where I-80 and I-5 intersect in northwest Sacramento. This is now Sacramento County.

I-5 Sacramento Area and North to I-5 / I-505 Junction.

Sacramento City Birding Spots
Note: *These listings begin south of the I-80/I-5 intersection (I-5 Exit 522) and go north.*

I-5 Exit 514. Reichmuth Park. Easy to reach from I-5, this park is south of US 50 in central Sacramento. Take Exit 514, go east a short distance to Gloria Drive and turn south. It is located at 6135 Gloria Drive. What you'll find: picnic areas, toilets, playing fields, and a nature area that is twenty acres of undeveloped open space next to heavily used playing fields. There are over 105 species recorded on eBird for this small park. Among birds you can expect are Wood Duck, Snowy Egret, Green Heron (year-round), Red-shouldered Hawk, Swainson's Hawk (spring and summer), Anna's Hummingbird, Nuttall's Woodpecker, Black Phoebe, Bushtit, House Wren and Spotted Towhee.

South of Sacramento, Worth Noting

I-5 Exit 485. *At Exit 485 off I-5, you can take CA 12 east to Lodi. This town hosts a Sandhill Crane Festival every November. A little further south along I-5 is the city of Stockton, which hosts the annual Central Valley Bird Symposium, also in November. In Stockton, the I-5 bridges over the San Joaquin River have large nesting colonies of White-throated Swifts.*

I-5 Exit 519. Sutter's Landing Park. This city park lies along the south bank of the American River, upstream (east) from its confluence with the Sacramento River. It's about 3 miles from the downtown exit, Exit 519 on I-5. The park entrance is at the north end of 28th Street, east of downtown Sacramento. Take any of the "letter" streets east until you get to 28th Street then turn north. What you'll find: benches, off-leash dog area, water. There's access to the riverside at many places. The strand is sandy and easy walking if the water is below the bankside trees and brush. In winter the river hosts Common Goldeneye in large numbers. Expect Great and Snowy Egrets, listen for the screams of Red-shouldered Hawk, keep an eye out for a hunting Peregrine and a fishing Belted Kingfisher. This is a good place to find Yellow-billed Magpie. Sometimes they are seen flying across the river trailing those splendid tail feathers. The park includes grasslands on reclaimed landfill and recently "constructed" hills. This open area attracts Black and Say's (winter) Phoebe, White-tailed Kite and Kestrel. The riparian thickets may hide House Wren, Golden-crowned and Lincoln's Sparrow in winter, and Anna's Hummingbird. Look for Bullock's Oriole and Black-headed Grosbeak in spring and early summer. Tree Swallows are here year-round.

I-5 Exit 520. Discovery Park. One of Sacramento's city parks, Discovery Park is located beside I-5 near downtown. From I-5, take the Richards Boulevard off-ramp (Exit 520), then go west to get to the south entrance of the park. Or, from Exit 521A follow the Garden Highway east from I-5 to find the north entrance. You'll see signs pointing out the way. This park covers 275 acres at the confluence of the American and Sacramento rivers. What you'll find: picnic areas, toilets, trails, a boat ramp, fishing and swimming.

Over 115 species have been reported to eBird from this park. Discovery Park is part of the American River Parkway and is the western trailhead for the Jedediah Smith Trail that runs 32 miles east to Folsom. Year-round there are Red-shouldered Hawk, Anna's Hummingbird, Nuttall's Woodpecker, Black Phoebe, Yellow-billed Magpie, Oak Titmouse, Bushtit and Spotted Towhee. Summer birds include White-throated Swift and Western Kingbird. Some uncommon winter visitors have included Ross's Goose and Tundra Swan.

I-5 Exit 522. Intersection of Interstates 80 and 5. From this point, if you take I-80 further east, you go around the northern part of Sacramento and then eastward into the Sierra Nevada. And if you keep on going you will eventually get to Lake Tahoe and then northern Nevada. If you take I-5 south, you go along the western edge of Sacramento, then into the Sacramento Delta and thence down the San Joaquin Valley.

Note: *If you traveled south down to I-5 Exit 514 you will need to backtrack north to the I-80/I-5 intersection. Now we can resume our northward journey on I-5, along the third side of the I-505/I-80/I-5 pie wedge.*

I-5 Exit 528. Airport Environs and **Fisherman's Lake.** Exit here for Airport Boulevard and the Sacramento Metropolitan Airport. Turn north from I-5. Birding the open areas outside the airport can yield some interesting birds, including Northern Harrier, Swainson's Hawk (spring and summer), Ferruginous Hawk in winter, Loggerhead Shrike, Horned Lark in fall, Burrowing Owl, and Long-billed Curlew (winter). A vagrant Great-tailed Grackle has been reported from here.

South of I-5 from this exit, you can take the airport access road east to **Power Line Road**, then turn south. On reaching Del Paso Road, turn east to reach **Fisherman's Lake** in about 2 miles. This can be a rich area for raptors, grassland birds and marsh birds. Among species you can find here are Common Gallinule (formerly Moorhen), Swainson's Hawk in warm months, White-tailed Kite, Northern Harrier, Red-shouldered Hawk, Prairie Falcon and Say's Phoebe in winter. Year-round birds include Black Phoebe, Nuttall's Woodpecker, Yellow-billed Woodpecker and Oak Titmouse. Numerous western sparrow species may be found here as well. EBird lists six dozen species for this location.

For birding along the Sacramento River levee, continue down Powerline Road to Garden Highway, which parallels the river and the levee. You will eventually reconnect with I-5 whether you turn east or west on Garden Highway, or return the way you came.

I-5 Exit 529. Vietnam Veterans Rest Area. Only southbound lanes afford access to this rest area. This stop gives you a chance to watch for the typical birds of the Sacramento River Valley. Raptors, waterfowl, Western Meadowlarks and grassland sparrows may be found here.

I-5 Mile 530. This bridge over the Sacramento River crosses the county line. From here, Yolo County is west of the river, Sacramento County to the east.

I-5 Mile 531. Now on the Yolo County (west) side of the river, you travel over the Yolo Causeway. Much of this lowland will fill with water in wet winters. I have seen thousands of geese on this stretch of freeway in winter: Snow, Ross's and Greater White-fronted. There can also many hundreds of dabbling ducks, especially Northern Pintail.

I-5 Exit 536. Cache Creek Settling Basin. Exit here onto County Highway E8 then, a little more than a mile north of the exit, turn east (right) onto Kentucky Avenue (County Road 20). At the east end of this road is the **Cache Creek Settling Basin.** County Road 103 runs along the west side of the basin. This settling basin is used to collect gravel and sand that comes downstream in Cache Creek. Its purpose is to prevent that sediment from reaching the Sacramento River and increasing the need for dredging.

Access each year depends on water levels. When it is accessible, the basin can provide rich birding in spring: Cinnamon Teal, Wood Duck, Northern Harrier, American Bittern, Black-crowned Night-heron, Green Heron, Snowy Egret, White-faced Ibis, Swainson's and Red-shouldered Hawk, Nuttall's Woodpecker, Ash-throated Flycatcher, Western Kingbird, Northern Mockingbird, Spotted and California Towhee have been reported here. This may be the best place listed in this book for nesting Blue Grosbeak, which is not abundant anywhere in California. Black-headed Grosbeak and Bullock's Oriole nest here.

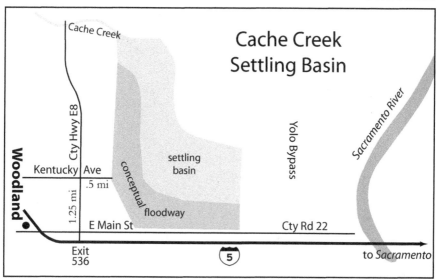

I-5 Exit 537. Exit here to take CA 113 southbound to the city of Davis. See Davis area listings earlier in this chapter.

I-5 Exit 538. Exit here for CA 113 eastward to the Sacramento River at Knight's Landing.

I-5 Exit 541. Exit onto CA 16 for Woodland.

I-5 Exit 548. Exit here for Zamora on County Road E10 and head west out of town (as described above under I-505 Exit 28). In winter the rural roads in this area may have Golden Eagle and Mountain Bluebird (see *I-5/I-80/I-505 Wedge Area Map* at beginning of chapter).

I-5 Mile 551. To the east on clear days you will catch your first look at Sutter Buttes, a circular complex of eroded volcanic lava domes that rises abruptly off the flat valley floor.

I-5 Exit 552. Here is where I-505 merges with I-5, south of the town of Dunnigan. We are done with the pie wedge and heading north in the Sacramento Valley.

Volcanos
The Cascade Range

Mt. Shasta is an active volcano. Its last eruption was in the late 1700s. It's 14,161 feet high, the tallest mountain along I-5 inside California. There are five glaciers on its slopes. From a 1980 U.S. Geological Survey publicaton:

> *Mount Shasta has erupted, on the average, at least once per 800 years during the last 10,000 years, and about once per 600 years during the last 4,500 years. The last known eruption occurred about 200 radiocarbon years ago. Eruptions during the last 10,000 years produced lava flows and domes on and around the flanks of Mount Shasta, and pyroclastic flows from summit and flank vents extended as far as 20 kilometers from the summit. Most Shasta eruptions produced large mudflows, many of which reached more than several tens of miles from Mount Shasta. Future eruptions like those of the past could endanger the communities of Weed, Mount Shasta, McCloud, and Dunsmuir, located at or near the base of Mount Shasta. Such eruptions will most likely produce deposits of lithic ash, lava flows, domes, and pyroclastic flows.*

All of the volcanos in the Cascade Mountains are capable of explosive eruptions. The Cascades volcano chain begins at the southern end with Mount Lassen, southeast of Mount Shasta and east of Redding. Two other California Cascade volcanos are Black Butte, which abuts I-5 south of Weed, and the Medicine Lake Highlands. As you head northward into Oregon the first Cascade volcano is Mount McLoughlin, 9,495 feet high. It's east of Medford and visible from I-5 around Central Point. If you are southbound, there's a highway sign pointing to Mount McLoughlin as you near Mile 35.

The most notorious of the Cascade volcanoes is Mount Saint Helens in southern Washington State. A spectacular eruption in 1980 killed 57 people and spewed ash that reached eleven states. Much of the central eruption zone is now part of a national park.

Perhaps the most explosive eruption we can clearly envision in the Cascades happened when Mount Mazama blew up 7,700 years ago. The remains of that ancient volcano are now Crater Lake. It is one of America's most scenic and geologically uneasy national parks.

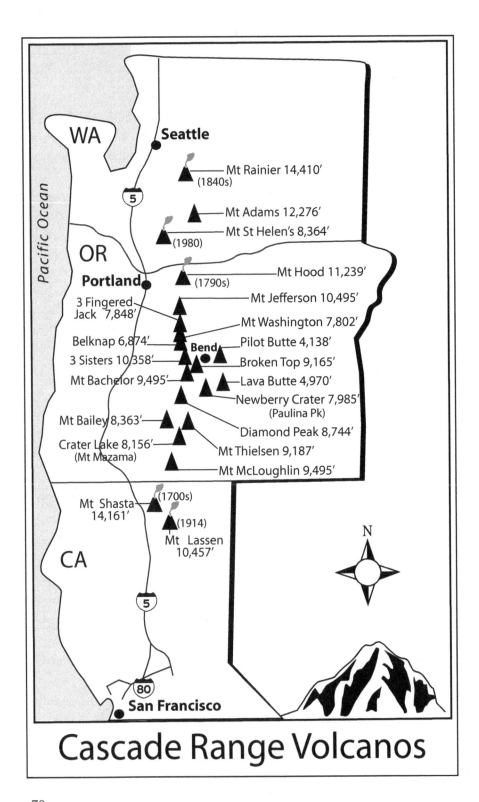

Cascade Range Volcanos

Mt Rainier 14,410' (1840s)
Mt Adams 12,276'
Mt St Helen's 8,364' (1980)
Mt Hood 11,239' (1790s)
Mt Jefferson 10,495'
3 Fingered Jack 7,848'
Mt Washington 7,802'
Belknap 6,874'
Pilot Butte 4,138'
3 Sisters 10,358'
Broken Top 9,165'
Mt Bachelor 9,495'
Lava Butte 4,970'
Newberry Crater 7,985' (Paulina Pk)
Mt Bailey 8,363'
Diamond Peak 8,744'
Crater Lake 8,156' (Mt Mazama)
Mt Thielsen 9,187'
Mt McLoughlin 9,495'
Mt Shasta 14,161' (1700s)
Mt Lassen 10,457' (1914)

WA
OR
CA
Pacific Ocean
Seattle
Portland
Bend
San Francisco
N

Volcanos from Northern California to Seattle

CALIFORNIA: <u>Most Recent Eruptions</u>
    Mount Lassen: 1917
    Medicine Lake: 1065
    Mount Shasta: ~ 200 years ago
    Black Butte: ~ 9,500 years ago

OREGON: <u>Most Recent Eruptions</u>
    Mount McLoughlin: ~ 20,000 years ago
    Mount Bailey: unknown
    Crater Lake: 7,700 years ago
    Mount Thielsen: ~ 300,000 years ago
    Diamond Peak: unknown
    Newberry Crater: ~ 1,300 years ago
    Lava Butte: created about 7,000 years ago from
        eruptions on the flanks of Newberry Volcano
    Mount Bachelor Volcanic Chain: probably 8,000 –
        10,000 years ago
    Pilot Butte: unknown
    Broken Top: probably 100,000 years ago
    Three Sisters: ~ 2,000 years ago
    Belknap: ~ 1,500 years ago
    Mount Washington: unknown, but the volcano is
        likely a few hundreds of thousands of years old
    Three-fingered Jack: unknown, but the volcano is
        likely between 500,000 and 250,000 years old
    Mount Jefferson: 40,000-50,000 years ago
    Mount Hood: 1790s

WASHINGTON STATE: <u>Most Recent Eruptions</u>
    Mount Adams: ~1020 (a thousand years ago)
    Mount St. Helens: 1980
    Mount Rainer: 1854

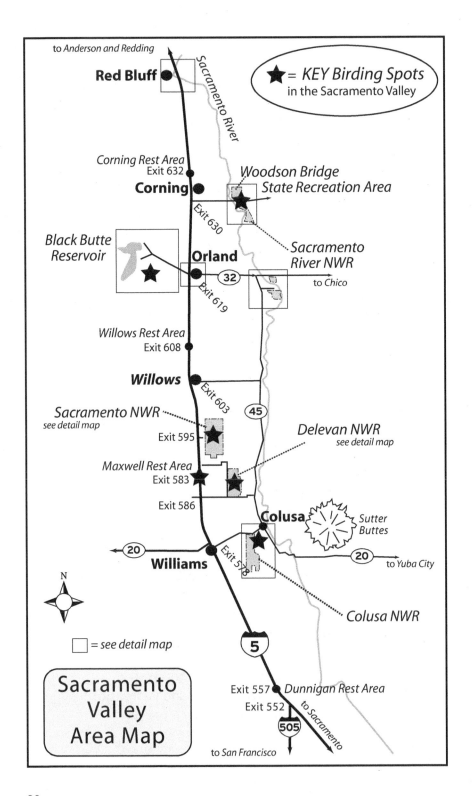

to *Anderson and Redding*

Red Bluff

Sacramento River

★ = *KEY Birding Spots*
in the Sacramento Valley

Corning Rest Area
Exit 632

Corning

Exit 630

Woodson Bridge
State Recreation Area

Black Butte
Reservoir

Orland
Exit 619

32

Sacramento
River NWR

to *Chico*

Willows Rest Area
Exit 608

Willows
Exit 603

45

Sacramento NWR
see detail map

Exit 595

Delevan NWR
see detail map

Maxwell Rest Area
Exit 583

Exit 586

Colusa

Sutter
Buttes

20

Williams
Exit 578

20

to *Yuba City*

N

Colusa NWR

☐ = *see detail map*

5

Sacramento
Valley
Area Map

Exit 557
Exit 552

Dunnigan Rest Area

to *Sacramento*

505

to *San Francisco*

Sandhill Crane

Chapter 6

The Sacramento Valley

Interstate 5
Yolo, Colusa, Glenn, Butte, Tehama, and Shasta Counties

Our route takes us up through the heart of the Sacramento Valley, from the junction of Interstate 5 and I-505 up to Anderson at the north end of the valley.

I-5 Mile 552. Here, just south of the town of Dunnigan, I-505 merges with Interstate 5. If you go south on I-5, you head toward Sacramento (see sections on Sacramento birding in Chapter 5). Heading northward, you are going toward Oregon and Washington State. For the next 190 miles, northbound I-5 roughly follows the Sacramento River, sometimes crossing the river itself. At the far north end of the Sacramento Valley (just past Redding), after you climb into the mountains around Mount Shasta, you will pass by the spring that gives birth to the Sacramento River. That spring is in a city park in the town of Mount Shasta (see Chapter 7).

I-5 Mile 557. Dunnigan Rest Stops. The Dunnigan Rest Stops offer an artificial environment of Australian eucalyptus trees, weeds from across the globe and huge trucks with their motors running. In spring, Cedar Waxwing flocks may stop by to hit the eucalyptus blossoms. In summer Western Kingbird, Mockingbird and Cliff Swallow may be around. Along the next 50 miles, be alert for possible soaring Swainson's Hawk overhead. They are much less common than the year-round Red-tailed Hawks. Starling, House Sparrow, Robin, American Kestrel and Yellow-billed Magpie are also possible.

I-5 Mile 558. In the northern end of Yolo County you will see almond orchards. In late summer expect large truckloads of tomatoes on their way to the processing plants.

I-5 Exit 559. County Line Road. If you leave I-5 at this road, you'll drive along the county line between Yolo on the south and Colusa on the north. Much of this land is used for growing rice. It is heavily farmed and irrigated. The flooded rice paddies afford some attractive habitat for wintering waterfowl, large wading birds and raptors. Brewer's and Red-winged Blackbirds, Starlings and Western Meadowlarks are abundant.

I-5 Mile 562. Watch for Swainson's Hawk in warm months, Yellow-billed Magpie year-round. The magpie will stand out because of its black-and-white plumage and very long tail. There are no Black-billed Magpies in the Sacramento Valley.

I-5 Exit 569. Hahn Road. From this exit you can bird just off the free-way next to a large farm storage elevator. You'll be walking along the edge of pistachio groves. The pistachio tree has rounded, dark glossy green leaves. Here I've found Lesser Goldfinch, Western Kingbird, House Finch and Brewer's Blackbird. If you choose to drive along the access roads here, you will pass through the Colusa Basin, where egrets and Great Blue Heron abound, and White-faced Ibis are common in summer. Double-crested Cormorant and White Pelican may use irrigation impoundments. Dabbling ducks will over-winter in flooded areas.

I-5 Exit 578. Colusa National Wildlife Refuge and **Colusa-Sacramento River State Recreation Area.** Take CA 20 from this exit and drive 6.3 miles eastward to the **Colusa National Wildlife Refuge** (NWR), a southern unit of the large Sacramento National Wildlife Refuge Complex. The headquarters is about a mile further east and then a short drive

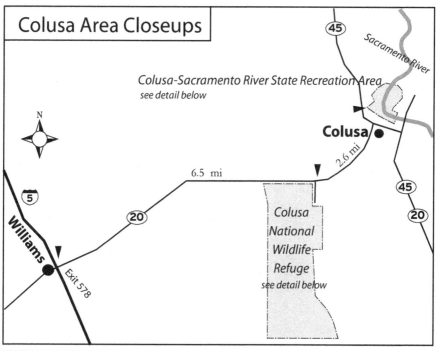

Colusa Area Closeups

Colusa-Sacramento River State Recreation Area
see detail below

Colusa

6.5 mi

2.6 mi

Williams

Exit 578

Colusa National Wildlife Refuge
see detail below

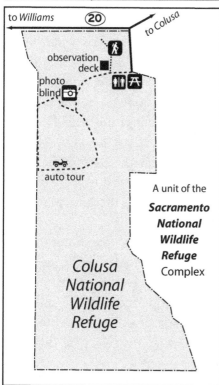

to *Williams* — 20 — to Colusa

observation deck

photo blind

auto tour

A unit of the
Sacramento National Wildlife Refuge Complex

Colusa National Wildlife Refuge

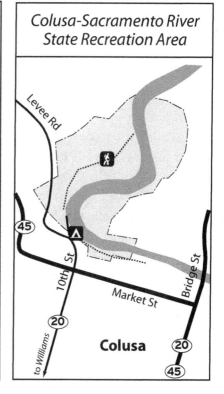

Colusa-Sacramento River State Recreation Area

Levee Rd

45

10th St

Bridge St

Market St

to Williams

20

Colusa

20

45

south of CA 20 on a dirt road. Look for a sign on CA 20 pointing the way. What you'll find: parking, toilets, a viewing platform, information kiosks, a half-mile hiking trail alongside a small slough and a driving loop. There is a photography blind, requiring reservation. Camping is not allowed anywhere on the Sacramento NWR lands.

This refuge was created in 1937 and is used by many waterfowl and shorebird species. From the viewing platform I saw my first-ever Falcated Duck, a brightly plumaged male with his bustle of long wing feathers trailing in the water. This rare Asian vagrant is one of the occasional surprises that find this winter oasis amid the farm fields and rice paddies of the area.

Wintering birds are often here in numbers. One late fall survey found Colusa had over 8,000 Coot, 1,500 White-fronted Geese, 3,700 white geese (Ross's and Snow), over 10,000 Pintails, 5,600 Gadwall, 9,300 American Wigeon (and some Eurasian Wigeon hidden in the flocks), thousands of Shoveler and Green-winged Teal and a couple dozen Cinnamon Teal. Common Gallinule are here year-round, as are Marsh Wren.

Further east on CA 20 is the town of Colusa on the Sacramento River, 9 miles from I-5. Colusa apparently marks the southern boundary of the known Sacramento Valley breeding range for the highly scarce and endangered California sub-species of Yellow-billed Cuckoo. Fewer than 100 pairs are believed to breed anywhere in the state, and the stretch of the Sacramento River from Colusa north to Red Bluff is probably the richest territory for this bird. If you take CA 45 north from Colusa, it will keep you next to or near the Sacramento River and afford some birding access to the riparian corridor favored by the Yellow-billed Cuckoo. At several points northward there are westbound roads that can take you back to I-5.

Just north of the town of Colusa is the **Colusa-Sacramento River State Recreation Area**. What you'll find: Picnic tables, barbeque stoves, parking areas, toilets, campsites, swimming, boating, and mooring facilities. There's a mile-long nature trail plus access to a 3-mile long hiking trail atop the levee on the west side of the Sacramento River, which includes access to a Colusa city park on the river near the center of this historic river town.

EBird shows over 110 species for this state recreation area, but not one report of a cuckoo. However, the area does have Blue and Black-headed Grosbeak in spring, White-faced Ibis, Ash-throated Flycatcher and Black-chinned Hummingbird in summer, plus a variety of migrants that pass along the river in spring and fall. And maybe you could be the first to report a cuckoo from here.

I-5 Mile 583. Northbound Maxwell Rest Area. If you're traveling north, don't miss the **Maxwell Rest Area**. Not only does it border rice fields, there are four irrigation ponds on the north end of the parking lot, just over the fence. During fall migration this can be a great 10-minute stop. One September day I counted scores of Western Sandpiper; dozens of Black-necked Stilt; a Northern Harrier over the fields; Barn, Cliff and Northern Rough-winged Swallows; Killdeer; Great Egret; Belted Kingfisher; White-faced Ibis; and swirling Red-necked Phalarope. In spring both American Avocet and Black-necked Stilt use these ponds, and an occasional Cinnamon Teal may stop by for a swim. Red-winged Blackbirds abound on the margins of the rice paddies. In summer there are Western Kingbirds. One reason this can be a rich spot for birds is that it's only a couple of miles as the ibis flies from the nearby Delevan Unit of the Sacramento NWR.

Yellow-billed Magpie is possible here–and anywhere in the Sacramento River Valley–though it's not abundant since the onslaught of West Nile virus. Also beset by habitat loss and poisoning of the ubiquitous California Ground Squirrel, California's endemic magpie is on the Audubon Society's Watch List. The only other California endemic bird species is the Island Scrub-Jay, found on one of the Channel Islands off Ventura in Southern California.

I-5 Exit 586. Take this exit for Maxwell Road and drive 2.6 miles east from I-5 to reach the **Delevan Tract** of the **Sacramento Wildlife Refuge Complex,** north of Maxwell Road. The entire Sacramento Valley NWR encompasses over 35,000 acres of restored wetlands. Delevan covers about 5,800 of those acres, much of it wetlands in winter. How about a small pond full of White-faced Ibis, about 30 feet from your car window? Delevan is nearly always worth the trip.

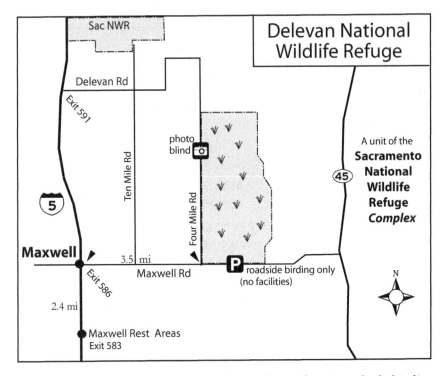

Delevan has no hiking trails and no toilets. This is roadside birding, but it can be rewarding. You'll need to try the side roads. On the left, if you're heading east from I-5 on Maxwell Road, is Four Mile Road (gravel). It heads north along the western edge of the refuge land. You will encounter numerous small ponds and creeks along here. It's a good spot to find White-faced Ibis in spring and summer. Stay on Maxwell Road and 3.2 miles from I-5 you'll come to a bridge that offers some vantage over the marsh. At 4.6 miles from I-5, you'll have come to the eastern edge of the refuge.

Delevan has nearly all the species found in the Sacramento National Wildlife Refuge complex. Most of the Cinnamon Teal counted in the entire refuge are found at Delevan. In fall and winter, it hosts thousands of several dabbling duck species, as well as good numbers of Ring-necked, Ruddy and Bufflehead. Pintail and Green-winged Teal can be especially abundant. It's a great place for your best-ever photo of the elegant male Pintail. In fall and winter you can count on plenty of shorebirds. About 200,000 ducks and another 100,000 geese winter here every year. Wintering waterfowl attract raptors, including Northern Harrier, Peregrine and Bald Eagle.

There are usually a small number of Yellow-headed Blackbirds nesting at Delevan in summer. It's a bird that's uncommon west of the Sierra in California. Look for them in willows along the edges of Delevan Road or the side roads. Black Phoebe, Western Kingbird, swallows, Nuttall's Woodpecker, Common Yellowthroat and Marsh Wren are other breeding birds here. Mammals include Mule Deer, Muskrat and American Beaver.

I-5 Mile 593. Here you cross the line between Colusa County on the south and Glenn County on the north.

I-5 Exit 595. Exit eastward onto Road 68 (Norman Road), then follow signs and turn north along the access road on the east side of Interstate 5. It's a little over half a mile to the entrance to the headquarters unit of the **Sacramento National Wildlife Refuge (NWR)**. An entrance fee is charged. What you'll find: There's a visitors center, toilets, a driving loop of 6.2 miles and a wildlife trail of 2 miles. Birding the trail will take you at least an hour, or you can linger until dark because winter bird counts here are in the hundreds of thousands. There's an elevated wildlife-viewing platform along the auto route with adjacent toilets. If you want to use photography blinds on this NWR, you'll need to make reservations ahead of time. Hunting of some birds is allowed on parts of the refuge.

This refuge unit covers 11,000 acres. It is the largest of the several refuges in the Sacramento Valley. Each of the refuges in this complex is called a "unit". This one stands in the Colusa Basin, west of the Sacramento River itself. The land is low. The waterways are lined with willow and cottonwood. It's flooded and marshy in winter, when the weather can be wet, with dense fog. In summer the area bakes into dry grasslands. The rich surrounding farmland, where rice, almonds, tomatoes and pistachios are grown, is irrigated.

Birding the **Sacramento NWR** in winter and fall is exhilarating. Thousands of Snow and smaller Ross's Geese form drifts along the edges of shallow lakes. This is the best place in the United States for seeing large numbers of wintering Ross's Geese next to their bigger, longer-beaked cousins. Both geese winter here, with midwinter totals topping a hundred thousand white geese most years.

Further north along I-5 the Ross's Goose can be rare because their migration route goes across the eastern portions of Washington and Oregon to and from their limited breeding grounds in north central Canada. This main reserve unit of the **Sacramento NWR** and the Delevan unit a few miles to the south (in Colusa County) get most of the white geese wintering in this NWR. Some can also be found on the Colusa unit. How good is the birding? One couple I know reported 35 species on an hour-long drive (in February) along the Sacramento unit auto loop without ever getting out of the car.

At the Sacramento NWR large numbers of dabbling ducks are to be seen along with Northern Harrier, American Pipit (winter only), Nuttall's Woodpecker, Black Phoebe, Bald Eagle, Peregrine, Red-tailed Hawk, Black-necked Stilt, and a small population of the scarce Tricolored Blackbird. The White-faced Ibis breeds here in summer and a few usually can be seen all winter. Look for the diagnostic flight pattern of this slender bird, with tail and head suspended below its arched back. In weak light these birds look black, while bright sun brings out the rust, copper and even iridescent tones. A typical waterfowl survey here between November and mid-March will find a half million birds or more. The most abundant duck here in winter is the elegant Northern Pintail, usually numbering over a quarter of a million. Winter counts for all units of the Sacramento NWR often top one million waterfowl. That many ducks and geese attract predators including Peregrine Falcon and Bald Eagle. Every winter some hardy Tree Swallows remain in the Sacramento River Valley, and they often fly back and forth over water that offers the best chance for insects on cold days. They can occur here and in other similar habitats.

In summer both Blue and Black-headed Grosbeak may be found, along with Bullock's Oriole, Savannah Sparrow, Black Tern, Lesser Nighthawk and Swainson's Hawk. Year-round residents include California Quail, Marsh Wren, California Towhee, Western Meadowlark, White-breasted Nuthatch, Bushtit, Oak Titmouse, Western Scrub-Jay and Yellow-billed Magpie. Virginia and Sora Rail are year-round, as is the Common Gallinule (formerly Moorhen), which here is at the northern edge of its range. Further north along I-5 the Gallinule becomes a vagrant only. The introduced Ring-necked Pheasant and Starling are abundant all year. In some summers, the Delevan unit of the NWR

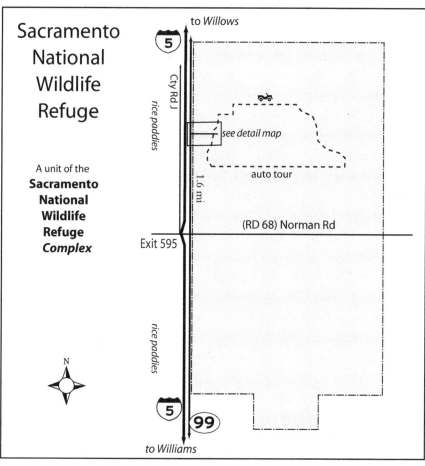

Sacramento National Wildlife Refuge

A unit of the
Sacramento National Wildlife Refuge *Complex*

to *Willows*

Cty Rd J

rice paddies

see detail map

auto tour

(RD 68) Norman Rd

Exit 595

1.6 mi

rice paddies

N

to *Williams*

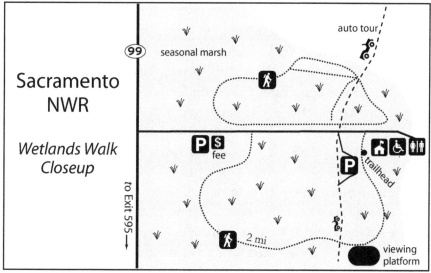

Sacramento NWR

Wetlands Walk Closeup

seasonal marsh

auto tour

P $ fee

trailhead

to Exit 595 →

2 mi

viewing platform

(see above) has a small breeding population of Yellow-headed Blackbird, not common this far south in the Central Valley of California.

Sandhill Cranes are not expected on the Sacramento Wildlife units near I-5. They are found further east at the Llano Seco unit of the NWR. But the **best** area for wintering Sandhill Cranes in Central California is south of Sacramento and north of Stockton around I-5 Mileposts 485-498, an area not covered by this book. There, cranes can be abundant along Woodbridge Road, which can be accessed from the local road that runs parallel to I-5 north of the intersection with CA 12.

In the Sacramento NWR, jackrabbits are abundant and fairly tame—useful if you want a photo of these long-eared denizens of the grasslands. Coyote and light brown California Ground Squirrel are also present.

If you don't have time to make the Sacramento NWR auto loop, try birding along County Road J which parallels I-5 on the west side heading north from this exit (595). In winter these flooded rice paddies may have ducks, Greater Yellowlegs or other shorebirds, White-faced Ibis (here in modest numbers in winter), egrets and raptors.

I-5 Mile 607. Watch for Western Kingbirds along the fencerows. Check for Red-tailed and Swainson's Hawk (spring and summer) soaring overhead. Cliff Swallows nest under every bridge and overpass along the freeway here.

I-5 Exit 608. Willows Rest Area. In spring, check the eucalyptus trees for possible nesting Yellow-billed Magpies. I have seen singing Blue Grosbeak in the fields adjacent to the southbound rest stop in early summer. This is a good area to look up for buteos, including Swainson's Hawk in warm months. They migrate out in September.

I-5 Exit 619. Orland. If you go west from Exit 619 you will be on County Road 200, Newville Road. Just off the freeway is a good spot for Yellow-billed Magpie: Turn onto County Road HH, just west of the freeway, and check the residential area. Going north on Road HH you soon dead-end at Road 12. Turn left along the canal, continuing to watch for the long-tailed, often vociferous, magpies that like this habitat. Here they find roofs to perch on, gardens and garbage cans to

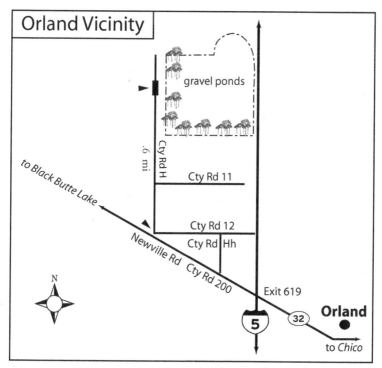

Orland Vicinity

gravel ponds

Cty Rd H

.6 mi.

to Black Butte Lake

Cty Rd 11

Cty Rd 12

Cty Rd Hh

Newville Rd Cty Rd 200

N

Exit 619

5 32 **Orland**

to *Chico*

check for morsels, small farms and old barns to pick over, and a wide variety of trees and shrubs. In short, this area is magpie heaven. Listen for their nasal "dweek-dweek" calls. Also present here are Mockingbird, Western Scrub-Jay, Brewer's Blackbird, Eurasian Collared-Dove and Mourning Dove.

If you continue west, either on County Road 200 (Newville Road) or on County Road 12, you will come to a three-way intersection of County Roads 200, 12 and Road H (Glenn Avenue), which heads north. Take Road H for 0.2 mile north of County Road 200, to Road 11, which heads east, back toward the freeway. It dead-ends at a seasonal marsh, which has waterfowl in winter.

If you go 0.6 miles on Road H north of Road 200, you'll come to a bridge and a break in a largely impenetrable line of eucalyptus trees. From this vantage point you have just enough elevation to can scope the large ponds for ducks, geese, heron, egrets and other water lovers. The ponds are the result of on-going gravel mining. The variety of birds is especially rich in fall and winter. Back on I-5, heading south, you pass near these same gravel ponds, but there is no place to stop safely for a look.

If you continue west on Newville Road for 8 miles you'll come to **Black Butte Lake**. What you'll find: toilets, campsites, showers, trails for hiking and biking, picnic areas, boating, fishing, but no electrical, water or sewer hook-ups. East of the lake, the road splits, and each branch leads to a different campground. The lake is a reservoir formed by a dam that was completed in 1963. The northern end of the lake is in Tehama County. Seven miles long, Black Butte Lake has a 40-mile-long shoreline. When full, its surface area is about 4,500 acres. The area is very steep so access to the lakeshore is limited.

EBird records show nearly 150 species here. Among them are wintering waterfowl and grebes, shorebirds on fall migration, wintering Bonaparte's Gull and White-tailed Kite. In summer, look for Ash-throated Flycatcher and Lesser Nighthawk. Year-round species include Nuttall's Woodpecker, Black Phoebe, Western Scrub-Jay, Yellow-billed Magpie, Oak Titmouse, Bushtit and California Towhee. Some tough birds to find include Grasshopper Sparrow and Lawrence's Goldfinch in spring.

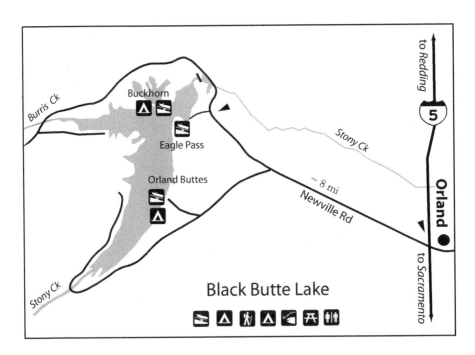

Heading east from Exit 619 at **Orland** is CA 32, which leads to the city of Chico in about eighteen miles. Chico hosts the Snow Goose Festival every winter.

Going east on CA 32, before crossing the river you can access two more units of the **Sacramento NWR: Capay and Phelan Island**. Both are a bit south of Hamilton City via CA 45 and border the west bank of the Sacramento River between river mile markers 191 and 194 (see *East of Orland* map). Capay is on County Road 23 and has three parking pullouts and a hiking trail. Dogs are allowed but must be leashed. Phelan Island can only be reached from the river itself. Both units are for day use only. Birds here are typical of the Sacramento riparian habitat.

By continuing east on CA 32, just before crossing the Sacramento River a half-mile east of Hamilton City you will find the smaller portion (of two) of **Bidwell-Sacramento River State Park**, which consists of two widely separated sections on opposite sides of the river. This one is the 25-acre **Irvine Finch River Access**, located in an old walnut orchard. One-fifth of the area is taken up with a large parking lot for boats, trailers, et al. Watch for the sign on the south side of the highway. What you will find: boat ramp, trail, picnicking, toilets, potable water. This spot is popular with rafters and inner-tube riders. No fee. It is an accessible spot to look for riparian species.

Back on CA 32 and across the Sacramento River you can find the **Pine Creek Unit** of the **Sacramento NWR**. This is about 10 miles east of Orland. The Pine Creek Unit has picnic areas, boat launch and trails. This 564-acre unit, located in Butte County, is owned by the United States Fish and Wildlife Service. The property has 31 acres of fallow land, 228 acres of restored native grass, and 33 acres of existing riparian habitat dominated by cottonwoods.

For more good birding nearby, visit the other (east bank) section of the **Bidwell-Sacramento River State Park**. What you'll find: picnic areas, toilets, trails, fishing and boating. The park charges an entrance fee. To reach this main part of the state park, from CA 32 turn south onto River Road, which follows the east boundary of the Pine Creek Unit. Travel south about one more mile to the Indian Fishery unit of this complex state park. Or, if traveling from Chico, take West

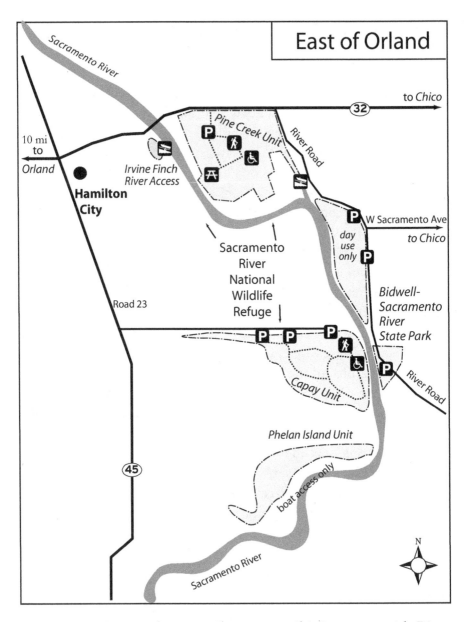

East of Orland

to *Chico*

32

10 mi
to
Orland

Pine Creek Unit

River Road

Irvine Finch
River Access

Hamilton
City

W Sacramento Ave
to *Chico*

day
use
only

Sacramento
River
National
Wildlife
Refuge

Bidwell-
Sacramento
River
State Park

Road 23

River Road

Capay Unit

Phelan Island Unit

45

boat access only

N

Sacramento River

Sacramento Avenue about 5 miles west until it intersects with River Road. Big Chico Creek will be to your left, Indian Fishery straight ahead, the Pine Creek Unit and CA 32 to the right.

Bidwell-Sacramento River State Park has access to the river for day use only. Here, the river is lined by ancient cottonwoods and oaks, a remnant of the riparian habitat that once spread across wetter portions of the Sacramento Valley. Over 150 species have been reported to eBird for this park. They include Wood Duck, Common Merganser, California Quail, Green Heron, Osprey, Red-shouldered Hawk, Acorn and Nuttall's Woodpecker, Black Phoebe, Western Kingbird, Yellow-billed Magpie, Oak Titmouse, Bushtit, Yellow-breasted Chat, Spotted and California Towhee, Black-headed Grosbeak, Lazuli Bunting, Bullock's Oriole. There is one intriguing report of Yellow-billed Cuckoo. Also reports of Lawrence's Goldfinch in August, after the breeding season.

In this area, the Sacramento River serves as county line: East of the Sacramento River you're in Butte County, west of the river is Glenn County.

I-5 Mile 622. This is the county line; Glenn County is to the south, Tehama County to the north.

I-5 Exit 630. Sacramento River Area. Exit onto South Street on the southern edge of Corning and travel east to **Woodson Bridge State Recreation Area.** It's about 6 miles from I-5 through some of the most venerable olive groves in America. You'll notice ancient olives with multiple trunks and twisted branches. The park itself is on the Sacramento River. What you'll find: Woodson Bridge has over 420 acres and nearly four dozen campsites, as well as toilets and trails. There's also a boat ramp into the Sacramento River.

South of Woodson Bridge on the opposite side of the road is the **Rio Vista Unit of the Sacramento River National Wildlife Refuge.** Among the hundred plant species in these two parks is the towering valley oak. The California black walnut, Oregon ash, black cottonwood, sycamore, and willow are also found here. In the riparian corridor there are elderberry, wild grape, and wildflowers in season. This is what much of the Sacramento Valley looked like before ranching and agriculture began here in the 19th Century. The small **Tehama County River Park** is at the east end of the bridge, with a walkway beneath the road, a boat ramp and picnic tables.

Bald Eagles winter on this stretch of river. Osprey are here all year. In spring the area comes alive. Expect to see Western Bluebirds, White-breasted Nuthatches, California Quail, summering swallows, Nuttall's, Acorn and Downy Woodpeckers, Western Scrub-Jay, Oak Titmouse, Spotted and California Towhee. During spring migration

I've seen all three species of goldfinch in a single large flock at Tehama County River Park. There is no evidence that Lawrence's Goldfinch actually nest near here.

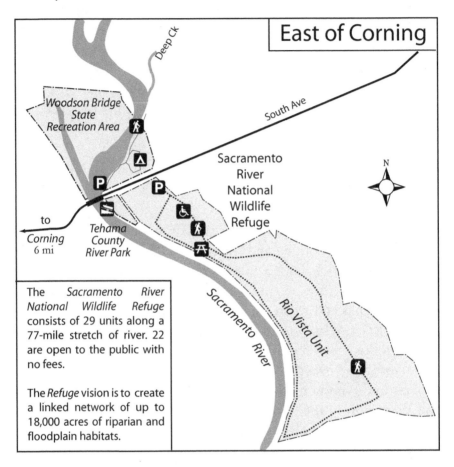

The *Sacramento River National Wildlife Refuge* consists of 29 units along a 77-mile stretch of river. 22 are open to the public with no fees.

The *Refuge* vision is to create a linked network of up to 18,000 acres of riparian and floodplain habitats.

EBird has limited data on Woodson Bridge but still lists more than 70 reported species. Rio Vista still has little eBird data as well, but the unit is home to Red-shouldered Hawk, Ash-throated and Pacific-slope Flycatchers in summer, Black Phoebe and numerous riparian species. The state's official website for Woodson Bridge claims nesting Yellow-billed Cuckoo, but you are far more likely to find a Yellow-billed Magpie.

I-5 Exit 631. Corning. This is the main exit for Corning, elevation 277 feet. You'll find a complete range of commercial services. Crows and Mockingbirds are often seen in town.

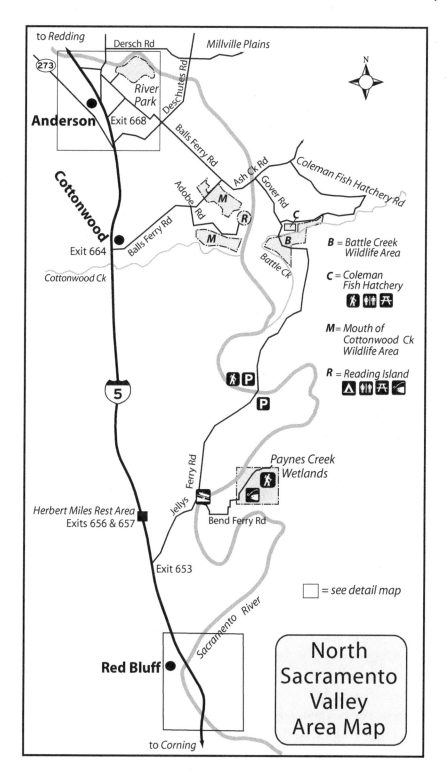

to *Redding*

Dersch Rd

Millville Plains

N

273

River Park

Deschutes Rd

Anderson

Exit 668

Balls Ferry Rd

Ash Ck Rd

Coleman Fish Hatchery Rd

Cottonwood

Adobe Rd

M

R

Gover Rd

C

M

Balls Ferry Rd

B

B = Battle Creek Wildlife Area

Exit 664

C = Coleman Fish Hatchery

Cottonwood Ck

Battle Ck

M= Mouth of Cottonwood Ck Wildlife Area

R = Reading Island

5

Paynes Creek Wetlands

Ferry Rd

Jellys

Herbert Miles Rest Area
Exits 656 & 657

Bend Ferry Rd

Exit 653

☐ = see detail map

Sacramento River

Red Bluff

North Sacramento Valley Area Map

to *Corning*

97

I-5 Exit 632. Corning Rest Areas. The rest areas feature large, wonderfully aged olive trees. Scrub-Jays, Crows and Mockingbirds are likely species here. North of the rest stops and south of Red Bluff, the pastureland may yield Western Meadowlark, Red-tailed Hawk, Turkey Vultures and Western Kingbirds in spring and summer.

I-5 Mile 648. Here, a couple of miles south of Red Bluff, is the first crossing of the **Sacramento River** north of the I-505 intersection, and you will cross a second time in less than another two miles. Watch for Osprey along the river. Between Red Bluff and Redding there are numerous places to get to the Sacramento River and adjacent lowlands and tributaries. This is a fine area for California riparian bird species in spring and summer.

I-5 Exit 649. Red Bluff Recreation Area. This pleasant stop is next to the Sacramento River, about 2 miles from I-5. Take Exit 649 at Red Bluff and head east on CA 36/99E. There will be a Forest Service sign on right. Take the first road to the right at the lights, which is Sale Lane, and drive 1.5 miles.

What you'll find: campsites, fishing, picnic areas, trails, toilets and showers, a visitors center, a boat launch and a salmon viewing plaza. The park is managed by the Mendocino National Forest. Fees are charged for some activities. From the fish viewing platform you can watch migrating salmon and steelhead from May 15 to September 15. Habitat variety here includes riparian forest, flowering grasslands, wetlands and oak woodlands. There is also a 2-acre demonstration garden of drought-resistant native plants.

Being so close to Red Bluff, this spot is birded heavily, and over 130 species have been reported on eBird. Migrating waterfowl abound, including Ross's Goose, Pintail, Canvasback and Hooded Merganser. Osprey, Bald Eagle, California Quail, Snowy Egret, Nuttall's Woodpecker, Anna's Hummingbird, Black Phoebe, Oak Titmouse and Yellow-billed Magpie are year-round residents. Both Vaux's and White-throated Swifts have been spotted here. Other birds reported at this site occasionally include Black-chinned Hummingbird, Lewis's Woodpecker (winter), Pacific-slope and Olive-sided Flycatchers, Blue Grosbeak, Lazuli Bunting and Tricolored Blackbird.

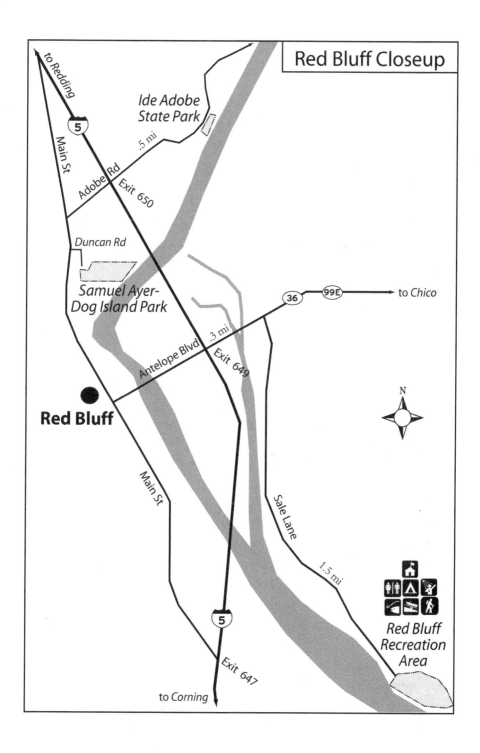

Red Bluff Closeup

I-5 Exit 650. Exit here and drive east on Adobe Road one-half mile to **William Ide State Historical Park** on the Sacramento River. This and other California state parks may be closed because of fiscal issues in the state. When open, it has toilets, picnic tables and drinking water. There are impressive old cottonwoods here and huge oak trees. Riparian bird species are present spring and summer: Bullock's Oriole, Black Phoebe, Oak Titmouse, Anna's Hummingbird, Bewick's Wren and Western Tanager in migration. Greater White-fronted Geese are among the migrating waterfowl that can be seen cruising along the Sacramento River.

Also from Exit 650, go west on Adobe Road to Main Street for **Samuel Ayer-Dog Island Park,** a city park in Red Bluff (see *Red Bluff Closeup* map) on the Sacramento River. Go south on Main, and finally go east a short distance on Duncan to Dog Island Park. Birding here can get you some California specialties like Western Red-shouldered Hawk, Vaux's Swift, Oak Titmouse, Nuttall's Woodpecker, Black Phoebe and Wilson's Warbler in summer.

I-5 Exit 653. Wetlands and Wildlife Areas on the Sacramento River. Exit onto Jellys Ferry Road, which goes northeast from I-5 and eventually crosses the Sacramento River. This route takes you to the **Battle Creek Wildlife Area** at Bloody Island as well as to **Paynes Creek Wetlands,** and eventually to Anderson and Redding. You'll cross from Tehama into Shasta County along the way.

Jellys Ferry Road passes through varied lowland habitat and can be a rich route for raptor watchers in late winter. Rough-legged and Red-Shouldered Hawk, Northern Harrier and White-tailed Kite have all been found here. The Red-shouldered Hawk hunts from tree or power line perches. The other three prefer open grassland. Other birds that have been reported along Jellys Ferry Road include Loggerhead Shrike, Oak Titmouse and California Thrasher.

About 3 miles after exiting I-5 at Exit 653 and turning onto Jellys Ferry Road you will come to Bend Ferry Road. If you turn right (east) onto Bend Ferry, you will cross the Sacramento River and then angle northeast. There is a public boat ramp and river access on the east end of this bridge. Go 2 miles on Bend Ferry Road and you'll reach the BLM's **Paynes Creek Wetlands**. What you'll find: toilets, trails, campsites, picnic areas, horseback riding, hiking, hunting, bicycling and a fishing pier. No fees are charged. There are 3,700 acres here to roam in, and numerous river access points. The area here includes a riparian corridor along Paynes Creek, which flows west out of the Sierra Nevada to join the Sacramento River at the Big Bend, between here and Red Bluff. That juncture is on BLM land. The habitat is riparian lowlands, oak forest, grasslands, ponds and wetlands.

Paynes Creek is on the Pacific Flyway and also gets mountain birds during fall dispersal and migration. Species reported here include Cinnamon Teal, Great-tailed Grackle, Yellow-headed Blackbird, Townsend's Solitaire, Mountain Chickadee, MacGillivray's and Nashville Warbler, Ferruginous Hawk in winter, Harrier, Red-shouldered Hawk, Common Gallinule, Black-necked Stilt, American Avocet, Wilson's Snipe, and wintering Lewis's Woodpecker. Acorn and Nuttall's Woodpecker are found in the oaks and cottonwoods year-round.

Returning to Jellys Ferry Road and turning north, you will eventually cross the Sacramento River in about 4.5 miles. This bridge is the first of two places along Jellys Ferry Road where you can access the river. At the north end of the bridge there's a trailhead for the Yana Trail, which goes along the north and eastern bank of the Sacramento. The other access is less than a half-mile north of the bridge; this is Oka Slough Trailhead, another trail that also goes east and passes Osprey Pond before it merges with Yana Trail about a mile downstream. This is a good place to bird for riparian woodland species.

About 5.5 miles north of the river crossing is the **Battle Creek State Wildlife Area**. It's 582 acres of riparian forest, and is on both sides of Battle Creek. It is managed by California Fish and Game. Like Payne's Creek, Battle Creek flows west out of the Sierra Nevada and into the Sacramento River. It joins the river just east of the town of Cottonwood. Shasta County lies north of the creek, Tehama County south of it.

EBird shows over 100 species reported from Battle Creek State Wildlife Area. Included are Wood Duck; Western Red-shouldered Hawk; California Quail; Sora; Virginia Rail; Common Gallinule; Wilson's Snipe (winter); Lewis's (winter), Acorn and Nuttall's Woodpecker; Black Phoebe; Hutton's Vireo; Bewick's and Western Marsh Wren; Spotted

Towhee; and Golden-crowned Sparrow (fall and winter). Osprey and Bald Eagle nest here. Mammals include American Beaver, Northern River Otter, Bobcat, and Coyote.

If you choose to continue north on Jelly Ferry Road rather than backtrack, you will eventually rejoin I-5 at either Cottonwood or Anderson. Follow the signs. The entire "loop" is approximately 21 miles.

I-5 Exit 656 (northbound) or **Exit 657** (southbound). **Herbert Miles Rest Area.** On both sides of I-5, the Herbert Miles Rest Area is surrounded by oak savannah. The northbound rest area also borders a seasonal creek. Summer birds at both rest areas include Robin, Killdeer and Bullock's Oriole. Killdeer sometimes breed in the areas without lawn. Look for young in April and May. Golden-crowned Sparrow is a wintering species. White-breasted Nuthatch, Acorn Woodpecker, Brewer's Blackbird and House Finch are year-round. Turkey Vultures and Red-tailed Hawks are often overhead.

I-5 Mile 663. At this point you cross Cottonwood Creek and another county line. Tehama County is to the south, Shasta County to the north.

I-5 Exit 664. Just after you cross Cottonwood Creek, take Exit 664 into the town of Cottonwood. Then go east on Route A17 (Fourth Street to Balls Ferry Road) to reach **Reading Island** and the adjacent **Mouth of Cottonwood Creek Wildlife Area.** This exit can also take you to **Battle Creek Wildlife Area** east of the river, and there you can go on to Jellys Ferry Road, the area described under the Exit 653 entry (see *North Sacramento Valley Area Map*).

Reading Island is on BLM land. Cottonwood Creek and Battle Creek are state owned; both are on the Sacramento River. Reading Island, located approximately 5 miles east of Cottonwood, offers access to the Sacramento River. What you'll find: a picnic area, group camping (permit required), vault toilets, and potable water. This is a great fishing site. It is also a great place for birding, hiking, backpacking and river rafting. The scenic area is comprised of oak, willow, cottonwood, blackberries and elderberries. Mouth of Cottonwood Creek Wildlife Area covers over 900 acres on the banks of the Sacramento, while Battle Creek Wildlife Area is about half that size, with 582 acres.

EBird shows over 100 species for this area, including Red-shouldered Hawk, California Quail, Cinnamon Teal, Sora, Virginia Rail, Common Gallinule, Wilson's Snipe and Nuttall's Woodpecker. Land birds you could find here include Yellow-billed Magpie, California Thrasher, Oak Titmouse and Yellow-breasted Chat. Ash–throated Flycatchers are seen here in spring as well. There's even one report of Phainopepla, which is at the very northern edge of its range in this part of the Sacramento Valley and scarce as a result. Lawrence's Goldfinch and western warbler species may pass through in spring.

I-5 Exit 668. Anderson River Park. In Anderson, exit onto **Balls Ferry Road**, going eastbound. After an elbow in the road, look for Dodson

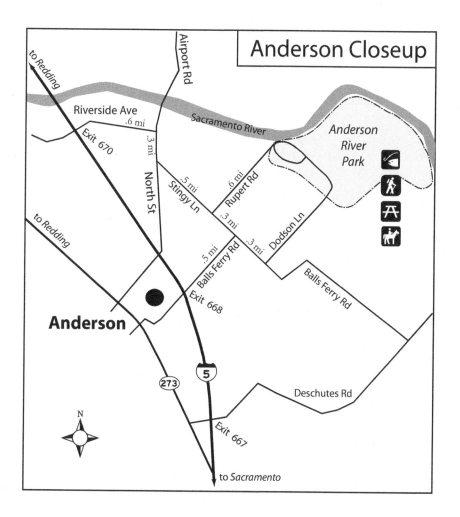

Road on the left, which leads into **Anderson River Park.** What you'll find: river access, picnicing, trails, toilets, frisbee course, playground, ballfields. It is on the west bank of the Sacramento River about 2.5 miles from the I-5 exit. Possible birds here include Osprey, California Thrasher, Yellow-billed Magpie, Acorn Woodpecker and Wood Duck. Bewick's Wren and Green Heron nest here. Cedar Waxwing, American Pipit and numerous warblers show up during migration. EBird shows nearly 100 species for this municipal park, open for day use only.

If you continue southeast on Balls Ferry Road past Dodson Road, your next major intersection is with Deschutes Road. If you turn left (northeast) onto Deschutes, you'll cross the Sacramento River. Then turn right on Dersch Road to bird on the **Millville Plains**, a mix of grasslands and oak savannah. This is a good area for Prairie Falcon in winter. Great-tailed Grackle, Ash-throated Flycatcher and Western Kingbird are here in warm months. Yellow-billed Magpie and Common Gallinule are here year-round. The distance from the I-5 exit to the intersection of Deschutes and Dersch roads is about 4 miles.

Woodpeckers

A variety of western woodpecker species can be found in the mountainous and forested areas of California, Oregon and Washington. The more widespread woodpeckers like Northern Flicker, Downy, Hairy and Pileated I have not included in the notes here.

Most regional specialties are present one season or another somewhere in Siskiyou County, CA, or in Jackson County, OR. The best way to find them is to inquire of local birders, and to know the habitat each species prefers. Here are some thumbnail notes that may be helpful.

Acorn Woodpecker: Sedentary resident in oak forests. Colonial and vociferous. Can be found in towns as well as rural areas. Not common in mountain terrain. Unlikely north of Portland.

Lewis's Woodpecker: Nomadic outside of breeding season, often in loose flocks in oak woodlands or open ponderosa stands, but unpredictable from year to year. Often seen in recently burned or logged habitat. Sometimes will winter in orchards.

Red-breasted Sapsucker: Found at low elevations in winter; breeds primarily in old-growth coniferous forests up to 7,000 feet. Also may be found breeding along streams where aspen or cottonwoods domi-

nate. May be found in towns and gardens in winter. Look for trees with parallel lines of sap holes the bird has drilled around the trunk of the tree.

Red-naped Sapsucker: Usually found only east of the Cascades in breeding season. Prefers forest with some deciduous trees.

Williamson's Sapsucker: A widespread woodpecker with disjunct breeding populations in dry forests. Prefers middle- and high-elevation coniferous forest or mixed forest with quaking aspen. Winters often in oak-juniper forest on dry side of mountains. The males and female have strikingly different plumage. Rare west of Interstate 5.

White-headed Woodpecker: A montane species rarely found below 4,000 feet elevation. Prefers open forest with large-cone pines and Douglas-fir. Not highly migratory but in winter may concentrate where cone crop is best. May visit suet feeders in winter.

Black-backed Woodpecker: Never common and highly particular about habitat. Prefers burned over and beetle-infested forest in dry climate. Rare in lower elevations or areas of heavy precipitation. Often changes breeding area from year to year. Unusual west of Interstate 5.

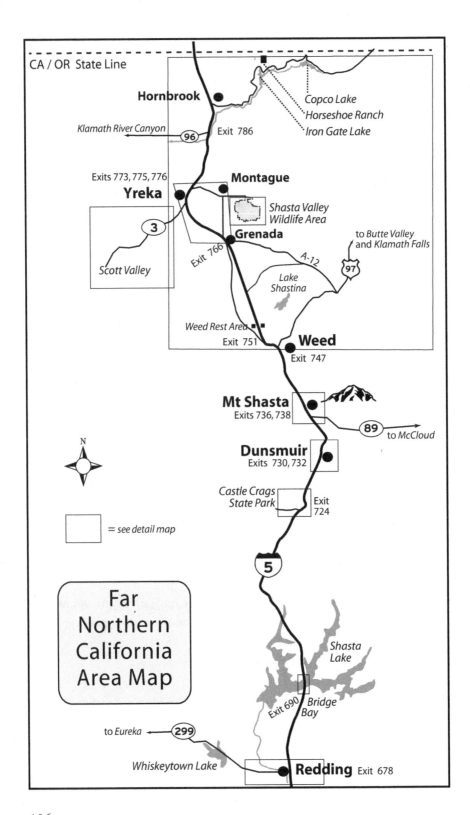

Far Northern California Area Map

Chapter 7

Far Northern California

I-80 / I-505 / I-5
Shasta and Siskiyou Counties

Redding and Environs. Winters are mild in this area, with most daytime highs above freezing. Summers here are hot and dry. From June through September the average daytime high temperature is over 90 degrees, and many days it tops 100. Many summer days, Redding is the hottest town in the Sacramento River Valley so birding is best done at dawn and dusk. Annual rainfall averages over 30 inches, mostly from October through May. From Redding south to Red Bluff there are numerous public access sites for the Sacramento River and its adjacent riparian forest and lowlands. These are excellent places for spring and summer birding.

I-5 Exit 678, West. Turtle Bay Vicinity. Turning west from Exit 678 puts you onto CA 44, which is carried on surface streets through Redding before heading out to Eureka on the north coast. In a couple of blocks CA 44 is signed Eureka Way.

Go west for a park complex that includes **Sundial Bridge, Turtle Bay Exploration Park, Redding Arboretum** and **Kutras Lake.** Follow the signs on CA 44 (Eureka Way) to Turtle Bay and Sundial Bridge (pedestrian only). Go right (north) on Auditorium Drive to get to the central part of Exploration Park and to the Sundial Bridge, which connects you by foot to the Arboretum on the other side of the

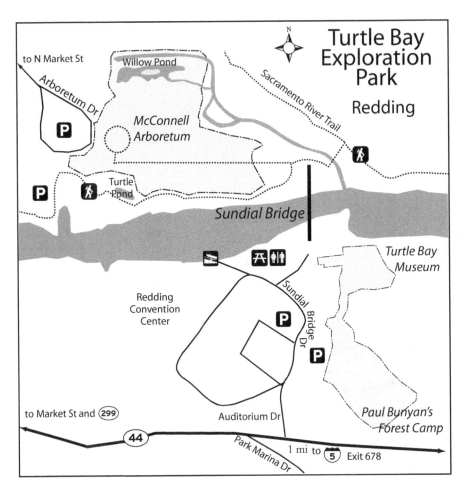

Sacramento River. There is park land on both shores of the river, affording protection to numerous huge valley oaks.

Birds here include Common and (wintering) Hooded Merganser; Turkey Vulture; Pied-billed Grebe; Green Heron; Great Egret; Great Blue Heron; Nuttall's Woodpecker; Anna's Hummingbird; Olive-sided, Pacific-slope and Ash-throated Flycatcher; Western Wood-Pewee; Black Phoebe; Warbling Vireo; Yellow-billed Magpie; Western Scrub-Jay; various swallows; Oak Titmouse; Bushtit; Orange-crowned, Yellow, Wilson's and MacGillivray's Warbler; and Common Yellowthroat. There are nesting Bald Eagles, as well. Many western migrants stop here, Townsend's Warbler in spring, for one.

In the same neighborhood, if you turn south from CA 299 onto Park Marina Boulevard you will come to **Kutras Lake**. (See *Greater*

Redding map.) The lake is east of the intersection of Park Marina and South Street. This may be the best spot in Redding for "ocean" birds, including wintering gulls, loons and mergansers. Other migrating birds you might see here include Barrow's Goldeneye, Red Phalarope and Greater Scaup. North of the lake, along Park Marina, is a small pond that often has wintering ducks such as Ring-necked. Palm trees in this area may shelter nesting Hooded Orioles in late spring and summer. This former southwestern desert denizen has expanded its range northward as parks and gardens now provide mature fan palms, which this oriole uses to weave its nest.

Another couple of miles farther west (after crossing Market Street, CA 44 ends and Eureka Way is signed CA 299), turn south onto Buenaventura Boulevard to visit **Mary Lake** (formerly Falk's Lake). Water runs into and out of Mary Lake via Jenny Creek, which flows eastward into the Sacramento River. The lake, which lies in a 17-acre

city park, is maintained by Redding. The lake has an installed aeration system to help curtail algae growth. Among the birds found here are Green Heron, Nuttall's Woodpecker, Black Phoebe, Hutton's Vireo, Anna's Hummingbird, Oak Titmouse, Bushtit, Spotted and California Towhee, White-crowned Sparrow and Lesser Goldfinch.

If you have plenty of time, you can explore nearby **County Road A16 (Placer Street)**, reached a short distance farther down Buenaventura. See *Greater Redding* map. It heads southwest out of Redding and passes through dry grassland and hills. Here you can find Golden Eagle. In spring and summer, Lark Sparrow, Grasshopper Sparrow and the hard-to-find Lawrence's Goldfinch may be present. The latter is particularly fond of chemise bushes.

With lots of time to spare, you can continue on CA 299 westbound out of town to eventually reach **Whiskeytown Lake National Recreation Area**. While Redding lies at 495 feet alongside the Sacramento River, Whiskeytown Lake's elevation is about 1,200 feet. Surrounding mountains are much higher. With a four-wheel-drive vehicle you can go to Shasta Bally peak, over 6,000 feet—the highest point in the park. The eastern (closest) end of Whiskeytown Lake National Recreation Area is 8 miles from I-5.

What you'll find: Whiskeytown is a fee area, with a visitors center overlooking the reservoir (open 10 a.m. to 4 p.m. September to May, otherwise, 9 a.m. to 6 p.m.), numerous camping and RV sites, toilets, trails, boat ramps, fishing, with some areas open to dogs on leash. CA 299 parallels the northern shore of the lake for several miles, depending on lake level. The lake will be at its annual low point in October, its highest in May. The area gets over 50 inches of precipitation during the wet season. One favorite birding spot is the Tower House Historic District, about 15 miles west of Redding on CA 299.

The reservoir's surface area is more than 3,000 acres, and the shoreline totals 36 miles. The Park Service describes eight major biotic communities found in this NRA, which covers more than 39,000 thousand acres. There are over 70 miles of hiking trails. Some trails are open to mountain bikes and horses. Much of it is forest or scrubland. There are four major waterfalls and one is wheelchair accessible. Here's what the government website has to say about biodiversity at Whiskeytown:

Western whiptail lizards, indicative of dry and arid Great Basin habitats, are found alongside species that represent the great Pacific Northwest forests—tailed frogs and Pacific yew trees. As you enjoy the park's many treasures, you may be surprised to discover the numerous species and habitats found here….More than 750 native vascular plant species are known to occur in the park along with at least 42 mammal species, 160 bird species, and 30 reptile and amphibian species.

EBird's records show over 100 species around Whiskeytown Lake, including Osprey, Mountain Quail, Band-tailed Pigeon, Olive-sided and Dusky Flycatcher, Black Phoebe, Western Wood-Pewee and Pacific-slope and Ash-throated Flycatcher. The forests and creeks here house the vireo trifecta: Cassin's, Hutton's and Warbling. The warbler selection is good for western birding. It includes Black-throated Gray, Nashville, Wilson's, Yellow-breasted Chat and Townsend's in passage. Other western specialties to be found here include Western Tanager, Oak Titmouse, Wrentit, American Dipper, Lazuli Bunting and Lesser Goldfinch. At higher elevations you could find Hermit Warbler in the tall evergreens.

I-5 Exit 678, East. From this exit, CA 44 is a highway heading toward Lassen National Park, the first few miles of which are a freeway. In east Redding (that is, east of the Sacramento River and of I-5) you'll find **Clover Creek Preserve.** Leave CA 44 at Exit 4 and turn south onto Shasta View Drive. The preserve's parking lot is at Shasta View and Venus Way (south of Hartnell Avenue, see *Greater Redding* map.) What you'll find: 2.5 miles of hiking and 2 miles of paved biking trails, drinking water, but no toilets. This 128-acre open space is owned by the city. It features a 6.7 acre lake within a 46-acre flood control basin. Plans call for about 40 acres of the entire site to be preserved "as is," with an additional 15 acres of new wetland and riparian areas, 25 acres of grassland/meadows that could be converted in the future to recreational areas, and 55 acres of blue oak habitat. EBird has scant data for the area, but riparian species may be found here, along with Yellow-headed Blackbird and Acorn Woodpecker.

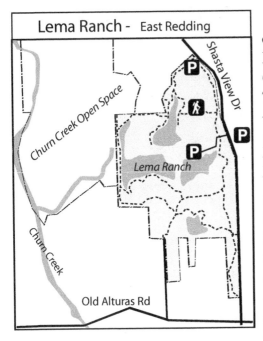

Lema Ranch - East Redding

Shasta View Dr

Churn Creek Open Space

Lema Ranch

Churn Creek

Old Alturas Rd

Another birding spot off of Shasta View Drive in east Redding, this one north of CA 44 Exit 4, is **Lema Ranch**. There are 200 acres here, privately held but open to the public for walking. What you'll find: toilets, drinking water, paved paths, and four constructed ponds. Dogs and bikes are not allowed. Lema Ranch is adjacent to Churn Creek Open Space (where dogs are allowed on leash). Grasslands and oak forest dominate the habitat around the ponds. The Wintu Audubon Society bird checklist for Lema Ranch includes 120 species, including Snow Goose, Tundra Swan, Cinnamon Teal, Redhead, California Quail, American Bittern, White-tailed Kite, Northern Harrier, Red-shouldered Hawk, Merlin in winter, Virginia Rail, Sora, Common Gallinule, Wilson's Snipe, Forster's Tern, Anna's Hummingbird, Lewis's Woodpecker, Nuttall's Woodpecker, Olive-sided and Ash-throated Flycatcher in spring, Black and Say's (winter) Phoebe, Oak Titmouse, and Spotted and California Towhee.

I-5 Exit 680. You might bird a bit around **Shasta College**, especially on the east side of the campus. To reach it, exit I-5 onto CA 299 eastbound and get off in 2.5 miles at CA 299 Exit 143, follow signs. The college pond has a variety of ducks in winter and spring. California Quail frequent the brushy areas. There are often Yellow-billed Magpies in the opens fields around the college.

I-5 starts to climb into the mountains soon after leaving Redding, crossing sprawling Lake Shasta.

I-5 Exit 687. Herbert Miles Rest Area. One on either side of freeway, both in open oak woodlands. Possible birds include Western Bluebird,

Acorn Woodpecker, White-breasted Nuthatch and Oak Titmouse.

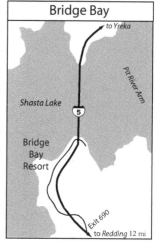

I-5 Exit 690. Shasta Lake. Exit here onto Bridge Bay Road. It takes you downhill to the large lakeside resort complex on **Lake Shasta.** They will not insist you pay the parking fee if you tell them you are simply going to the store. What you'll find: toilets, shopping, parking, boating, houseboat rental, fishing, motel, and restaurant. I've seen an Osprey squealing from a treetop in the parking lot. Osprey nest uphill from Exit 690 overlooking this parking lot. Also possible here are swallows in summer, especially Northern Rough-winged. Scrub-Jay, Killdeer, Cliff Swallow, Bald Eagle, Savannah Sparrow and Anna's Hummingbird are possible here as well.

I-5 Exit 694. Rest areas. Steller's Jays can be expected here. The northbound rest area offers views into the canyon to the east. Osprey sometimes nest on the utility pylons in this area.

I-5 Exit 724. The Castella exit gets you to **Castle Crags State Park.** There is an admission fee, and a possibility that it could be closed due to state budget woes. What you'll find: The park offers swimming and fishing in the Sacramento River, hiking in the back country, and views of Mount Shasta to the north. There are 76 developed campsites and six environmental campsites. The park is named for its glacier-polished crags, looming at 6,000 feet. The exposed cliffs are granite, isolated after softer metamorphic rocks that surrounded them eroded away.

As you come off of I-5 you have two choices: turn east or turn west. You can go east on Castle Creek Road, downhill to Frontage Road, then north until you see Riverside Road on your right. Turn there and cross the Sacramento River bridge, following Riverside as it angles north, paralleling the river. A half-mile from the interstate overpass, you will see the Castle Crags riverside picnic ground on your left. It's open from Memorial Day through Labor Day. A foot trail and footbridge connect the picnic area to the uphill section of the park. If you want

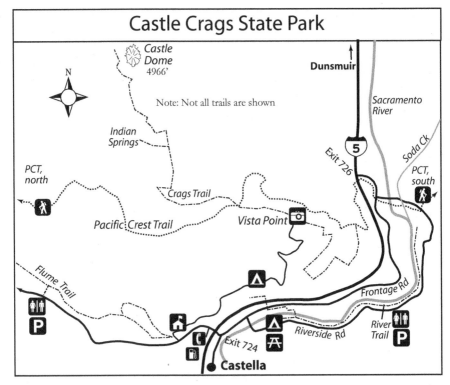

more riparian birding, continue on Frontage Road north for 2 miles then rejoin I-5 at Soda Creek Road via Exit 726.

If you go west at Exit 724, you will be on Castle Creek Road and in 0.2 mile come to the main park entrance on your right (north). The road into the park goes more than two crooked miles upslope into dense forest. Castle Crags State Park has 28 miles of hiking trails, including a 2.7 mile access trail to Castle Crags Wilderness, part of the Shasta-Trinity National Forest. The trail up into the Crags is over 5 miles long and gains over 2,000 feet in elevation—not a leisurely stroll. Some of the park's trails, however, are nearly level. There is even one trail specifically for dogs and their friends.

However, if you bypass the main entrance and continue west on Castle Creek, you can access two additional trails. There are another 2.4 miles of paved road that parallel the creek. A mile from the park entrance there is a parking area and trailhead at Red Barn. Go past that and continue another 1.5 miles west on Castle Creek Road to the trailhead and parking area for Dog Trail, which leads straight into the

Castle Crags Wilderness.

There is live oak in the lower elevations. Throughout there are broadleaf trees such as bigleaf maple, vine maple, cottonwood, willow and Pacific dogwood. Conifers are western yew, Port Orford cedar, incense cedar, sugar pine, ponderosa pine, Douglas-fir, white fir and lodgepole pine, with red fir, Jeffery pine and weeping spruce (Brewer spruce) nearer the Crags summit. Poison oak is also common at lower elevations. Signs warn of poison oak and bear raids on campers' food.

In summer, the temperature can hit 100 in the daytime, but nights are cool. Winters are mild, with little snow at the base of the Crags but rainfall is heavy; the park gets over 100 inches some years.

Birds to be found here include Cooper's Hawk, Northern Pygmy-Owl, Western Screech-Owl, Great Horned Owl, Band-tailed Pigeon, Mountain Quail, Flicker, Pileated Woodpecker, Raven, Steller's Jay, and Black-headed Grosbeak in warm months. Truly lucky hikers may catch a glimpse of the elusive Mountain Quail, or hear the male's sharp single-note call. There are three breeding hummingbirds: Anna's, Rufous, and the smallest bird in North America, the Calliope Hummingbird. Flycatchers include Olive-sided, Pacific-slope near the river, and Willow, plus Black Phoebe and Wood-Pewee. There are Cassin's Vireo in the evergreen forest, while Hutton's and Warbling Vireo, MacGillivray's and Yellow Warbler are along the streams. Look for three jays—Steller's, Scrub and Gray at higher elevations–and three chickadees—Mountain, Black-capped and Chestnut-backed. Nearly any western warbler species can occur during migration, including Townsend's and Black-throated Gray high in the canopy. Western Tanager and Bullock's Oriole nest here. Other possible birds include both kinglets, Lazuli Bunting, Cassin's Finch at high elevation and Spotted Towhee. If you hike toward the summit you could find Hermit Warbler, Dusky and Hammond's Flycatcher (difficult to tell apart), and perhaps even a Northern Goshawk. Peregrine nest near the summit. In May migrant warblers can include Wilson's and Nashville. Yellow-breasted Chat nest in the brush along the river. There'll be Green-tailed Towhee in high elevation brushland.

There's very little data in eBird for Castle Crags so please contribute your findings. The visitors center has copies of a park bird list. It was originally typed, so it predates computers by a bit. It originally had outdated names like "Sparrow Hawk" and "Traill's Flycatcher."

The list has been updated by hand over the decades, with much of the information drawn from a single four-day visit by a birding couple in 1988! This park needs your birding data. Please put any observations into eBird. Castle Crags deserves a realistic bird list.

The **Pacific Crest Trail (PCT)** crosses I-5 at Castella and passes through the Castle Crags Wilderness Area. The PCT is 2,650 miles long, from Mexico in the south to Canada in the north. Just north of the Oregon-California border near Siskiyou Summit, the PCT again crosses I-5 as it moves between the Cascades on the east and the Siskiyou Mountains on the west.

I-5 Exit 726. Soda Creek Road. If you exit here and go south on Frontage Road, which parallels I-5 and the Sacramento River on the east side, you will get in some riparian forest birding as you approach **Castle Crags State Park,** and access all the places described for Exit 724.

I-5 Mile 728. This is the county line between Shasta County on the south and Siskiyou on the north.

I-5 Exit 730. Dunsmuir. Exit here for both of Dunsmuir's city parks. You can cruise through town on Dunsmuir Avenue and return to I-5 at Exit 732. Elevation: 2,350 feet. The town gets over 60 inches of precipitation in an average year. From November through March the nights are often freezing, but daytime temperatures often top 50. In July and August the average daytime high is around 90, with nightly lows averaging 70.

Tauhindauli Park is directly beneath the I-5 bridge over the Sacramento River. See *Dunsmuir* map for directions. Northern Rough-winged Swallows nest under this bridge. What you'll find: There are no toilets here. Dogs are allowed on leash, but there is no camping.

At the north end of town on Dunsmuir Avenue, **Dunsmuir City Park** has an old-fashioned baseball field with wooden bleachers (Babe Ruth played here once). There are Robins, Juncos, Northern Rough-winged Swallows in season, Crows, Ravens and possible Dippers along the Sacramento River, which is about 25 feet wide at this point and still quite swift. This park has fishing, a botanical garden, toilets, a children's playground, and a single tennis court plus river access. Dogs are allowed on leash, but there is no camping.

Continue north on Dunsmuir Avenue to get to Hedge Creek Falls and to return to I-5 at Exit 732.

I-5 Exit 732. The small park at **Hedge Creek Falls** is right at the end of the Exit 732 off-ramp. On exiting, turn right at the stop sign on Dunsmuir Avenue. The park is next to a large metal industrial-style building. The park is heavily wooded with ponderosa pine, Douglas-fir, oaks, and cottonwoods along the creek. In May, creamy bracts of blooming dogwood glow in the forest's shadows.

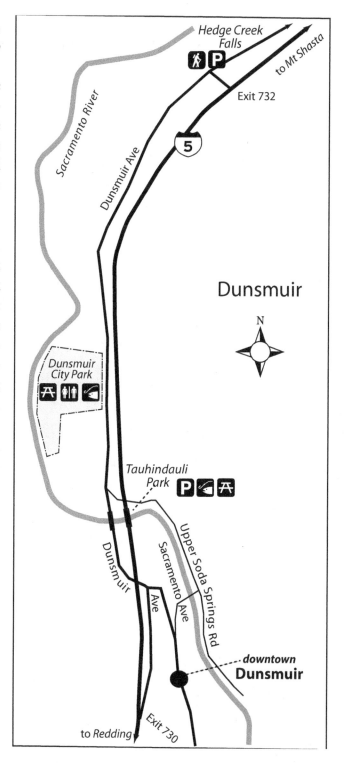

The hike down the switchbacks to the falls is moderately steep and about 200 yards long. There are multiple shelves of falling water; the longest drop is about 30 feet, and you can stand behind that fall, looking down on the creek and ravine below. A trail takes off downstream from behind the falls. Here you get true mountain music: the tympanic rhythm of the falling water and the upbeat melody of the singing Dipper. The woods may shelter Hermit Thrush in summer, Varied Thrush in winter. Regulars here include Pacific Wren and Downy Woodpecker, Red-breasted Sapsucker, Pileated Woodpecker, Western Tanager, Pacific-slope Flycatcher and Black-headed Grosbeak.

Inquire locally to see if the trail to nearby **Mossbrae Falls** is open. If it is, you might see nesting Black Swift there from late June to August.

I-5 Exit 736. McCloud and the McCloud River. Exit here onto CA 89 and drive east toward the old mill town of **McCloud** and the **McCloud River** area for some rich birding. About five miles east of I-5 on CA 89 you are at Snowman's Summit. What you'll find: parking and toilets. A spring walk on the woodland trails here can yield warblers, Green-tailed and Spotted Towhee, Western Tanager, Thick-billed Fox Sparrow, Mountain Chickadee and all three local nuthatches.

It is 10 miles from Exit 736 to McCloud, and then the side roads off CA 89 can take as much time as you can spare to seek out montane forest birds like Cassin's Vireo, Olive-sided Flycatcher and American Dipper. The McCloud Falls (Upper, Middle and Lower), a short distance off of CA 89, are a popular and worthy side trip.

I-5 Exit 738. Mount Shasta. This exit takes you into central Mount Shasta City, elevation 3,561 feet. On exiting, a turn west onto Lake Boulevard will take you to the Sisson Museum and still-operating fish hatchery in a mile, and in another couple of miles, to Lake Siskiyou, with it's fine circumvent-the-lake trail.

An east turn onto Lake Boulevard from Exit 738 leads to downtown. At the traffic signal on Mt. Shasta Boulevard, turn left (north) toward the city park, reached in 1.7 miles. See more details under Exit 740.

This is also the way to Road A10 (Everitt Memorial Highway), a road that climbs far up the south slope of Mount Shasta, California's tallest volcano. Shasta rises to 14,179 feet. This road winds 14 paved miles up the mountain from its starting point in downtown Mount Shasta City and stops at around 7,860 feet elevation. Most of Mount Shasta is public land (national forest and a wilderness area) and has numerous hiking trails and campgrounds. Weather on this mountain can be treacherous at any season so don't lightly set off to hike to the glaciers.

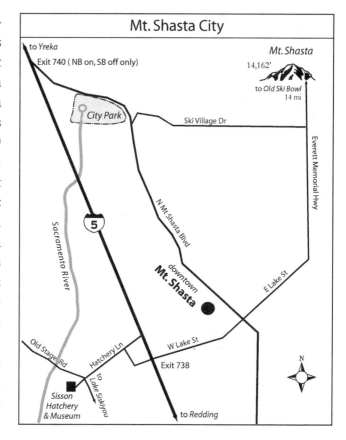

Birds that you might find in this area include Williamson's Sapsucker; White-headed and Lewis's Woodpecker; Pileated Woodpecker; three Empidonax (Pacific-slope, Dusky and Hammond's Flycatchers); Olive-sided Flycatcher; Cassin's Vireo; Gray Jay; Clark's Nutcracker; Mountain Chickadee; Mountain Bluebird; three thrushes (Varied, Hermit and Swainson's); Black-throated Gray, MacGillivray's, Hermit and other western warblers; Green-tailed Towhee; and Cassin's Finch. There's a small population of breeding Gray-crowned Rosy-Finch.

I-5 Exit 740. This exit is closer to City Park but the offramp is for southbound traffic only. There is a northbound onramp. Drive south toward town for 0.8 mile to the entrance to the **Mount Shasta City Park** (on your right). What you'll find: toilets, playgrounds, picnic areas and trails. Dogs are allowed. The park covers 26 acres of lawn and forest. Here the headwaters of the Sacramento River pour forth from Big Springs. There are multiple springs in the park, the largest about 20 feet across. At its source the Sacramento River is about 15 feet wide as it flows beneath an arched wooden footbridge. This bridge leads onto trails that wind past other spring outlets and through the dense woodland. The spring water comes from the snow-covered slopes of Mount Shasta. The park has Dipper, Robin, Yellow-rumped Warbler, Song Sparrow, Western Tanager and Black-headed Grosbeak.

I-5 Mile 742. Black Butte. The elevation of Black Butte Summit on Interstate 5 is 3,917 feet. The actual peak, to the east of the freeway, reaches 6,325 feet. This relatively small, mostly rock-sided volcano is a flank vent of Mount Shasta. The trees and bushes rooted here seem constantly beleaguered by falling volcanic boulders. A trail leads to the top, where a fire lookout once stood.

I-5 Exit 747. Klamath Basin, Shasta Valley, and Butte Valley. Exit onto US 97. This highway will take you northeast across the east side of **Shasta Valley** (I-5 follows the western edge of Shasta Valley, see Mile 752), over a pass then across **Butte Valley,** and eventually to the Klamath Basin, near Klamath Falls, OR. All are IBAs. Shasta Valley has nesting Sandhill Cranes and Forster's Terns. **Butte Valley National Grasslands** is the best place in northeastern California for good views of pronghorn. Seventy miles north of Weed is Klamath Falls in Oregon. It has a bird festival every February ("Winter Wings"), to which birders are drawn in part by the dozens of Bald Eagles and Rough-legged Hawks that winter there. In Klamath Falls, Link River is an excellent spot for a concentration of waterfowl in winter when the limited patches of open water are surrounded by otherwise frozen lakes. There are always Barrow's Goldeneye in the crowd, and many Bald Eagles watching for an easy meal.

Without traveling so far afield, in about 10 miles north on US 97 you can turn left onto Big Springs Road (A29), which will take you to **Lake Shastina,** which has a housing development and golf course on the east side of the lake. This lake is behind a small dam constructed on the Shasta River, which empties into the Klamath River further north.

From Big Springs Road turn left onto Jackson Ranch Road, then

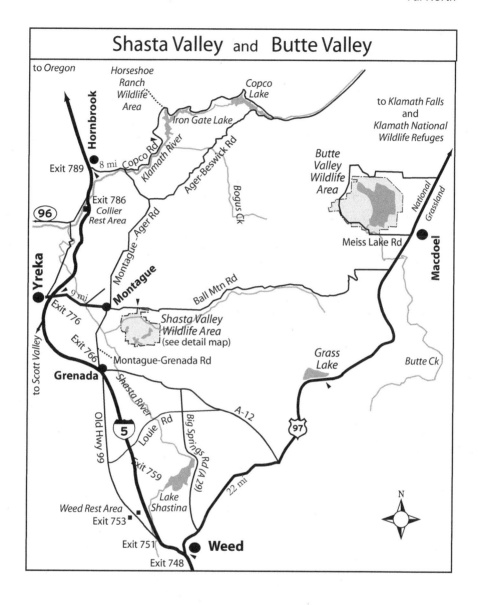

Shasta Valley and Butte Valley

to *Oregon*

Horseshoe Ranch Wildlife Area

Hornbrook

Copco Lake

Iron Gate Lake

to *Klamath Falls* and *Klamath National Wildlife Refuges*

Exit 789 8 mi

Copco Rd

Klamath River

Ager-Beswick Rd

Bogus Ck

Butte Valley Wildlife Area

(96)

Exit 786 Collier Rest Area

Montague-Ager Rd

Macdoel

National Grassland

Meiss Lake Rd

Yreka

9 mi

Exit 776

Montague

Ball Mtn Rd

Exit 766

Shasta Valley Wildlife Area (see detail map)

Montague-Grenada Rd

Grass Lake

Butte Ck

Grenada

Shasta River

Old Hwy 99

(5)

Louie Rd

Big Springs Rd (A-29)

A-12

(97)

Exit 759

22 mi

Lake Shastina

Weed Rest Area Exit 753

Exit 751

Weed

Exit 748

N

right onto the road to the public boat launch on the south end of the lake. This lake is a good spot for shorebirds and waterfowl in the fall. Five grebe species, Common Loon, Pectoral Sandpiper and Redhead have been seen here. This is Black-billed Magpie territory, and Townsend's Solitaire are possible in the juniper and other trees.

On Big Springs Road north of Jackson Ranch Road follow signs to the Community Center, which is west on Driftwood Lane. Here you can see the bird activity at the earthen dam on the north side of the lake. EBird shows over 60 species reported for Lake Shastina from only a few checklists.

If you continue further northward on Big Springs Road past Lake Shastina, you will cross the eastern stretch of Louie Road. If you take Louie Road west from here, you will rejoin I-5 at Exit 759. The grasslands here can be good for Loggerhead Shrike in summer. Cattle herds may be attended by *icterid* flocks including Tricolored Blackbirds. Or, to avoid more freeway driving, you can continue north to County Road A12, then go west to rejoin I-5 at Exit 766.

Shasta Valley Wildlife Area is north of here just outside of the little town of Montague but is not easily reached from juncture—see Exit 766 and Exit 776.

I-5 Exit 751. Old Highway 99. Exit here to take the more leisurely "old road" north for several miles towards Yreka and the Oregon border. Old Highway 99 can also be accessed via Exits 759 and 766.

I-5 Mile 752. Traveling north of Weed you cross the Shasta Valley, which sits between the Cascades on the east and the Klamath Mountains on the west. This plateau is generally over 2,200 feet in elevation. This is Black-billed Magpie country. Also expect Red-tailed Hawk, Harrier on migration, Brewer's and Red-winged Blackbird, Western Kingbird and Western Meadowlark. You will not find Yellow-billed Magpie north of Redding.

I-5 Exit 753. Weed Rest Areas. Here you can expect Ring-billed Gull and an occasional California Gull. In the winter this area can be quite cold and windy, often staying below freezing all day long. If you exit for the rest stops, from either side of the freeway you can go a little bit south onto Edgewood Road. Turn left (east) toward the small Shasta River, a tributary of the Klamath River to the north. Just east of the freeway and north of Edgewood Road is a large boulder pile. Check it for Yellow-bellied (name not a slur) Marmots and California Ground Squirrels on the lookout for Red-tailed Hawk.

0.7 mile east from the freeway overpass is the intersection of Edgewood and Slough Roads. Just east of the T-intersection, Edgewood Road bridges the Shasta River. In late spring and early summer look for a breeding colony of Northern Rough-winged Swallows. In summer, the short-grass fields have American Kestrel, Western Scrub-Jay, Savannah Sparrow and Western Meadowlark. Barn Swallows work the whole area in season. If you drive north on Slough Road you parallel the Shasta River and its riparian corridor for almost half a mile until the river meanders away from the road. Here you may find warblers, vireos, Bushtit and Bewick's Wren in the warm months.

I-5 Exit 759. Louie Road. At this exit the habitats you'll find are sage steppe on the uplands and wet, marshy grassland on the flats. Most of the area is cattle ranches, but birdlife is plentiful in warm months. Drive west from I-5 on this rural road in spring, and swallows, Killdeer, Western Meadowlark, and Cinnamon Teal are likely. It is a good spot for Loggerhead Shrike in late spring and early summer. They hunt from the fence posts and you may get a good picture through an open car window, but they flush easily. Check the blackbird flocks for Tricolored. If you're northbound, you can increase your birding time by driving to the west end of Louie Road, then turning north on Old Highway 99. Follow it north to Grenada and rejoin I-5 at Exit 766.

I-5 Exit 766. From this Grenada exit you can head south on Old Highway 99, which parallels the freeway on the west side, and rejoin I-5 at Louie Road Exit 759, as mentioned above. Tricolored Blackbirds are possible here in all seasons. Ferruginous Hawks winter here. Western Meadowlarks abound, and on sunny days they sit atop wires and fence posts.

From the east side of the freeway here at Exit 766 you can take a "shortcut" to the **Shasta Valley Wildlife Area.** Take A12 east and very shortly turn north onto Montague-Grenada Road. When you reach Montague in about 6 miles, turn right on CA 3 and in 1.5 miles you will be there. Note that you can also reach the wildlife area from Yreka via CA 3 (Montague Road) at Exit 776.

What you'll find: toilets in the parking areas (in warm months check carefully for possible hornet nests inside), fishing and boating (electric motors only) in Bass Lake, an auto tour with several pullouts. Checklists for wildlife are usually available at the first entry gate. The refuge is in the rain shadow of Mount Shasta but has lakes, marsh and over 4,600 acres of open space.

EBird shows 140 species reported for this site. The state staff has collected records for 256 species, and that includes breeding Sandhill Cranes. During waterfowl hunting season, hunters have access on Wednesday, Saturday and Sunday. Among birds occasionally seen here are Trumpeter Swan; Red-necked Grebe; Barrow's Goldeneye; American Bittern; Northern Shrike (winter); Loggerhead Shrike; Long- and Short-eared Owl; Merlin; Common Tern; Mew, Sabine's and Glaucous-winged Gull; Vesper and White-throated Sparrow; and Lapland Longspur (winter). Forster's Tern, Northern Harrier and Black-billed Magpie nest here annually. Yellow-headed Blackbirds abound in warm months. Bank Swallow colonies are sporadically spread across arid parts of the Western United States. Here check the gully east of Trout Lake for insect-hawking Bank Swallows. There is good dragonfly watching on the bridge over Little Shasta River near Parking Lot 2.

After birding here you can head west on CA 3 and follow the signs through the town of Montague to rejoin I-5 in Yreka, 6 miles to the west.

I-5 Exit 770. Easy Street. If you can spare twenty minutes in spring or early summer, exit here. On the west side of the freeway turn right (north) onto Easy Street and drive 0.2 mile. To the west, right alongside the road is a wetland around **Brazie Pond**. See *Yreka Vicinity* map. In rainy years it encompasses several acres. In April and May I often get an icterid bonanza here: in addition to the widespread Brewer's and Red-winged Blackbird, look for the buttery flash of the larger Yellow-headed Blackbird, which only becomes common east of the Sierra Nevada or Cascade Mountains. Best of all, there is often a flock of Tricolored Blackbird. Watch for the white shoulder bar on this bird, which has a very limited range and declining population. Finally, listen for the Western Meadowlark singing from the surrounding grasslands. Now it's your five-species icterid bonanza. It may take you about two minutes once you're out of your car.

Other marsh lovers you can see here include Mallard, Gadwall, Shoveler, Bufflehead, Green-winged Teal, American Wigeon, Ruddy Duck, Canada Goose and Coot. Swallows flying over the water can include Barn, Cliff, Tree and Northern Rough-winged. Crows and Ravens are often about as well. Both Mule Deer and California Ground

Squirrel are often found in the grass bordering the marsh.

I-5 Exit 773. Yreka. Elevation: 2,595 feet. The town receives an average of 20 inches of precipitation, much of it in light winter snows. Night-time lows are often below freezing November through February. In July and August highs can be above 90 degrees. Summers are dry with the occasional wet thunderstorm. In warm months Cliff Swallows and Ring-billed Gulls often circle over the town of Yreka, which has the full spectrum of business and tourist services.

From Exit 773 you can go south on CA 3 toward Fort Jones in Scott Valley. About 4.5 miles from I-5 you will be in the hills, and locals say the highway crews use the pullouts at steep slopes here for

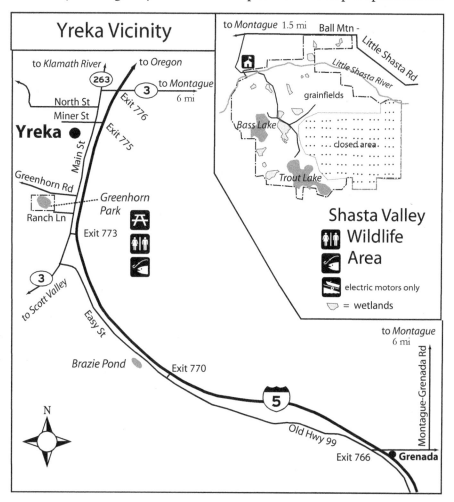

dumping road kill. If a deer or two has been unlucky, you may find a large circle of interested birds: Turkey Vultures (in warm months), Black-billed Magpies, Ravens, Golden and Bald Eagles are most likely.

If you continue to Fort Jones (15 miles from Yreka), you can bird the **Scott Valley,** which is rich in raptors in winter. Scott Valley extends south and southeast from Fort Jones. (See *Scott Valley* map.) If you do bird this valley, the best way back to I-5, unless you have half a day to spare, is back through Yreka.

You can find Rough-legged Hawks, Ferruginous Hawks, all four western falcons, Harrier, Bald Eagles and numerous Golden Eagles hunting the fields and pastures of the valley. Maps, information, and toilets are available at the Ranger Station on the west end of Fort Jones, right along CA 3. Also in Scott Valley, watch for Wilson's Snipe, California Quail, Acorn Woodpecker and Loggerhead Shrike.

Also from Exit 773, west side of freeway, turning north on South Main Street (CA 3) will take you to Yreka's shady **Greenhorn Park.** From South Main turn left (west) onto Greenhorn Road and go 0.6 mile to the entrance to Upper Greenhorn Park. This Yreka city park has two parts, designated Upper and Lower, with Greenhorn Reservoir as the centerpiece. Lower Greenhorn Park is accessed either on foot around the lake from Upper Greenhorn or via Ranch Lane, which also turns off of South Main Street. What you'll find: parking, toilets, play areas, picnic areas, a paved trail all the way around the lake including handicapped-accessible fishing areas. A trail system is being developed. The Ditch Trail in the park is level once you reach the large municipal water tank that's visible from the Lower Greenhorn parking lot. In warm months Lazuli Bunting and Black-throated Gray Warblers are breeding in this hillside habitat. Greenhorn Park covers 400 acres, while the reservoir has a surface area of over 20 acres.

Birds here include Pied-billed Grebe, Belted Kingfisher, California Quail, Red-breasted Sapsucker, Common Nighthawk, Vaux's Swift, Cassin's, Hutton's and Warbling Vireo, and numerous wintering waterfowl, including Wood Duck and Green Heron. Caspian Terns visit to fish. Pacific and Bewick's Wren, Brown Creeper, Bullock's Oriole, Western wood-Pewee and Black-headed Grosbeak are here in breeding season. Western Bluebird, Townsend's Solitaire and numerous western warblers come through on migration. EBird shows nearly 90 species.

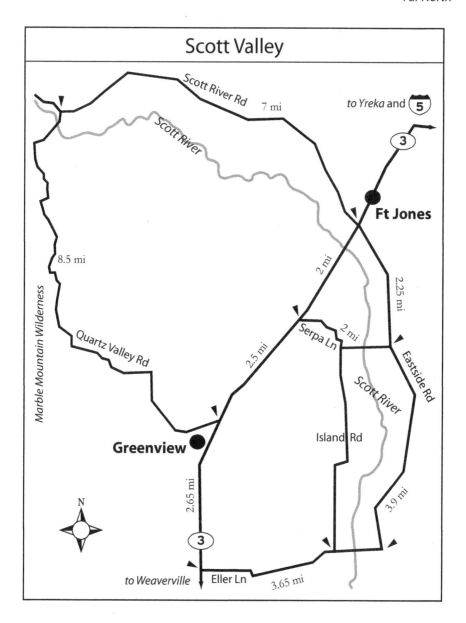

Scott Valley

Scott River Rd   7 mi

to Yreka and (5)

(3)

Scott River

Ft Jones

8.5 mi

Marble Mountain Wilderness

2 mi

2.25 mi

Quartz Valley Rd

Serpa Ln   2 mi

2.5 mi

Eastside Rd

Scott River

Greenview

Island Rd

N

2.65 mi

3.9 mi

(3)

to Weaverville   Eller Ln   3.65 mi

Continuing north on Main Street will take you to the other Yreka area sites listed under Exits 775 and 776.

I-5 Exit 775. Upland from Yreka. Take this central Yreka exit, go west of the freeway to Main Street (CA 3). Go north on Main, then left (west) onto North Street. Follow North Street to the upper edge of Yreka where it ends at Humbug Road at a T-intersection. Turn right (north).

After passing two large water tanks the road turns to dirt and is now called Yreka-Walker Road (County Road 7J001), going steadily uphill.

The habitat here is scrub oak and ceanothus ("buck brush") brushland, very hot and dry in summer. Species that can be found here as you climb higher include California Thrasher, Western Scrub-Jay, Oak Titmouse, Ash-throated Flycatcher (breeding), Golden-crowned Sparrow (cold months), Wrentit, Bushtit, Lazuli Bunting, and California and Spotted Towhee. Blue-gray Gnatcatcher are here in breeding season. In the deep side canyons with trees, you may find Calliope Hummingbird, Hermit and Nashville Warbler, and Lazuli Bunting in late spring and summer.

There is quite a network of dirt roads in this area and the signage is sparse. You can pick up a Forest Service map at the Klamath National Forest Supervisors Office on South Main Street before you head up here. Without a map or a local guide, it would be best to head back down the hill to Yreka before venturing too far.

I-5 Exit 776. Montague and Shasta Valley. Exit here and go east on CA 3 (Montague Road) for Montague and upper **Shasta Valley**. Birding the Montague area in spring and summer can yield many species. This area has nesting Sandhill Cranes. See Exit 766 entry for details on **Shasta Valley Wildlife Area.**

If you go west from Exit 776 to the west side of I-5 (or if you just proceeded north through Yreka on Main Street), you can take CA 263 (also called the State of Jefferson Scenic Byway) north. This road roughly parallels the freeway and goes along the lower Shasta River, crossing it several times. At 7.3 miles from the edge of Yreka, you can take Hudson Road down under one of the historic concrete bridges then park and walk the edge of the road. Look for Dipper along the river and Canyon Wren on the talus slopes. Each year the Yreka Christmas Count gets Canyon Wren from this road.

Where CA 263 (see more under entry for Exit 786) ends at the intersection with CA 96, the Shasta River flows into the Klamath. Atop the large bluff west of this intersection, Peregrines have been seen hunting. They may also nest on the cliff.

You can turn west down CA 96 to bird the Klamath River just as far as you want; the highway follows the river for over 100 miles. (See more details under the Exit 786 entry.) Or, you can continue 2 miles north on CA 96 to the end of this highway to rejoin I-5 at the Collier Rest Area, Exit 786. For this short distance you will be following the Klamath River. Common Merganser and Wood Duck nest along the Klamath, and Osprey, Bald Eagle and Double-crested Cormorant fish the river.

I-5 Exit 778. This is a vista point, accessible from southbound lanes only. This is not a worthwhile birding stop, but offers fine views toward the southeast across the volcanic plateau to Mount Shasta. Just south of this vista point you cross the Shasta River.

I-5 Mile 782. Anderson Grade Summit. Elevation: 3,067 feet. Note the oak forest on the steep mountainsides.

I-5 Exit 786. Randolf Collier Rest Area. Exit I-5 from either direction to reach the rest area. This is a 5-acre roadside park between the freeway on the east and the Klamath River on the right. The rest area's artificial forest includes tulip, redbud and cherry trees in amongst ponderosa pine and incense cedar. This exit also marks the start of CA 96, a highway that follows the Klamath River through its winding canyon most of its way to the Pacific Ocean, about 175 miles away by road. The elevation at the rest area is below 2,000 feet. The surrounding Klamath Mountains rise to 7,500 feet.

Around the rest area, the river is lined with a narrow strip of riparian habitat dominated by cottonwoods and willows. As you move upslope, oak dominates. This is prime habitat for breeding Lewis's Woodpeckers. You may see their crow-like flight across the river from the rest area. Or walk to the south end of the lawn area and go through a gap in the fence. Then you can approach a grove of oaks with one large cottonwood. Lewis's Woodpeckers feed and nest here on the same side of the river as the rest stop. As many as twenty woodpeckers may be seen here in the spring. They do not overwinter here.

In late spring and early summer look, or listen, along the river for the voluble Yellow-breasted Chat. Spring and summer bring Western Tanager; House Finch; Yellow-rumped, Yellow and Orange-crowned Warbler; Lincoln's Sparrow and Song Sparrow right next to the river;

Downy Woodpecker; White-breasted Nuthatch; and Western Kingbird. Both Lesser and American Goldfinch nest in the area. Ring-billed Gulls, California Quail, Crows and Ravens are year-round birds at Collier Rest Area. An occasional California Gull may appear among the Ring-bills. It will have a darker mantle and is slightly larger. The rest area work crews regularly see and hear Wild Turkeys, an introduced species. Along the river you may find Common Merganser, Wood Duck, Green Heron, Bald Eagle and Osprey. EBird has limited data on this site but shows over five dozen species in spring and summer.

If you continue downstream (roughly southwestward) on CA 96 you will parallel the Klamath River. Two miles from the Collier Rest Stop you will come to CA 263 which winds through the Shasta River canyon, mentioned in the above entry for I-5 Exit 776. This scenic route is the "back way" to Yreka. The canyon, the rugged hills, the mountain river; it's classic western scenery. CA 263 follows that small river and crosses it several times on historic bridges, including two elegant concrete arches. Birds along there can include California Thrasher along the stream, Spotted Towhee on the brushy hillsides, Canyon Wren on roack faces, Peregrine hunting from atop rock outcroppings. From the CA 96/CA 263 junction it is 8 miles to Yreka, where you can rejoin Interstate 5 at Exit 776 or 775.

For more birding downstream along the Klamath River, at the CA 96/CA 263 junction turn west on CA 96. In about 4 miles (6.5 miles west I-5 Exit 786), you come to **Tree of Heaven Campground** on the river (might be closed in winter, but you can walk in). Here both Rock and Canyon Wrens may be found on bouldered slopes below the roadway. EBird has limited data on Tree of Heaven, but lists five dozen spring species including Wood Duck and Common Merganser (both breed along the river), Vaux's and White-throated Swifts, Red-breasted Sapsucker, Pileated Woodpecker, Western Tanager, Black-headed Grosbeak, Wilson's Warbler, Yellow-breasted Chat and Spotted Sandpiper. The campground has a short interpretive wildlife trail and handicapped accessible river access for swimming, rafting or fishing.

If you try some of the roads that go north, upslope, from CA 96, you'll be in the northernmost known breeding range of the California Thrasher. In winter the juniper scrub often holds large flocks of Townsend's Solitaire, who love juniper berries.

CA 96 continues southwestward until it ends at CA 299, halfway between Redding and the Pacific Ocean to the west. Along the way CA 96 follows the Klamath River for miles, providing access to several small towns and countless big mountains, the habitat growing lusher the further west you travel. This highway gives you the chance to enter three major wilderness areas: the Marble Mountains, the Siskiyou Wilderness and the Trinity Alps. It also passes by the Hoopa Indian Reservation near where the Trinity River flows north and empties into the Klamath River. All along the Klamath River are Common Merganser, Wood Ducks, Osprey in summer, Bald Eagle, Belted Kingfisher and the birds that thrive in riparian habitat.

An excellent guide for birding the Klamath River Valley is Bob Claypole's *Klamath River Bird Finder* (see the bibliography).

I-5 Exit 789. Iron Gate Dam and Copco Lake. If you're northbound, exit here at Hornbrook for the road to Iron Gate and Copco Lakes, both formed by dams on the Klamath River. Follow signs for Copco Road, which takes you roughly eastward to Iron Gate Dam. As you head east out of Hornbrook, listen for California Thrasher in spring on dead-end side roads along Copco Road. It's about 8 miles east from I-5 to **Iron Gate Dam** and **Lake**.

Both Iron Gate and Copco dams are operated by Pacific Power Company to generate electricity. On the way up, there are numerous pullouts along the river for birding. Just below Iron Gate dam, the fish hatchery is worth a visit during the fall salmon migration season. There are picnic tables and toilets and a walking tour. The dam is at 2,343 feet elevation, and the lake covers 845 acres when it's full. There are three small campgrounds around Irongate Lake.

From Iron Gate it is another ten miles alongside the lake to Copco Dam and Lake. See *Shasta Valley and Butte Valley* map. At Copco Lake there are boat rentals available.

Birds around the Iron Gate and Copco reservoirs include numerous wintering waterfowl, both eagles, Northern Pygmy-Owl, Black-billed Magpie, Oak Titmouse, Golden-crowned Sparrow (cold months) and Lesser Goldfinch.

There are three small campgrounds around Irongate Lake and numerous pull-outs along the river for birding. At the fish hatchery just below Irongate Dam are picnic tables and toilets. Following the road along the north side of the lake you will find picnic areas with lake views. The dam is at 2,343 feet elevation, and the lake covers 845 acres when it's full. Birds around the Iron Gate and Copco reservoirs include numerous wintering waterfowl, both eagles, Northern Pygmy-Owl, Black-billed Magpie, Oak Titmouse, Golden-crowned Sparrow (cold months) and Lesser Goldfinch.

Horseshoe Ranch Wildlife Area, over 9,000 acres of publicly owned land administered mostly by the California Department of Fish and Game, can also be reached from this route. It is located another couple of miles beyond Irongate Dam but well before Copco Lake. As you go along the north side of Irongate Lake watch for the entrance sign on north side of the road. It's an easy hike up a gated dirt road alongside a creek to the grassy historic ranch site. The habitat is oak woodland, grassland, and creek-side forest. Camping is allowed, but there are no facilities. Some species reported at Horseshoe Ranch Wildlife Area are Golden Eagle, Lewis's Woodpecker, Common Poorwill, Common Nighthawk, Mountain Quail, Ash-throated Flycatcher, Oak Titmouse, Rock Wren, Western Tanager, Black-headed Grosbeak, Bullock's Oriole, Lazuli Bunting and Lark Sparrow.

I-5 Exit 790. Just west of the freeway is a modest farm pond with well-eatablished willow fringe. This pond may yield interesting birds, including vagrant ducks, Green Heron in warm months and Great-tailed Grackle which is expanding its range northward.

I-5 Mile 791. Not see many birds on this stretch but there are Turkey Vultures spring to fall, as well as American Kestrel and Common Raven.

I-5 Exit 796. This northern-most exit off I-5 in California takes you to the town of Hilt. In warm months look for Cassin's Vireo, Bullock's Oriole, Western Kingbird and Western Wood-Pewee in woods and brushlands around this community. For complete information on birding the side roads between here and Mount Ashland or here and the Klamath River area, see *Klamath River Bird Finder,* by Bob Claypole.

I-5 Mile 800. You are at the California-Oregon border.

Great Gray Owl (GGO)

The Great Gray is North America's tallest owl, though both Great Horned and Snowy Owls usually weigh more. Much of the Great Gray's bulk is plumage, including its long tail. This owl ranges across mostly boreal forests in Canada and Alaska. It has a limited breeding range in the Lower 48 States including Yosemite, Yellowstone and portions of the Cascades in central and southwestern Oregon. It's found in the mountains of central and eastern Washington or the higher portions of the Oregon Cascades. Thus Jackson County, Oregon, is the most likely spot for this owl along the entire route of Interstate 5. The bird is a regular breeder in the Cascades east of I-5. It also breeds in the Siskiyous in central Jackson County, Oregon. The Great Gray Owl is also found in the northern reaches of Europe and Russia.

The Great Grey Owl hunts along the edges of bogs and meadows, often surrounded by dense forest. If in winter food is scarce in the bird's normal range, it will move southward. It often winters where snow is deep and the surface crust is thick. With its immense strength the bird breaks through the crust and catches rodents it hears moving beneath the snow. The Great Gray is a rodent-hunting specialist.

The Great Gray's wingspan is over four feet, but it still flies as silently as smaller owls. Each owl or nesting pair has a proportionately large range, so it is never easy to find; it's a boon when a nest or roost has been discovered by local birders. The Great Gray Owl rarely breeds before it's three years old. It will build a nest, usually on top of a broken tree trunk, or take over one abandoned by raptors. This owl will also use man-made nest platforms that in dense old growth forest should be at least forty feet off the ground. At maturity the Great Gray Owl's major enemy is the automobile owing to night collisions. Ravens and Great Horned Owls are their major predators, taking eggs and nestlings.

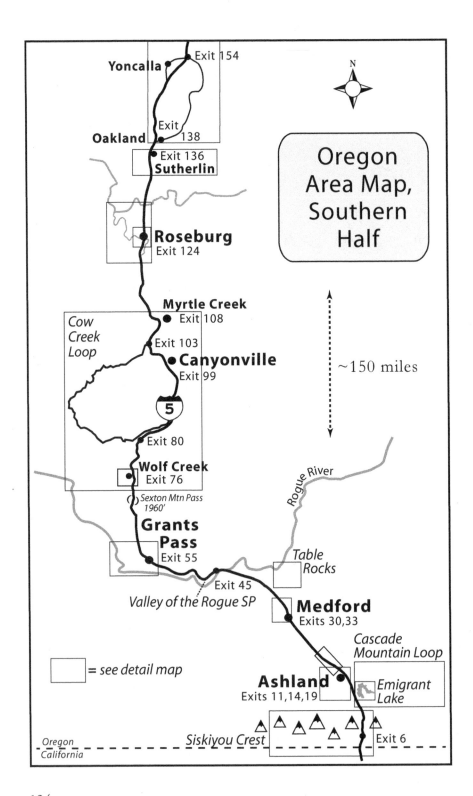

Yoncalla • Exit 154

N

Oakland Exit 138

Exit 136 • Sutherlin

Oregon Area Map, Southern Half

Roseburg • Exit 124

Myrtle Creek • Exit 108

Cow Creek Loop

Exit 103
Canyonville •
Exit 99

5

~150 miles

Exit 80

Wolf Creek • Exit 76

Sexton Mtn Pass 1960'

Rogue River

Grants Pass • Exit 55

Table Rocks

Exit 45
Valley of the Rogue SP

Medford • Exits 30,33

Cascade Mountain Loop

= see detail map

Ashland • Exits 11,14,19

Emigrant Lake

Siskiyou Crest

Exit 6

Oregon
California

Mountain Quail

Chapter 8

Southern Oregon

I-5, Ashland to Oakland
Jackson, Josephine and Douglas Counties

A few miles north of the California-Oregon state line you climb to the Siskiyou Pass at 4,310 feet. This Oregon mountain pass is the highest elevation anywhere on Interstate 5. Heavy snowfall may temporarily close this pass between November and April. During the snow season, you need to carry tire chains and their use may be occasionally required. This area of Jackson County gives you the quickest access to high elevation species on this entire route.

Note that the exit numbering has restarted at the state line.

I-5 Exit 1. Exit here (possible only if you're northbound) for Old Highway 99 South which winds northward up the south slope of the Siskiyous. If you continue north of Old OR 99 from Exit 1 you will come to Exit 6 on I-5 and the east end of Mt. Ashland Road. En route you will pass the beginning of the Forest Service Road to the base of Pilot Rock, the thumb-shaped monadnock clearly visible east of I-5 in this area. If you are heading south on Old OR 99 you can rejoin I-5 at Exit 1. You cannot access the northbound lanes at Exit 1.

The habitat around Exit 1 is arid brushland with very dry, hot summers. Here are scattered western junipers, always a sure sign of aridity in this part of the U.S. On side roads in the BLM lands here you may find Spotted Towhees, Blue-gray Gnatcatchers (spring and summer), Bushtits, California Quail. At higher elevations there are Mountain Quail. This area may have a breeding population of Black-throated Sparrows. Check local sources for recent sightings.

I-5 Exit 6. Exit here for **Mount Ashland Road** and access to **Pilot Rock Road.** To reach either, from the west side of I-5 turn back south on Old Highway 99 paralleling the freeway. Mount Ashland itself rises 7,533 feet above sea level. That's the highest point in the geologically ancient Siskiyou Mountains. To the east, the Cascades are much newer mountains and many top Mount Ashland in elevation, but they are further from I-5.

Shortly after exiting the freeway you will reach Mount Ashland Road on your right. If you choose to drive up Mount Ashland Road, set your trip odometer to .00 as you turn onto it. The mileage points given in this section assume that you've done that.

Once you're on Mount Ashland Road it's almost 9 miles one way to the large parking lots at the Mount Ashland Ski Lodge and then another mile to mountain meadows at about 6,500 feet elevation. There are numerous good birding spots along Mount Ashland Road. EBird shows a hundred species recorded here.

Facilities: In spring, there are no facilities except parking and hiking trails. Once the snow melts and the roads clear, there are toilets at the campground beyond the ski lodge. The road is plowed to just beyond the ski area in winter.

Mt. Ashland Road

1 mile. At a little more than a mile from the start of Mount Ashland Road you can stop amidst scattered houses to check for Red-breasted Sapsucker in trees and listen for calling Mountain Quail in spring. Black-headed Grosbeak nest here at about 4,500 feet, but they don't go much higher. At the start of Colestin Road (which heads south and downhill toward California and eventually to I-5 at Hilt), you can bird for Hermit and other warblers, Mountain Chickadee, Ducky Flycatcher and Lazuli Bunting in spring. Juncos will likely be the most abundant bird on any visit to Mount Ashland.

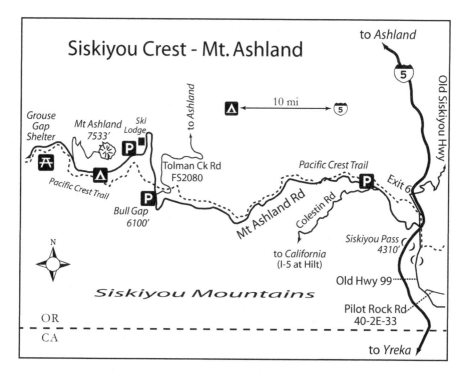

Siskiyou Crest - Mt. Ashland

to Ashland

Grouse Gap Shelter

Mt Ashland 7533'

Ski Lodge

P

to Ashland

10 mi

5

Tolman Ck Rd FS2080

Pacific Crest Trail

P

Exit 6

Pacific Crest Trail

P

Bull Gap 6100'

Mt Ashland Rd

Colestin Rd

Siskiyou Pass 4310'

N

Old Siskiyou Hwy

to California (I-5 at Hilt)

Old Hwy 99

Pilot Rock Rd 40-2E-33

Siskiyou Mountains

OR

CA

to Yreka

3 miles. At this point there's a steep rock face on the right hand side. This is good habitat for Green-tailed Towhee, Lazuli Bunting, MacGillivray's Warbler in the draw, and Hermit Warbler and Western Tanager in the tallest conifers. Forest edges may have calling Dusky and Willow Flycatchers in warm months. They are usually not high in the trees. Western Wood-Pewee climb much higher, and the occasional Olive-sided Flycatcher will call from the tip of the tallest conifer. If you seek an Olive-sided, study the simple, memorable three-note call. It's usually your best cue to scope the treetops for the bird. Golden-crowned Kinglet, Cassin's Vireo and Yellow-rumped Warbler are also more likely in the canopy. In the deepest woods there are Hammond's Flycatchers, often hard to spot unless they're calling. Orange-crowned Warblers abound in brushy areas as well.

6 miles. (This is actually near a milepost marked "7".) At Bull Gap parking area (elevation 6,100 feet) you can pull off the right side (north) of Mount Ashland Road. Here you may walk the trails and check along the roadside for possible White-headed Woodpecker, Dusky Flycatcher and Mountain Chickadee. One spring, Dusky Fly-catchers nested in a bush just north and downslope from the gravel parking area. White-headed Woodpecker usually nest in vertical dead snags. Cassin's Finch may be found among Pine Siskins. The gregarious Evening Grosbeaks are sporadic in this area at any season. Listen for their baby-chick peeping calls.

Taking this dirt road (Forest Service Road 2080) downhill will eventually get you all the way into Ashland but this is not advisable without a good map. Read more details under entry for I-5 Exit 14.

When you've gone **8.5 miles** up Mount Ashland Road, you'll reach the ski lodge parking lots. Mountain and Western Bluebird and Chipping Sparrow often nest in open areas around the ski lodge. The striped-backed mammals are mostly Golden-mantled Ground-squirrels. Green-tailed Towhee nest in the brush on the slope below the parking lots. In brushy margins of forest groves there are Red-breasted Sapsucker.

At **9 miles** up Mount Ashland Road, you'll come to the small pullout next to the campground toilets. Check here for Red-breasted Sapsucker. In spring or early summer, it's wonderful to walk further along the dirt road as it heads westward from here. You may want to drive, then walk, move the car forward, walk some more, and so on. Townsend's Solitaire may sing beautifully from treetops in spring. Later they can be hard to locate in the trees. These brushy meadows have Lazuli Bunting, Lincoln's Sparrow, MacGillivray's Warbler, Sooty Grouse and Green-tailed Towhee. Dusky Flycatcher, Cassin's Vireo and Hermit Warbler are likely in the scattered groves of mature trees. Most of the large soaring birds will be Red-tails, Ravens and Turkey Vultures; however, Goshawks are possible. Gray Jays are seen here occasionally. Sooty Grouse and mountain beaver live in these meadows. In late summer the adult grouse may perch on a rock to overlook their browsing young. In summer the wildflowers bloom in profusion, as there is only a short growing season so many species bloom at once.

At **11 miles** up Mount Ashland Road, two gravel Forest Service roads intersect. To get to Grouse Gap, go left (downhill) on FS 20, a Forest Service road. In this area, you're at 6,500 feet, and you can find nesting Nashville and Orange-crowned Warbler, Lazuli Bunting, Green-tailed Towhee, Mountain Bluebird, and Chipping and Lincoln's Sparrow. American Kestrel nest up here. Check blossoming brush for Calliope, Rufous and Allen's Hummingbirds.

From the slopes of Mount Ashland an array of Forest Service roads continue much further west and even south into California, but you should get a detailed area map before traveling further from the freeway. The roads west of the Mount Ashland Ski Lodge are usually snow-blocked from early winter until June.

Pilot Rock Road turns off of Old Highway 99 beyond (south of) the Mount Ashland Road turnoff. (If you happen to be heading north on Old Highway 99 from I-5 Exit 1, you will reach this road in about 5 miles.) As you go south on Old Highway 99 it goes under the freeway, through the "old" Siskiyou Pass and then comes to Pilot Rock Road heading off to the east. The road is also named FS 40-2E-33 (Forest Service Road). Be advised: this is a very rough, unimproved road and not easily driven in a low-slung car. In spring this is a good place to hear and perhaps even see Mountain Quail. In the brush and scattered woods you may also find Lazuli Bunting, Chipping Sparrow and Green-tailed Towhee. Once you reach the denser woodlands expect Mountain Chickadee, Hermit Warbler and Hermit Thrush. MacGillivray's Warbler nest in the damp gullies. Watch for their beloved willows. Ruffed Grouse breed in the dense underbrush of the forest. You can hear the males ruffling their feathers in May. If you hike the short trail into the wilderness area beneath Pilot Rock you may not find many birds, but the spring wildflowers are exceptional. This thumb-shaped rock knob is just over 5,900 feet high. It was a crucial navigation marker for American Indian and pioneer travel in this rugged area. Old Highway 99 continues south and will hit I-5 at Exit 1.

Back to **I-5 Exit 6,** if you turn east and drive past Callahan's Lodge you will head sharply downhill (north) on Old Siskiyou Highway, a "back way" into Ashland, OR. In fall or winter, watch the roadside for Varied Thrush that will flush and fly up into the trees. When you come to the railroad, you can walk the tracks in either direction for Steller's Jays and Golden-crowned Kinglets in all seasons, plus possible woodpeckers. You will eventually reach OR 66, and that road will lead either to Ashland (turn west) or to Emigrant Lake and the Cascade Loop (turn right, see I-5 Exit 11 entry).

I-5 Exit 11. If you are northbound, Exit 11 gives you the quickest access to **Emigrant Lake** and **Cascade Mountain Loop** east of I-5. Take Siskiyou Boulevard north from the exit toward Ashland. Turn right on Crowson Road, which takes you under I-5 and over to OR 66. You can turn either right (south) or left (north) on 66 to do the Cascade Mountain Loop.

A right turn will first take you by Emigrant Lake, a large reservoir that is usually full in spring and fairly low in late summer. Low water provides good mudflats at the south end. These attract migrating shorebirds in late summer.

The north end of Emigrant Lake can be exceptionally windy in any season. Before reaching the entrance to the recreation area (Emigrant Lake Road), the short Corp Ranch Road is good for Acorn Woodpeckers and Western Bluebirds, and provides a nice place to watch for soaring Golden Eagles. They make use of the thermals around the steep rocky mesa east of the road as it catches all the wind that comes across the Siskiyou Pass and wafts over Emigrant Lake.

About 2 miles south of Crowson Road on OR 66 you will see a sign that marks the entrance to **Emigrant Lake Recreation Area** (a county park). What you'll find: toilets, picnic areas, trails, playground, fishing and boat ramps open year round for day use, and campground, RV hook-ups, water slide, swimming in summer only. According to eBird, the Emigrant Lake perimeter and adjacent fields have yielded over 175 species to birders.

The pastures around the entrance to the Emigrant Lake Recreation Area often have large flocks of Canada Geese. In fall and winter, these flocks may have Greater-white Fronted, Snow or Cackling Geese as well. One Christmas Count had over a hundred Cackling Geese here. In summer, watch the fields and fence lines to your left for Western Kingbird, Western Bluebird and Lesser Goldfinch.

When you enter the park you'll be in a mixture of native oak forest and gardened parkland. This habitat supports Acorn Woodpeckers, Oak Titmouse, White- breasted Nuthatch, Western Bluebird, Spotted Towhee, Scrub-Jay and Brewer's Blackbird year-round. In winter you may see both kinglets and clouds of Juncos, Golden-crowned and Fox Sparrows. Yellow-rumped Warblers are common in passage. From

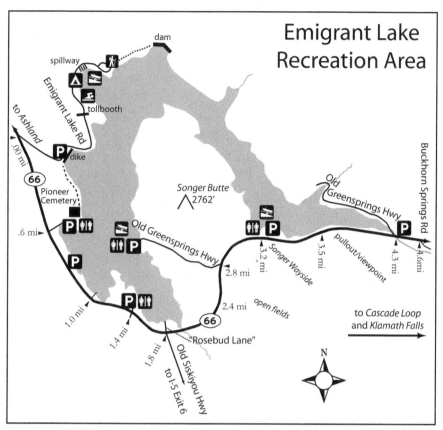

March through September you may spot Osprey perched or hunting over the lake. One February morning a Golden Eagle passed close overhead as our birding group stood along the road by the boat ramp. Bald and Golden Eagles can be seen around or over the lake any time of year. Both species breed nearby.

As you turn up the hill toward the rowing club building left of the road, check the berry tangle on that side. In winter, the thicket shelters sparrows, including Golden-crowned and an occasional White-throated or Lincoln's. When the road levels out and goes along above the lake look for Western Bluebirds, goldfinches, House Finches, and any birds on the lake. Any time of year there can be Acorn Woodpeckers in the oaks on the hillside to the left; Lewis's Woodpeckers may join them in the winter and early spring.

As early as mid-February Sandhill Cranes may be seen or heard migrating north over the lake after crossing the Siskiyou Pass. They move southward past here in late September. A few may stop at the south end of the reservoir. Cranes are often quite high in the sky on migration so listen for their bugling calls overhead.

Year-round birds that can be seen anywhere around Emigrant Lake include Great Blue Heron, Red-tailed Hawk, Red-shouldered Hawk, both eagles, California Quail, Acorn Woodpecker, Western Meadowlark, Western Scrub-Jay, Crow, Raven, Western Bluebird, Spotted Towhee, Lesser Goldfinch and Brewer's Blackbird.

Out on the water look for Western Grebe from fall to spring, and Common Merganser year-round. Eared and Horned Grebe may occur during both migration seasons. Wintering ducks can include Ruddy, Bufflehead, Lesser Scaup, Ring-necked and Green-winged Teal (mostly at the shallow south end of the reservoir). Coots winter here annually. Along the lakeshore in the sparse willows you may find Yellow Warbler, Yellow-rumped Warbler and other spring migrants.

When you reach the cement spillway just past the large boat ramp, look to the north and watch for Golden Eagle. They often launch themselves from the steep bluffs in that direction, uphill from the yellow Tuscan-style mansion. The boat ramp area may attract migrating shorebirds in late summer, including Western and Spotted Sandpiper.

As you pass through the RV parking area toward the end of the road, watch for bluebirds. In spring there may be Lazuli Bunting, Chipping Sparrow and various swallows. Take the trail toward the dam, going parallel to the lake with the RV area to your back. In spring, you can find Olive- sided Flycatcher (in treetops) and Orange-crowned Warblers (in the brush). Both Rock and Canyon Wren have been seen along this trail. The Rock Wren even comes down out of the hilltop boulders to feed around the houses above the lake. Western Grebes frequent this deeper end of the lake outside the breeding season.

Emigrant Lake

For birding the rest of Emigrant Lake by foot, bike or car, return to OR 66. Set your trip odometer to .00 where the entrance road joins OR 66. The mileages given in this section assume that you've done that.

OR 66, 0.6 miles (from Emigrant Lake entrance road intersection). Just south of the mailbox for 5825, take the dirt road on your left, heading east. It runs along the top of a steep-sided berm. Below the road level, on your left, is a berry tangle with aged apple trees. Here are California Quail, Spotted Towhee and Scrub-Jay. In winter you should find sparrows: Fox, Lincoln's, Golden-crowned, White-crowned and resident Song. Cedar Waxwings love the fruit they find in this thicket. In August, this brushy area will harbor Black-headed Grosbeaks and Western Tanager as they prepare for migration. Some falls Lewis's Woodpeckers gather here to feed. I've seen Pacific-slope and Willow Flycatchers here on passage in late summer. On your right, you overlook the marshy edge of one finger of the reservoir. In wet winters the water will reach to the bottom of the road's berm. By early autumn—before the rains begin—it will have receded a hundred yards or more. Green Herons hunt here, nesting in the willows along the lake's western high-water shoreline. They do not winter here.

At the end of this short road is a parking lot and toilet. Nearby is the pioneer cemetery, with graves dating back to the 1850s. In summer look for Ash-throated Flycatcher; Western Kingbird may be found here. Year-round birds in this spot include Oak Titmouse, Spotted Towhee, Lesser Goldfinch, Western Bluebird, Scrub-Jay, and Bushtit. Winter birds include Juncos and Golden-crowned Sparrows. Spring migrants may include various warblers, Warbling Vireo and American Goldfinch.

The summer gulls are usually Ring-billed. Occasionally a Caspian Tern will pause on passage. Usually a few Common Loons stop on the lake in September. At any time this can be a good raptor watching spot. Here I've seen the ubiquitous Red-tailed Hawk, also Red-shouldered Hawk, White-tailed Kite, Peregrine, Bald Eagle, Golden Eagle, wintering Merlin and Prairie Falcon (taking a cold bath). From March through October, look for Turkey Vulture and Osprey. Look south toward the oak-covered knolls for perching Bald Eagles. The eagles also frequently stand right along the water line far away from the nearest humans. Especially in fall and winter, check the shoreline and lake for peeps, dowitchers, Spotted Sandpiper, ducks, grebes, Great Egret, Tundra Swan, Snow and Cackling Geese. The geese also graze the adjacent pastures along OR 66.

1 mile. At about a mile along OR 66 from the zeroing point, a dirt road leaves OR 66 and runs down toward the lake shore. In summer this road is passable. It will take you near the lake's receding edge, dropping as water is drained off the reservoir for irrigation. The road is not suitable for low-slung cars. The willows and brush in the draws can attract numerous wintering birds. Watch wires and fences for Western Kingbird in summer and late spring.

1.4 miles. Here you will see another dirt road on your left, next to a row of mailboxes. This road goes down to a gravel parking lot with a toilet building. The road is locally known as Quarry Road as it leads to a defunct quarry on the shore of the lake. The brush here harbors sparrows and both towhee species found at this elevation. It's the best spot around Emigrant Lake for California Towhee. The Spotted Towhee is everywhere around the lake. The oaks and scrub also have Acorn Woodpecker, Western Bluebird, White-breasted Nuthatch, Oak Titmouse and Lesser Goldfinch. The predominant chickadee in this area is the Black-capped at low elevation, but Chestnut-backed may occur in winter. Flickers and sparrows should be around in winter. One winter I found a vagrant Phainopepla in the oaks here. In summer you may find Ash-throated Flycatcher. Walk toward the lake and expect both Green (spring and summer) and Blue Heron. There are at least two small heronries in the vicinity. Great Egrets show up in late fall. In fall the dried lake bed above the waterline attracts passing American Pipit flocks. The edge of the irrigation-lowered lake will harbor shorebirds on their southward migration in August and September: Western, Baird's, Pectoral and Least Sandpiper, Spotted Sandpiper and Semipalmated Plover are regular birds of passage. Some years, Red-necked Phalarope stop here.

The trail that leads north from this parking lot to the oak-covered knoll passes along the steep, treacherous edge of a rock quarry. The quarry will be on your right (east side) as you head up the knoll toward its crest. There's always water in this quarry, even when a land bridge cuts it off from the main reservoir. Quietly check it for fishing Belted Kingfisher any time and for more secretive ducks in fall and winter. Green-winged Teal, American Wigeon and Ruddy Ducks are most often at this shallow end. Bald Eagles often use the taller oaks on this hill to scan the lake for fish or for Osprey to steal from. You might see White-tailed Kite hunting in this area as well.

At **1.8 mile** you'll see Old Siskiyou Highway coming in on your right. This road winds southerly up through the forest toward I-5 Exit 6 and Siskiyou Pass, another two thousand feet up in elevation. In winter Varied Thrush can be spotted in densely shaded spots along the roadside. On your left, Old Siskiyou Highway dead-ends at traffic barriers and disappears beneath willows and eventually the lake surface. As you face north along this short piece of abandoned roadbed, there is a dense tangle of feral hedge roses on your right. Because of this, the stub road is now called "Rosebud Lane" by local birders. Among the roses you may find finches and sparrows in winter, bush rabbits and California Quail year-round. In summer and fall, walk beneath the willows to the open land beyond. In autumn "Rosebud Lane" leads through the willows into the dried mudflats. This gives you great viewing of the shallow end of the lake. Migrant grebes, terns, gulls and even Common Loon are most likely in this area. Migrant shorebirds found along the lake here can include Solitary and Pectoral Sandpiper. The willow thickets may harbor several Green Herons at one time in spring and summer. They migrate south for winter.

There's a trail that begins at the old farm shed along the abandoned road and heads east toward Hat Creek with its riparian trees. South of OR 66 here both Red-shouldered Hawks and White-tailed Kites have nested. Bewick's Wrens inhabit the willow thickets around the lake and the creek that flows through this area. There is a small Blue Heron rookery about a quarter mile south among the trees on a hillock there. Just east of the creek behind the houses there is a small pond that shelters Bufflehead and other wintering waterfowl.

2.4 miles (OR 66 Milepost 7) At 2.4 miles, watch the open fields for Western Meadowlark, Western Bluebird, Lesser Goldfinch and Western Kingbird in spring and summer. Red-tailed Hawks hunt here. California Ground Squirrels and Black-tailed Jackrabbit abound.

2.8 miles. Turn left onto **Old Greensprings Highway Spur,** another road that disappears beneath the lake. It is 0.7 miles from the turn off

OR 66 to the parking lot and toilet building that sit just above the high water mark. In late summer you can drive all the way to the lowered lake level. This is a good spot for winter waterfowl viewing. I've seen Merlin and Tundra Swan along the shoreline, and Lewis's Woodpecker on the oak-covered slopes uphill. The hedges along the houses hold California Quail, Western Scrub-Jay, sparrows, California Towhee, finches, goldfinches. Western Bluebirds are regular in the open fields. Ground squirrels scurry along the road in mild or hot weather. If you walk south along the lake and pass through the willow thickets you may approach some of the migrating shorebirds in fall. This southern end of the lake is frequented by resident Common Mergansers year-round. Wintering Merlin and Prairie Falcon are most likely along this shore of the lake. In late summer and fall the lake level is low enough to allow you to walk south (left from end of submerged road) through willow thickets and get close to the rich mudflats where many migrants gather in August to October. I have gotten within fifty yards of loafing Caspian Terns and feeding Pectoral Sandpiper with a quiet approach along the shore.

Back on OR 66 at 2.8 miles, you will see an aluminum gate (southeast of OR 66) facing across the highway from the entrance to Old Greensprings Spur. If you walk past this gate you will be immediately in a more arid brushy habitat. The dirt road leads to an old, abandoned section of OR 66. Here you may encounter Blue-gray Gnatcatcher in spring or summer as well as the usual mix of dry oak forest inhabitants. A small swale choked with willows attracts migrating *Empidonax* flycatchers and warblers.

3.2 miles. Songer Wayside. Here is another old road disappearing beneath the lake's surface. What you'll find: a parking lot and toilets. Good views of the southeast finger of the lake. Red-shouldered Hawks and Acorn Woodpeckers are regular here. Also Common Mergansers may retreat to this part of the lake if it's windy or there are too many boats in the broader waters. Check the rock outcroppings far above the lake for possible perched Golden Eagles surveying their kingdom.

3.5 miles. Pull off on the lake side for a view of the southeastern finger of the lake. This is a good spot for diving ducks in fall and winter.

4.3 miles. Turn left here onto another section of the **Old Greensprings Highway** just after (east of) the OR 66 bridge over Emigrant Creek. This road runs about a half mile along the shore of the easternmost finger of Emigrant Lake. Quietly check beneath the bridge for American Dipper.

The willows along lower Emigrant Creek here and at the shallow end of the lake attract migrants in spring and fall. I've seen dozens of Western Tanager here as they begin to collect for fall migration. In the fields upslope, look for Lark Sparrow, Western Meadowlark, Lesser Goldfinch, Western Kingbirds and Bluebirds. In the willows, Downy Woodpecker, and Bewick's Wren are year-round. Spring and summer bring Western Wood-Pewee and Bullock's Oriole. About 100 yards along this segment of Old Greensprings Highway the pavement ends. Look due west (straight ahead) for a nest platform used most years by Osprey.

4.6 miles. There will be an intersection on your right (south side) with Buckhorn Springs Road. This dirt road parallels Emigrant Creek for some distance. At the bridges, look for Dipper. Along the road, Tree and Barn Swallow, Western Bluebird, Kingbird, Acorn Woodpecker, Black- headed Grosbeak, Lesser and American Goldfinch, Pine Siskin (winter), and White-headed Woodpecker.

To get back to I-5, retrace your route, or continue east on OR 66 for the **Cascade Mountain Loop** in reverse, or counter-clockwise. The following entry for Cascade Mountain Loop describes the route from I-5 in a clockwise direction (see *Cascade Mountain Loop* map).

I-5 Exit 11 or Exit 14. Cascade Mountain Loop. This loop can easily take half a day or longer, depending on your birding pace. If you're coming from the south and leave I-5 at Exit 11, turn right onto Siskiyou Boulevard, a mile further on turn right again on Crowson Road, go under I-5 and take a left onto OR 66. Go about 0.3 mile north (left) and turn east (right) onto Dead Indian Memorial Road.

If you are coming from the north, you will need to take Exit 14. Take the overpass left across I-5 and head east on OR 66. In half a mile you will come to the foot of Dead Indian Memorial Road. Turn left.

In addition to roadside birding, along the way there are side roads, trails, boat rental and ramp, campsites, RV hook-ups, cafés, toilets and picnic grounds, but most of these public facilities are around the mountain lakes over fifteen miles from I-5 Exit 14. This route will take you from about 2,200 feet of elevation to over 5,000 feet, so expect a temperature drop of ten degrees or more in any season. The mountain lakes can be quite windy on summer afternoons.

Cascade Mountain Loop

From either direction, as you turn onto Dead Indian Memorial Road, set your trip odometer to .00. The mileage points given in this section assume that you've done that. We will travel in a clockwise direction.

1 mile. Dead Indian Memorial Road here parallels Walker Creek on the right, with steep and grassy slopes on the left. The low-elevation riparian forest includes alder, oak, cottonwood and willow. Oak Titmouse, Bullock's Oriole, Bushtit and Spotted Towhee are among birds that nest in the trees. On the grassy hillsides you may spot Western Kingbird and Lark Sparrow in summer. Western Meadowlark, Lesser Goldfinch and Western Bluebird are year round. California Quail live where there is dense brush. Some winters there are Black-billed Magpies in this area.

2.8 miles. Here are pull-outs with clear views. Golden Eagles are among possible raptors here. The grasslands can have Western Kingbird, Lesser Goldfinch and Lark Sparrow. California Ground Squirrel may perch on fence posts. Western Scrub-Jay is the dominant species in this mixed habitat.

4.6 miles. Another convenient pull-out, this one overlooks oak woods, and has a view across the valley to Mount Ashland, the tallest peak in the Siskiyou Range. There may be Acorn Woodpecker, Black-headed Grosbeak and Chipping Sparrow in the oaks.

5.2 miles. Here there's a pull-out on a grassy knoll dotted with gnarled oaks. Park next to the aged wooden cattle chute and corral

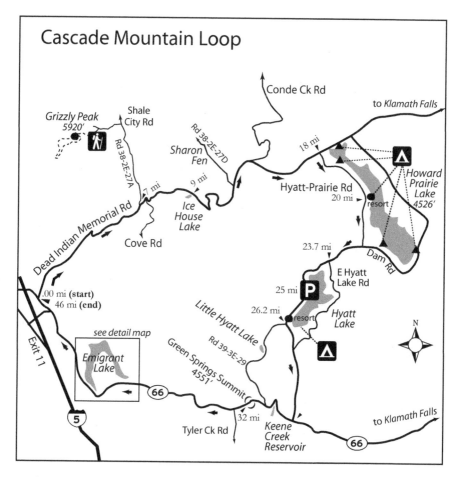

Cascade Mountain Loop

and walk around. Winter birds I've seen here include Northern Shrike, Lewis's Woodpecker and Northern Pygmy-Owl. Summer birds here can be Lark and Chipping Sparrow, Ash-throated Flycatcher in the trees, Western Kingbird and Violet-green Swallow who both nest in cavities in the old trees. Year-round birds in the area include Western Bluebird and Meadowlarks.

7 miles. Shale City Road heads north from the left side of Dead Indian Memorial Road. In this area you may find Common Nighthawk (spring), Sooty Grouse, Hermit Warbler and Lewis's Woodpecker (winter). If you head up Shale City Road, conifers begin to dominate the woods. Here are Northern Pygmy-Owl, Pileated Woodpecker, Mountain Quail and Western Wood-Pewee. About 4 miles up the road, a gravel road in spring and summer will take you another mile to the trailhead for Grizzly Peak. It is closed during snow season, usually December–May. In late spring, walking this dirt road may afford you sounds of Mountain Quail calling. The hike to the top from the Grizzly Peak Trailhead is a 5-mile round-trip. That mountain's elevation reaches 5,922 feet on this eastern front of the Cascades. It has open meadows that often hold Great Gray Owl. There is limited data on eBird for this mountain but species that have been seen here include Gray Jay, Green-tailed Towhee, Red-breasted Sapsucker, Townsend's Solitaire, Cassin's Finch and Gray-crowned Rosy-Finch. One morning in August I was pleased by dense flocks of migrating warblers and a small group of Ruffed Grouse feeding next to the trail. Wildflowers are prolific here in spring. If you drive the whole lonely Shale City Road loop in late summer look for Mountain Quail feeding along the road.

7.3 miles. Here Cove Road drops down to the right. Cove Road has no outlet apart from Dead Indian Memorial Road. It winds more than two miles along the steep slopes. In this open woodland along Cove Road there are Ruffed Grouse, Spotted Towhee and, in summer, Western Tanager. In damp spots check for Pacific-slope Flycatcher and MacGillivray's Warbler.

8 miles. In this high elevation oak forest Lewis's Woodpecker is possible in winter. Expect Acorn Woodpecker and California Quail. Listen for Mountain Quail on steep slopes. Where elderberry and ceanothus are near the road listen and look for Lazuli Bunting from May through summer. They like these brushy mountain meadows.

9 miles. On the right hand side of the road there is a wide gravel pull-out. At the bottom of the steep cliff is a tarn, Ice House Lake. The area often has a variety of forest birds in spring: Red-breasted Sapsucker, Western Tanager, calling Mountain Quail, thrumming Ruffed Grouse on the slope across the pond from the road.

10 miles. There's a pullout on the right (south) side here next to a stream. The steep slope left of the road may have nesting Green-tailed Towhee and Western Wood-Pewee. Check this shady creekside for MacGillivray's Warbler in spring.

13 miles. The pullout here overlooks a mountain meadow below. Elk are possible here. Birds in this habitat include Lazuli Bunting, Western Tanager, Spotted Towhee and Steller's Jay. Above the ridge to the north of Dead Indian Memorial Road I have seen soaring Goshawk. You can take the dirt road up the ridge on the left (north) side of the road. This is Conde Creek Road. In winter this area can have flocks of Cassin's Finch, Red Crossbill and Evening Grosbeak. About a mile up Conde Creek Road there's a clearing where you can park to look and listen. Williamson's Sapsucker, Green-tailed Towhee and Lazuli Bunting have nested here regularly.

16 miles. Dead Indian Memorial Road takes you into the grassy meadows of Howard Prairie. This area above 4000 feet, is snow covered November until April most years. In spring, many Wilson's Snipe winnow before nesting. Vesper Sparrows nest here, at the southwestern extreme of their range. Both sparrow and snipe may sit on roadside fence posts in May. Raptors possible here include Goshawk, Bald Eagle, Red-shouldered Hawk and American Kestrel. Some winters a Rough-legged Hawk may appear here. Sandhill Cranes stop here on migration; one crane family always nests in the area and feeds in these meadows. They are often present starting in March with snow still covering the ground. The cranes are gone by the end of September usually.

17.2 miles. On the left (north), a narrow dirt road runs alongside an irrigation ditch. The ditch is the Conde Creek Canal while the road has no official name. It can provide good birding in spring: Green-tailed Towhee, woodpeckers, Lazuli Bunting, flycatchers, Red-breasted Nuthatch, Chipping Sparrow.

17.3 miles. Here is the intersection of Dead Indian Memorial Road and Hyatt Prairie Road. Stop and use your scope if you have one. Mountain Bluebirds regularly use the bird box on the large wooden sign southwest of the intersection. Expect Vesper and Savannah Sparrows and Sandhill Cranes. Harrier is possible over the lakeside marshes southeast of the intersection. Along the shore of Howard Prairie Lake there may be geese, ducks and shorebirds. I've seen a half dozen species of shorebirds here in September, including Black-bellied Plover and Long-billed Curlew. Osprey and Bald Eagle are regular at Howard Prairie and Hyatt lakes in warm months. A flock of non-breeding White Pelicans summer here.

If you continue east for just over a mile on Dead Indian Memorial Road, on your right you will see **Lily Glen Campground,** outfitted for horses and riders. What you'll find: There are toilets and trails here, and fees are charged for parking and camping. This is good spot to look for Common Merganser on the lake, Mountain Bluebird (especially near the horse manure piles), Vesper Sparrow, Hermit Warbler and Cassin's Finch. There may be a large Cliff Swallow colony here. In late afternoon check all meadows in this area for possible Great Gray Owls.

18 miles. Turn right (south) onto Hyatt-Prairie Road. Here's a cattle crossing with a gravel pullout on the left (east). This is another good spot for scoping the lakeshore and intervening wet meadowland. White Pelicans are around the lake in warm months. They do not nest here. The Sandhill Cranes that nest locally may be foraging in this meadow. Canada Geese will be abundant in warm months.

19.3 miles. Grizzly Creek Campground. What you'll find: hiking trails, a boat ramp, camp sites, picnic areas and toilets. Fees are charged for daily use and camping. This is a good spot for Steller's Jay, Mountain Chickadee, Hermit Warbler and Yellow Warbler in the lakeshore willows. Western Wood-Pewee and Red-breasted Nuthatch nest in forest. The gulls over the lake are most likely Ring-billed with a pale mantle. The tree squirrels at this elevation are the small, dark brown Douglas Squirrel.

20 miles. The entrance to **Howard Prairie Lake Resort** is on the left (east). The resort and its facilities are open from April 15th through October 31st. What you'll find: toilets, camp sites, hiking trails, RV camp, boat rental and ramp, swimming, fishing, dogs allowed, a store and a café. Elevation here is about 4,500 feet. Golden-mantled Groundsquirrels are abundant here and often come beg at the outdoor dining area of the café or at campsites.

In spring this can be a magical birding spot. I've seen a Hermit Warbler on the ground next to the café, a Mountain Chickadee nesting in a box on the patio, and a White Pelican loafing on the boat dock. In fall this lake can attract many interesting birds on migration or dispersal: Red-breasted Merganser far from the ocean, Common Gallinule far from its range, Clark's Grebe in fall, warblers and shorebirds on their way south. Gray Jays have been seen in the campground north of the café. Regular birds here include Common Merganser, Osprey, Bald Eagle (nest on the island northeast of the marina), Western Tanager, Pileated Woodpecker, Red-breasted Sapsucker, Dusky Flycatcher, Western Wood-Pewee, Vaux's Swift, Golden-crowned Kinglets, Spotted Sandpiper on the lakeshore. During autumn migration the variety of ducks and shorebirds increases. Caspian Tern are regular late summer birds. Juncos are abundant in the forest here.

It is faster to return back the way you came if you want to return to I-5. But if you continue south on Hyatt-Prairie Road you can complete the Cascades Loop.

Continuing on the Cascade Mountain Loop

If you continue on this Cascade Loop, set your trip odometer to .00 at the intersection of Howard Prairie Lake Resort entrance and Hyatt-Prairie Road. The mileage points given in this section assume that you've done that.

1.1 miles. At this point the road on your left– appropriately named Howard Prairie Dam Access Road–takes you to Howard Prairie Lake Dam. It is also FS 38-3E-42 (Forest Service designation). About a mile down this dam road is **Willow Point Campground.** What you'll find: toilets, camp sites, a trail and a boat launch. There is a small marshy area near the campground entrance and good forest birding at the campground. Look for Dusky Flycatcher, Western Tanager, woodpeckers, Spotted Sandpiper, ducks, Bald Eagle and Osprey. Further along this road open areas may have nesting White-headed Woodpeckers in logged or more open areas. If you want to continue northeast on this road arm yourself with a good local road map.

3.7 miles. East Hyatt Lake Road is a dead-end road that goes southeast past numerous cabins and some meadows that may have a Great Gray Owl.

3.8 miles. Buck's Divide Road heads west into the national forest. Hyatt Lake reservoir is on your left (east). On or above the lake you may see Osprey, Bald Eagle, Common Merganser, Double-crested Cormorant, and feeding swallows. If you walk or drive slowly along Buck's Divide Road, you may find Great Gray Owl in small meadows, flycatchers (including Hammond's), Cassin's Vireo, Hermit Warbler, Mountain Chickadee and House Wren. Hyatt Lake is just over 5,000 feet in elevation.

5 miles. Marked by a simple sign bearing only an image of binoculars, there's a small paved pullout on the left (east of the road) with a couple picnic tables and a toilet. The parking lot is only a couple feet above the elevation of Hyatt Lake when it's full. The forest here is dominated by ponderosa pine and Douglas-fir with some incense cedar. Willows may cluster along the lakeshore. I've seen Short-tailed Weasel hunting around the parking area. Just offshore is a large dead tree used by a nesting colony of Double-crested Cormorants. They're so close to shore you can hear their grunts and snorts. Spotted Sandpiper may be along the shoreline. Next to the lake and across the road in the woods you may find Williamson's Sapsucker, Cassin's Vireo and Yellow-rumped Warbler.

6 miles. The dirt road on the left goes to Hyatt Lake Resort. Some of the buildings may have bird feeders in warm weather.

6.2 miles. The unpaved road on the right (west) is Old Hyatt Lake Road (Forest Service 39-3E-29). It runs downhill next to Keene Creek, the natural outlet for Hyatt Lake. This is a good birding route after the snow melts. Little Hyatt Lake is about 2 miles from Hyatt Lake Road, and then it's another 3 miles before Old Hyatt Prairie Road ends back on OR 66.

Along here you can expect Olive-sided and Dusky Flycatcher, Cassin's and Warbling Vireo, Mountain Chickadee, MacGillivray's Warbler in willow thickets, Dipper nesting near the dam of Little Hyatt Lake, Mountain Bluebirds and Vesper Sparrow in meadows, nesting Osprey, Lazuli Bunting in brushy areas, Cassin's Finch, possible Mountain Quail.

10 miles. Hyatt Lake Road ends at the Greensprings Resort on OR 66. What you'll find: lodging and a café. There is also a visitors center here for the Cascade-Siskiyou National Monument. Heading left (east) on OR 66 takes you toward the Klamath Basin and upper Klamath River. Heading right (west) takes you downhill toward I-5 and Ashland, OR and will complete the loop drive.

11 miles. Now westbound on OR 66 you soon come to **Keene Creek Reservoir**. It attracts ducks on migration. I've seen Barrow's Goldeneye here along with Common Goldeneye, Lesser Scaup and Bufflehead. The highway is kept open all winter but the reservoir may freeze over.

12 miles. At **Green Springs Summit**, you've reached an elevation of 4,551 feet. From here you can see Mount Ashland to the west, and Pilot Rock to the southwest along the Oregon-California border. Just beyond this summit on the left, Tyler Creek Road winds downhill through forest and farms to Buckhorn Springs Road just south of Emigrant Lake. If you descend Tyler Creek Road from conifer to oak woodlands to grasslands there are numerous good birding spots, especially a roadside pond.

Western Wood-Pewee, Lesser Goldfinch, Warbling and Cassin's Vireo, Spotted Towhee, and Rufous Hummingbird are here as well. If you turn south on Buckhorn Springs Road (at the foot of Tyler Creek Road) it climbs southward into dry brush land where the Blue-gray Gnatcatcher nests. It's near the northern end of its range here. Orange-crowned Warbler, Lazuli Bunting and Rufous Hummingbird frequent the same brush, which is largely manzanita and ceanothus.

As you head further down on OR 66 toward Ashland and I-5, watch the highway mileposts. Between MP 14 and 13 there is a vertical rock face blasted away for the roadbed. On the downslope side of the road is pullout with a high chain-link fence to prevent you from going over the edge. This rock face may have breeding Rock Wren. Between MP 12 and 11, there is another pullout on the downslope side of the road. This particular pullout has auto access blocked by a metal gate. If you walk the area you can find scavengers ranging in size from Black-billed Magpies to Bald Eagle. This is where the highway crews often dump roadkill deer carcasses over the steep side of the pullout.

17 Miles (Milepost 10) OR 66. Here is a large dirt pullout across from a farm gate and large utility poles. In this open oak forest in the autumn, Goshawk is possible, as well as Western Bluebird and Meadowlark, White-breasted Nuthatch, Acorn Woodpecker and Chipping Sparrow. In some winters, Lewis's Woodpeckers congregate here. Black-billed Magpies may be on the hillsides here in fall and winter. Golden Eagles cruise these slopes in search of jackrabbits and other prey.

Continue west on OR 66 to the starting point at Dead Indian Memorial Road. From there, retrace your route to I-5, or cross over I-5 at Exit 14 and head into Ashland on Ashland Boulevard.

I-5 Exit 14. If you're southbound, exit here onto OR 66 east for **Emigrant Lake** and/or the **Cascade Mountain Loop.** (See I-5 Exit 11 entry). If you go west onto **Ashland Boulevard** you can get to birding spots in and around the town of Ashland.

About 1.5 miles from I-5 on Ashland Boulevard you can turn left at the first signal onto **Tolman Creek Road** and head south for some birding in the Siskiyou Mountains. (You can also reach Tolman Creek Road via I-5 Exit 11.) You will be driving up the north slopes of Mount Ashland.

Tolman Creek Road

If you take Tolman Creek Road, set your trip odometer to .00 when you cross Siskiyou Boulevard. The mileage points given in this section assume that you've done that.

After Tolman Creek Road crosses Siskiyou Boulevard, it climbs past housing into more rural habitat, passes a large rock quarry on the right (at 1.1 miles) and then climbs steeply to over 3,500 feet. If you have a good map and good weather you can take this route up the northeast slope to Mount Ashland. Don't try it without a dependable map, such as a Rogue River National Forest Map, because the roads are poorly marked and maintained and you might get lost where there is no cell service. This road (having become Forest Service 2080) connects with Mount Ashland Road at the Bull Gap parking area (see entry for I-5 Exit 6).

2.3 miles. There are pullouts on the left with treetop views on the right. This is a fine spot for Calliope Hummingbird in spring. They like short trees and dense, blooming manzanita, which cover the steep slope here. Manzanita is the evergreen shrub with round, pale green leaves. The Calliope is the smallest breeding bird in North America. Other birds likely here include Olive-sided Flycatcher in spring, Western Tanager, Band-tailed Pigeon, Black-headed Grosbeak and Nashville Warbler.

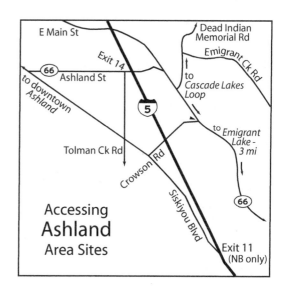

2.7 miles. At 2.7 miles from Siskiyou Boulevard there's a paved pullout on the left. Park here and walk the manzanita-lined road. The forest here is largely oak and madrone, with occasional tall ponderosa or Douglas-fir. Birds to expect in spring and summer include Calliope Hummingbird, Band-tailed Pigeon, Western Tanager, Nashville Warbler, Bushtit, Spotted Towhee, Blue-gray Gnatcatcher and Steller's Jay. Some winters there are Varied Thrush feeding on the roadside.

3.1 miles. Here is an iron gate, closed when the upper road is snowed under. You are now on Forest Service Road 2080 and entering the Rogue River National Forest. At 3.2 miles is a trailhead where you can park and walk up into the forest. At 3.7 miles the pavement ends and the forest thickens. Here are Hermit Thrush singing in spring, Red-breasted Sapsucker, possible Pacific-slope Flycatcher in the wet draws. After several miles, FS 2080 ends at Mount Ashland Road at the Bull Gap pullout (about 6,100 feet elevation), about 2 miles down from the ski lodge parking area.

Into Ashland. After leaving the freeway at Exit 14, continue west on Ashland Boulevard until it merges into Siskiyou Boulevard. Turn right onto Siskiyou Boulevard to visit birding spots in Ashland. You will pass Southern Oregon University on your left.

Proceed a few blocks to the stop light at Mountain Boulevard; turn right again and drive about half mile for **North Mountain Park.** After you crest a small hill, you'll be able to see downhill to the large baseball diamonds. After you enter the parking lot, on your right you'll see a Victorian house with a porch facing the parking lot. Park as near to the Victorian house as possible. The Victorian house is the City of Ashland's Nature Center, where you can get a wildlife checklist for the park. On the porch is a frequently updated list of birds and wildlife seen in and around North Mountain Park.

What you'll find: hiking trails, toilets, recreation areas, children's play area, a herb garden and a nature trail. There is a bird feeding station in winter and early spring. The park consists of 38 acres along Bear Creek, and there are a few more acres of open space along the creek across Mountain Boulevard. That is the town's Riverwalk Open Space. Both areas have small ponds that attract Black Phoebe, Green Heron in summer, Sora and Virginia Rail in fall. Birding here can be rewarding in any season. EBird shows 150 species recorded in this park. Green Heron, Yellow-breasted Chat, Wrentit, California Quail, Western Kingbird, Acorn Woodpecker, Western Wood-Pewee, Warbling Vireo, Bewick's Wren, Black-headed Grosbeak, Bullock's Oriole, Yellow Warbler, Tree Swallow, California and Spotted Towhee, Anna's Hummingbird and Western Screech-Owl are among the breeding species here. Bushtits also nest here. Their woven nests are shaped like teardrops with a single, central strand of grass connected to the limb above. The woven nests of orioles here have two points of connection to the supporting limb. Oak Titmouse are regular visitors. Perhaps the star of the avian show: vocal Yellow-breasted Chat along Bear Creek and the small ponds in the park. They arrive in early May.

In fall and spring any of the possible warblers, flycatchers or vireos may show up. Raptors in winter can include Merlin, Cooper's and Sharp-shinned Hawks and White-tailed Kite. All the local finches are possible here including Cassin's in winter. One winter a Rusty Blackbird joined the neighborhood Icterid flock. Also you may pish out a wintering Pacific Wren. Golden-crowned Sparrows crowd the ground beneath the feeders in fall and winter. Across Mountain Boulevard, along the creek, there is open space with three ponds. Sora are occasional here. In early summer you may see Common Nighthawks at dusk fly-catching high above Bear Creek. And watch for Vaux's Swift among the daytime swallows. Lesser Goldfinch are abundant all year, while Pine Siskins and Purple Finch are winter visitors. Check the ball diamonds' lawn for possible birds of interest. Besides the usual Killdeer, Canada Geese

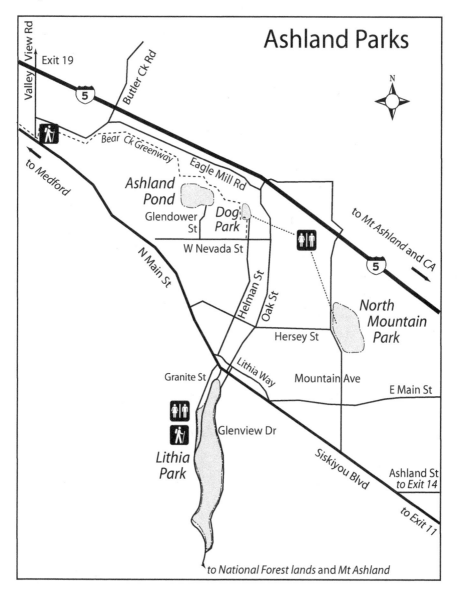

and Robins, one winter a handful of Wilson's Snipe decided to occupy deep left field. Because of the rich habitat, almost any species can show up: Lewis's Woodpecker in May, Evening Grosbeak and Olive-sided, Willow, Dusky, Hammond's and Pacific-slope Flycatchers.

Ashland Pond is a little-known gem of a place. This rich little birding spot can be reached from either Exit 14 or Exit 19. (See *Ashland Parks* map.) At the metal gate where the trail to the pond begins, there are often sparrows and finches in the brambles and willows. The whole loop around the pond is less than half a mile. Here Ashland Creek flows parallel to Bear Creek, forming a damp, lush riparian corridor before the two streams converge at the far end of the pond. A small stone divergence dam sends Ashland Creek water flowing through Ashland Pond in all seasons. What you'll find: There's a trail but no other facilities here on this undeveloped piece of Ashland city park land. Dogs are allowed on leash.

EBird lists over 145 species recorded here, including Redhead, Cinnamon Teal and Eurasian Wigeon. Wood Duck and Hooded Merganser have bred in the vicinity and raised young in the pond. There is a loud and active colony of Acorn Woodpeckers here. Breeding birds include White-breasted Nuthatch, Bullock's Oriole, Black-headed Grosbeak, Bewick's Wren, Wrentit, California Quail, Red-tailed Hawk, Cooper's Hawk, American Kestrel, Northern Flicker and Downy Woodpecker.

In winter there's a *Zonotrichia* flock that often includes White-throated Sparrow in addition to White-crowned and Golden-crowned. In migration, most of the western flycatchers, warblers and vireos are possible here. Waxwings can be abundant in fall, and a Belted Kingfisher usually stays all winter, as the pond rarely freezes solid owing to the flow of creek water. In spring and summer the flock of swallows overhead can be large and often includes some Vaux's Swift. Southbound swallows in fall often feed here at dawn and dusk. Harrier (winter), White-tailed Kite, Merlin (winter) and Red-shouldered Hawk will hunt in this area as well. When Evening Grosbeaks are in the area they may be found in peeping flocks in the trees here.

Muskrat and river otter can be seen here at times. You may notice chewed tree trunks along the creeks–signs of beaver. Their nocturnal habits keep them almost invisible.

I-5 Exit 19. Bear Creek Greenway and **Ashland Pond.** If you are southbound, take Exit 19 for access to **Bear Creek Greenway** or **Ashland Pond** (see above). Exit 19 is also the quickest (least congested) approach to **Lithia Park**, if you want to find local Dippers. See *Ashland Parks* map for various routes.

For the Greenway, on exiting turn left (south) on Valley View Road. Before crossing the bridge over Bear Creek, turn left onto Eagle Mill Road where you will find a small parking lot just after leaving Valley View Road. The **Bear Creek Greenway** is a paved path along the creek, and thus is popular with local bicycle commuters. It extends along Bear Creek all the way from Ashland to Central Point north of Medford and can be accessed in a number of places. It can be a good place for the usual riparian species. What you'll find here: There are no toilets at the Exit 19 parking area. It is about 2 miles north on the trail from here to Newbry Park, and 2 miles south on the trail to the Ashland Dog Park near Ashland Ponds. Both of these accesses have toilets.

Butler Creek Road. Turn onto Eagle Mill Road from Valley View Road (as above). Drive about 0.5 mile, then go left onto Butler Creek Road. That will take you north on an overpass above I-5, a few hundred yards south of the Exit 19 bridge. See *Bear Creek Greenway* map. Once you reach the farmland beyond the freeway, check the farm pond on your right for wintering ducks. Check the fields and treetops along the road for White-tailed Kite. A pair often hunts here in all seasons. It is best to retrace your path to get back to I-5 once you've birded along Butler Creek Road.

Lithia Park, reached from any of the I-5 Ashland exits but perhaps most easily from Exit 19, runs into the heart of Ashland. See *Ashland Parks* map. There are two species of considerable interest in Lithia Park: Dippers and Wood Ducks. At least two pair of American Dippers nest and reside along Ashland Creek from downtown up into the Siskiyous. Anywhere from the Water Street Bridge upstream to the upper end of Lithia Park, Dippers may be found along Ashland Creek year-round. They may be heard singing even during snowfall. Wood Ducks often gather in significant numbers in Lithia Park's upper duck pond outside of breeding season. The males are in their brightest plumage from

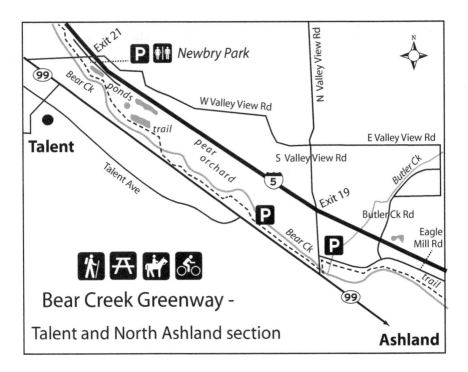

Bear Creek Greenway -

Talent and North Ashland section

January to May. Some winters the irruptive Varied Thrush is common in the most shaded parts of Lithia Park. Some winters Cedar Waxwings can be abundant if the berry crop is good. Red-breasted Sapsucker have nested in Lithia Park.

On the west and south, Lithia Park is bounded by Granite Street. A walk along that street may garner you Wild Turkey, Western Screech-Owl in owl boxes, Band-tailed Pigeon (spring and summer, lured to garden feeders), Black-headed Grosbeak, Steller's Jay and Red-shouldered Hawk. In winter there is often a calling Hutton's Vireo along this street.

MacGillivray's Warbler may be found in the dense brush uphill from the swimming reservoir at the end of the park farthest from the town center. Glenview Road parallels the park's upper east side. Some side trails are accessible from that road and there, Cedar Waxwing, Townsend's Solitaire and Western Bluebird may be found eating madrone berries in fall. Rarely, Mountain Quail are forced down to these trails during heavy winter snows. In the dense underbrush you may find Spotted Towhee, MacGillivray's Warbler, Nashville Warbler in the treetops, and Western Tanager. Check the tops of tallest evergreens for possible Pileated Woodpecker, Golden-crowned Kinglet (winter) and Merlin (winter only).

I-5 Exit 21. Exit here for another section of **Bear Creek Greenway** and **Lynn Newbry Park.** Take an immediate turn south at the west end of the freeway bridge onto Siskiyou View Road to enter the park. What you'll find: toilets, trails, picnic table. The creekside trail here is paved and used heavily by bicyclists. There are also ponds with overgrown borders where shy ducks feel protected. See *Bear Creek Greenway* map.

EBird shows nearly 110 species for this area. Common Mergansers may be seen on Bear Creek; the other waterfowl are found on the ponds. Nesting birds here include Wood Duck, California Quail, American Kestrel, Anna's Hummingbird, Western Wood-Pewee, Black-headed Grosbeak, Bushtit, Bewick's Wren, Wrentit, Bullock's Oriole and Lesser Goldfinch. This can be an especially rewarding place to bird in May when migrants and residents are in song and setting up territories. The most likely wintering waterfowl are Gadwall, Shoveler, Bufflehead, American Wigeon and Ring-necked and Wood Ducks.

I-5 Exit 22. The exit here is for southbound traffic only. It goes to a rest stop that is especially useful when the Siskiyou Pass, about 15 miles further south, is closed during a winter snowstorm. Truckers and motorists may stop here until the highway is reopened, usually within a few hours. In summer you can walk across the grassy field toward Bear Creek and bird the riparian strip there for Bullock's Oriole, Black-headed Grosbeak, Acorn Woodpecker.

I-5 Exit 30. North Medford. If you exit here you can drive about 5 miles to a somewhat rough, weed choked but dependable spot on the north edge of the Medford airport for wintering **Short-eared Owls.** You can also get there from Exit 33. See *North Medford* map. The field where these owls winter is full of dense grass, teasel and severe burr-carrying weeds. Wear an outer layer that does not pick up burrs. The soil is sticky with clay and can form heavy layers on the bottom of your boots. It is best if there are several people as you can fan out and work across the field toward the airport to flush these diurnal owls. Do not have a coronary if you flush a loud, wing-slapping Ring-necked

Pheasant. Western Meadowlark, Harrier, Western Bluebirds, various sparrows and an occasional Say's Phoebe are other birds you may find here November to March.

I-5 Exit 33. Exit here for several birding spots in the north Medford/ Central Point area of Jackson County: **Bear Creek Greenway, Ken Denman Wildlife Area, Lower Table Rock, Touvelle State Recreation Area, Whetstone Savannah.** What you'll find: Touvelle has picnic areas, trails, toilets, and an entrance fee is charged. Denman also charges an entrance fee; toilets are near the headquarters, and there are numerous trails. Lower Table Rock has toilets and trails. Whetstone—owned by the Nature Conservancy—has only vague trails, nothing more. The Greenway is only a trail, but commercial services with facilities are adjacent to the parking area.

This section of **Bear Creek Greenway,** in Central Point, was regularly birded for years. See *North Medford* map for access points. The eBird list here runs to over 120 species. In addition to brush and riparian habitat along the creek, there are gravel ponds that attract wintering ducks. If you go south on this trail there's Mingus Pond with a roofed viewing overlook. Some species seen here over the years include Blue-winged Teal, Canvasback, Black-crowned Night-heron in winter, Northern Harrier, White-tailed Kite, Peregrine, Prairie Falcon, Merlin, both yellowlegs, Vaux's Swift, Rufous Hummingbird, Harris's Sparrow and Great-tailed Grackle. Resident species include Wrentit, Bushtit, Spotted Towhee and Lesser Goldfinch.

For the other birding sites, see *North Medford* map for access and *Table Rocks and Rogue River* map for details.

Denman State Wildlife Area. This state wildlife management unit is part of a complex nature preserve. Part of it is open and accessible, some lies behind locked gates. There are wetlands, riverside forest, grasslands and many choices of trail in nearly 1,800 acres of open space on both sides of the Rogue River. The northern portion of Denman connects to Touvelle State Park via trails. What you'll find: There are toilets at

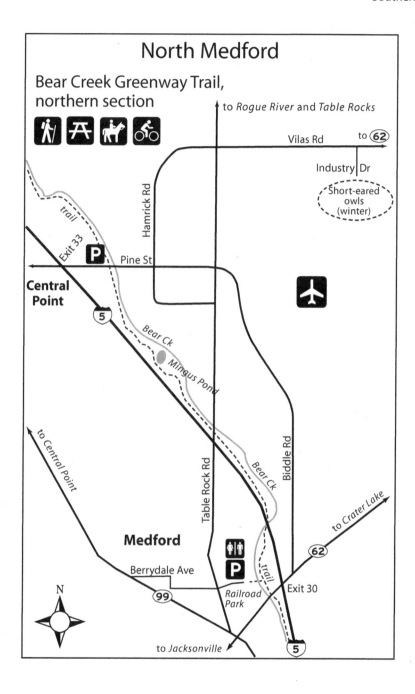

North Medford

Bear Creek Greenway Trail, northern section

to *Rogue River* and *Table Rocks*

Vilas Rd   to 62

Industry Dr

Short-eared owls (winter)

Hamrick Rd

trail

Exit 33

P

Pine St

Central Point

5

Bear Ck

Mingus Pond

Biddle Rd

Bear Ck

Table Rock Rd

to *Central Point*

Medford

Berrydale Ave

to Crater Lake

62

N

99

P

Railroad Park

Exit 30

trail

to *Jacksonville*

5

Denman in the Whetstone Pond parking area which is adjacent to the headquarters building. An entry fee is charged.

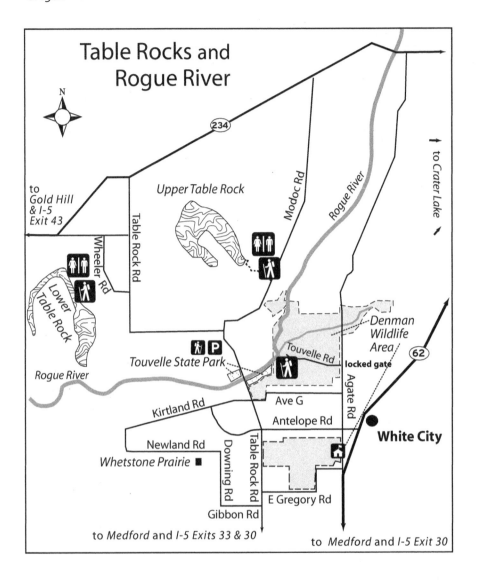

Table Rocks and Rogue River

Over 130 species have been reported to eBird from portions of Denman. In winter the waterfowl can be thick in the ponds and marshes; seventeen species of waterfowl have been reported, including Cinnamon Teal in spring. This is good area to find Osprey in summer, Merlin in winter. Great Horned Owl and Pileated Woodpecker nest on Hall Tract near Little Butte Creek. Resident species include Acorn Woodpecker, Black Phoebe, Oak Titmouse, Bushtit, Brown Creeper, Marsh Wren, Spotted and California Towhee, Western Meadowlark and Lesser Goldfinch. Tree Swallows are especially abundant along the

Rogue River, even over-wintering some years. Lewis's Woodpecker and Harrier are possible in winter.

Lower Table Rock. This is part of a preserve of over 4,500 acres that includes nearby Upper Table Rock. The area is jointly owned by the Nature Conservancy and the Bureau of Land Management. What you'll find: Facilities are limited to toilets (at the parking lot) and trails with occasional benches. Dogs are not allowed.

The Lower Table Rock trail from the parking lot to the rim of this butte is 1.75 miles. The change in elevation is from about 780 feet to just over 2,000 feet. The trails and expanse of the flat-topped table rock afford several more miles of hiking and birding. The butte harbors numerous vernal pools that are home to rare flora as well as numerous amphibians and birds. From the east and south sides of the butte you have great views of the Rogue River Valley below.

EBird shows 110 species for Lower Table Rock. The lower end of the trail moves through open oak savannah. Here you may find Ash-throated Flycatcher (spring), Western Bluebird, Blue-gray Gnatcatcher, Western Meadowlarks in the grassy areas and nearby farmland, Acorn and Lewis's Woodpeckers (winter), California and Spotted Towhee, Oak Titmouse and White-breasted Nuthatch. Table Rock is not far from the northern edge of the California Towhee's range. They can be readily found here feeding on the ground. Violet-green and Tree Swallows often fly along the butte's face, taking advantage of the updrafts. Turkey Vulture and Osprey often soar past in spring and summer. Before you reach the rim, the trail takes you through dense oak and madrone woodlands with scattered large conifers. Year-round birds here include Bewick's Wren and Anna's Hummingbird. In spring this forest can be alive with bird song: Hutton's, Cassin's and Warbling Vireo (a vireo trifecta), Nashville Warbler, Lesser and American Goldfinch, Western Wood-Pewee and Pacific-slope Flycatcher, Blue-gray Gnatcatcher near the northern edge of its breeding range. On top of Lower Table Rock you may find Rock Wren along the cliff face, Wilson's Snipe, Harrier, Lazuli Bunting (spring), Lark Sparrow, Wrentit, Orange-crowned Warbler and other birds that are drawn to the seasonal wetlands, brush or rock faces. Peregrine regularly nest on one of the rock faces of Lower Table Rock, usually on the southeast side facing over the river.

Touvelle State Recreation Area consists of two units on opposite sides of the Rogue River. It includes over 50 acres of oak woodland, grassland and riverbank. A trail runs from Touvelle east into the neighboring Denman Wildlife Area. What you'll find: a boat launch, picnic grounds, toilets and trails. An entrance fee is charged.

EBird shows over 130 species recorded here. In spring, Touvelle is a nest-watchers paradise. A large Great Blue Heron colony nests in the large cottonwoods across the Rogue, just north of the main parking lot. An Osprey pair often nests on a pole near the park entrance off Lower Table Rock Road. Dozens of Cliff Swallows build their mud condos on the underside of the bridge across the Rogue River. Tree and Violet-green Swallows seem determined to use every abandoned woodpecker cavity for their nests. They have to compete with Western Bluebirds. There is a permanent colony of Acorn Woodpeckers.

Wintering birds can include Lewis's Woodpecker and many Golden-crowned Sparrow. Belted Kingfisher and Common Merganser are regular along the river. Osprey fish here all summer. Year-round birds are Great Horned Owl, Bewick's Wren, Wrentit, Spotted Towhee, White-breasted Nuthatch, Brown Creeper, Lesser Goldfinch and Oak Titmouse. This is the best place in Jackson County for Creeper.

Whetstone Savannah is a 150-acre preserve owned by the Nature Conservancy. It is a remnant of the open oak forest and grassland that once dominated the flat areas where the summers are hot and arid and the soil is thin over geologically recent lava flows. Though it is level, the area can be rough hiking, and there are numerous wet potholes in winter. Spring wildflowers here can be spectacular. Whetstone is a recognized IBA.

EBird shows 75 species for this area. Birds you might encounter include Northern Harrier, White-tailed Kite, Peregrine (especially check nearby power poles), Red-shouldered Hawk, Vaux's Swift (summer), Lewis's Woodpecker (spring and winter), Ash-throated Flycatcher (spring), Spotted and California Towhee and Lark Sparrow. Golden-crowned Sparrows abound in winter. This is one of the northernmost spots to find Northern Mockingbird along I-5. North of here this species is uncommon.

I-5 Exit 45. Exit here for **Rogue River Rest Area** and **Valley of the Rogue State Park**. What you'll find: picnic areas, trails, toilets, campsites, RV sites, and a boat launch. The state park charges an entrance fee. The park has extensive Rogue River frontage and a trail over a mile long along the bank.

EBird shows over 75 species from just a few observers. Among the birds you can find here: Common Merganser, California Quail, Anna's Hummingbird, Red-breasted Sapsucker, Black Phoebe, Violet-green Swallow (summer), Bushtit, Wrentit and Spotted Towhee. Spring birds include Yellow-breasted Chat, Lazuli Bunting, Bullock's Oriole and Swainson's Thrush.

I-5 Mile 51. Here you will cross into Josephine County.

I-5 Exit 61, West. If you exit Interstate 5 at the Merlin exit, Exit 61, you can visit a wildlife rehabilitation center and a riverside park with good birding. Both are west of I-5. See *Grants Pass Vicinity* map.

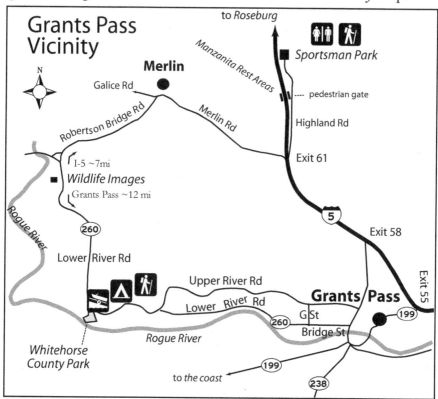

Wildlife Images, the only licensed wildlife rehabilitation center in southwest Oregon, is about 8 miles west of I-5 Exit 61. What you'll find: toilets, guided tours and a visitors center with a shop. There are resident eagles and other raptors at this facility, as well as smaller birds being prepared for release. There are also numerous mammals including bears and cougars. Wildlife Images provides tours that you can book in advance. Resident wild birds here include fairly tame and easy-to-photograph Wood Ducks.

About 4 miles farther down Lower River Road from Wildlife Images is **Whitehorse County Park.** It's about 12 miles from Exit 61 on I-5. The park can also be reached from Grants Pass Exit 55 to the south by heading west on G Street, but traffic on that route is likely to be much heavier.

What you'll find: campsites and RV hook-ups, picnic areas, trails, a boat ramp, a playground, and fishing. An entrance fee is charged. Whitehorse is on the north bank of the Rogue River. There's riverside marshland, forest and grassy areas for birding. EBird records for this park show over 110 species, including Wood Duck, Common Merganser, Osprey, Bald Eagle, Red-shouldered Hawk, Spotted Sandpiper, Vaux's Swift, Belted Kingfisher, Acorn Woodpecker, Pileated Woodpecker, Red-breasted Sapsucker, Olive-sided Flycatcher, Pacific-slope Flycatcher, Violet-green Swallow (summer), Swainson's Thrush (spring), Bushtit, Wrentit, Lazuli Bunting, and a dozen species of western warblers including Black-throated Gray on migration. In fact, this park may be as close to a sure thing for Pileated as anywhere along the Oregon stretch of I-5. One winter, a wandering Brant set down on the river, far from the Pacific where you'd expect it.

I-5 Exit 61, East. If you turn east from I-5 Exit 61 you will see Highland Road. If you follow it 2.2 miles north, you will enter **Sportsman Park,** maintained by Josephine County. What you'll find: toilets, visitors center, picnic tables and trails. Sportsman Park was designed and has facilities for archery and gun practice, but on weekdays the park is usually quiet. No actual hunting is allowed. There's a pond on the right shortly after you enter the park and numerous trails lead through the woods. The forest is mostly oak and madrone with scattered ponderosa pine and incense cedar. It's a good site for Rufous and

Anna's Hummingbird, Ash-throated Flycatcher around the oaks, Oak Titmouse, California and Spotted Towhee, Blue-gray Gnatcatcher and Lesser Goldfinch. Oak Titmouse, Gnatcatcher and California Towhee are all near the north end of their range here. There's no eBird data for this area.

I-5 Mile 63 (northbound). **Manzanita Rest Area,** with picnic areas and toilets is just north of Exit 61. The rest stop is named for the manzanita bushes that, along with ceanothus, form much of the undergrowth in this dry oak forest habitat. Manzanita means "little apple" in Spanish. These bushes produce berries beloved by thrushes, sparrows and other fruit eaters. Both the rest area and adjacent Sportsman Park (see above) are worth birding. It's a mile walk from the rest area to Sportsman Park along fairly quiet Highland Road, which can also be reached from Exit 61. There's a pedestrian entrance to and from Highland Road through a wire mesh gate at the back of the rest area. Be aware that Sportsman Park was designed specifically for gun and archery enthusiasts.

(Southbound) This rest stop borders several acres of accessible oak forest west of the truck parking area. In summer look for Ash-throated Flycatcher and Blue-gray Gnatcatcher. Year-found residents are Bushtit, Oak Titmouse, Scrub-jay, Spotted Towhee and White-breasted Nuthatch.

I-5 Mile 69. Sexton Mountain Pass. Elevation 1,960 feet. Sexton Mountain, east of I-5, is over 3,850 feet at its peak. You may see Ravens soaring overhead in these mountains.

I-5 Exit 72. Exit here and go east into Sunny Valley. It's about half a mile to the **Grave Creek Covered Bridge,** where there is a parking pullout. In summer this creek bottom has a large colony of Tree and Violet-green Swallows. The riparian corridor will have nesting Bullock's Oriole, Black-headed Grosbeak and Warbling Vireo. There are no facilities at the bridge, but there are businesses and a museum near I-5.

I-5 Exit 76. Wolf Creek. Wolf Creek County Park affords a chance to bird riparian habitat. It's less than 2 miles from I-5. What you'll find: toilets, trails and picnic areas. There are Bullock's Orioles, Black-

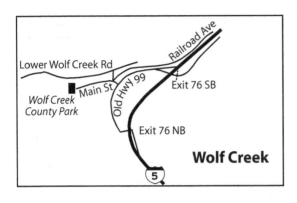

Wolf Creek

headed Grosbeak, vireos and warblers here in warm weather. In the hamlet of Wolf Creek, the Wolf Creek Inn is a State Heritage Site.

I-5 Mile 79. Stage Road Pass, elevation 1,830 feet. This is the county line between Josephine County on the south and Douglas County on the north. Note: Douglas County is named for United States Senator Stephen Douglas of Illinois, who supported Oregon's statehood. The abundant Douglas-fir in this area is named after David Douglas, a British plant collector and explorer, who discovered many new western American plants for science in the early 19th Century. The Douglas Squirrel found in dense forests of the Northwest is also named for the explorer, not the senator.

I-5 Exit 80. Exit here for the 45-mile-long **Cow Creek Loop,** which will take you to the town of Glendale then through ranchland and into habitat where you can find Wrentit, Cassin's and Hutton's Vireo, Hermit and Black-throated Gray Warbler, Pacific-slope Flycatcher and Swainson's Thrush. All are breeding birds here, but only the Hutton's and Wrentit stay past late summer. There are public waysides and campgrounds along the route, which follows Cow Creek through the foothills of a range that reaches 4,000 feet elevation. See the *Cow Creek Loop and Vicinity* map for directions if you have time for this loop. You will rejoin I-5 at Exit 103. Note that you can also pick up the loop at Exit 88 (Azalea), which will add another 5 or so miles onto the trip.

I-5 Exit 81 (northbound). **Cow Creek Rest Area.** Both Hermit and Varied Thrush may be seen on the ground here in spring, beneath the dense canopy of the Douglas-fir.

I-5 Mile 90. Canyon Creek Pass. Elevation 2020 feet. This is highest elevation along I-5 north of the Siskiyou Pass.

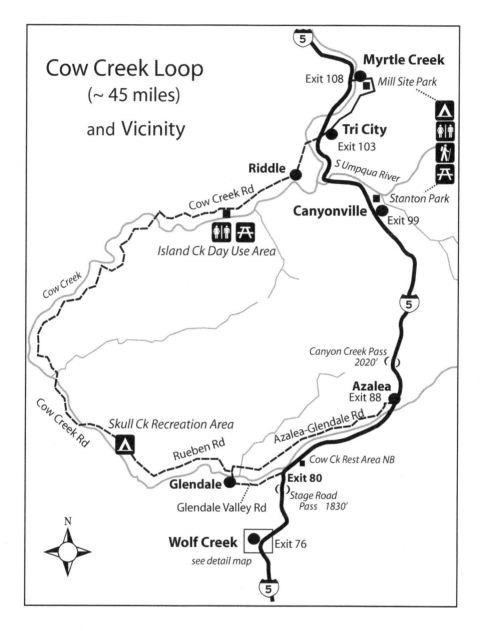

Cow Creek Loop
(~ 45 miles)
and Vicinity

I-5 Exit 99. Stanton Park. Exit here at Canyonville. Head north paralleling I-5 on the east side going past Seven Feathers Casino to the north end of town and **Stanton Park**. What you'll find: RV and traditional campsites, playground, toilets, picnic areas, showers and a trail. Dogs allowed on leash. This park is along the South Fork of the Umpqua River. Here you can find Wrentit, Bushtit, Spotted Sandpiper, Green

Heron, Common Merganser and woodpeckers, including Pileated. Just east of the RV campsite there is a short dirt trail down to the gravel beach along the river. Here you can look for Kingfisher, Common Merganser, Bald Eagle, Osprey (spring and summer). You can find swallows feeding over the river on warm nights. If you take Stanton Park Road north parallel to I-5 you will pass an Osprey nest platform on the right (east) near the river. This is about a mile north from Exit 99. It is frequently used by Osprey and is very difficult to see from the interstate but is clearly visible if you're on the local road. You can rejoin northbound I-5 at Exit 101. Then another mile north there's an often-used Osprey platform west of I-5.

I-5 Mile 103. Starting here and continuing for a few miles, I-5 parallels the **South Umpqua River**. Look for Great Egret in winter and Common Merganser. You may spot Turkey Vultures roosting in riverside cottonwoods along this stretch of highway.

I-5 Exit 108. Exit here for **Myrtle Creek** and go east on North Main Street. There is a city park just 0.6 miles from the exit. The first crossroad is Fourth Avenue. Turn right (west) here and go downhill alongside Millsite Park. There are hook-ups for RVs, playground, toilets and a chance to bird alongside the South Fork of the Umpqua River. At the bottom of Fourth Avenue a trail goes past some large boulders, crosses the railroad tracks and then parallels the river both to the north and south. The south trail branch forms a loop with the railroad tracks that will bring you back to the end of Fourth Avenue. The trail passes through a bottomland forest of cottonwoods with a few maple and madrone.

Spring birds may include Cliff Swallow and Vaux's Swift on and around the highway bridge across the South Umpqua, Bullock's Oriole and Black-headed Grosbeak. In winter look for Lewis's Woodpecker, both kinglets, Townsend's Warbler and Golden-crowned Sparrow. Red-shouldered Hawk, American Kestrel, Wrentit, Spotted Towhee, Song Sparrow, American Crows and Western Scrub-Jay are resident. Common Merganser nest along the river where Osprey and Bald Eagle sometimes fish. Best birding here is late winter and spring.

I-5 Mile 110. Along this stretch of I-5 you will see several Osprey nest platforms. The platforms are not used annually by Osprey. The bird is possible anywhere along the Umpqua River branches from March until October.

I-5 Exit 112. South Umpqua Rest Areas on both sides of I-5. There's another Osprey nesting platform nearby but I've never seen this one in use.

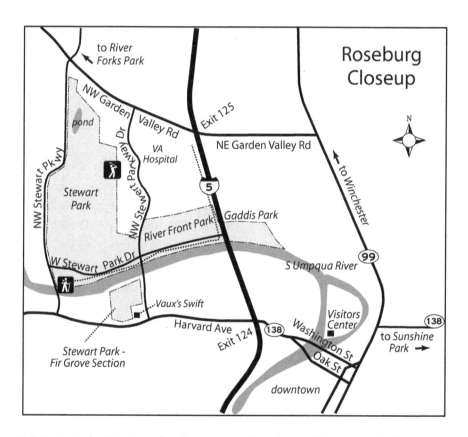

I-5 Exit 124. Exit here for downtown **Roseburg.** The annual Christmas Count here usually totals about 110 species. From mid to late September you can watch Vaux's Swifts coming to roost in the clay chimney behind the Umpqua Valley Arts Center at 1624 West Harvard Avenue. The Umpqua Valley Audubon Society hosts "swift watches" during that time. There is parking off NW Stewart Parkway Drive just north of Harvard. The pottery shed chimney is clearly visible at that point.

Annual wintering birds around Roseburg include Lincoln's and Golden-crowned Sparrows, Townsend's Warbler, Varied Thrush (most years), both kinglets, Pacific Wren, Hutton's Vireo, Black Phoebe and Anna's Hummingbird. Occasional wintering birds include Northern Shrike, Say's Phoebe, Virginia Rail, Rough-legged Hawk and Merlin. Summering birds along the Umpqua River will be Osprey, Common Merganser and Green Heron, Bullock's Oriole and Yellow Warbler.

Three city parks offer convenient birding stops in Roseburg. See *Roseburg Closeup* map.

Riverfront Park is located along the north bank of the South Umpqua River, west of I-5 on Stewart Park Drive. This 45-acre park has more than a mile of river frontage. Much of Riverfront Park is undeveloped, with mature Douglas-fir, ponderosa pine, madrone and oak trees. What you'll find: toilets, picnic areas, playgrounds, fishing, boat ramp and trails. Day use only. No dogs allowed from May 15 through September 15.

Adjacent **Stewart Park** covers over 200 acres. What you'll find: a butterfly garden, two wildlife ponds, a few acres of wetlands and complete recreational facilities. Birds you can find here include Green Heron, Anna's Hummingbird, wintering Merlin, Acorn Woodpecker and Bewick's Wren. In spring you may find Yellow-breasted Chat and Bullock's Oriole.

Both of these parks are reached by turning west off I-5 Exit 124 onto Harvard Drive. Turn north onto NW Stewert Park Drive and cross the river to reach the parks.

Also accessible from Exit 124 but east from I-5 is **Sunshine Park**. It is located five miles out OR 138 (Diamond Lake Boulevard). It has 85 acres of playing fields and open space. Here in spring you may find Black Phoebe, Violet-green among the swallows, Chipping Sparrow, Black-headed Grosbeak and Bullock's Oriole.

I-5 Exit 125. If you exit here onto Garden Valley Road and head west, you can find some birding spots in the **Umpqua River Valley**. See *Roseburg Vicinity* map. Near Melrose you can find Great Blue Heron, wintering Northern Shrike, Wood Duck, summering Western Kingbird, Wrentit and Lazuli Bunting. Follow the map to **River Forks Park,** on the east bank of the Umpqua. This park is about six miles from I-5. What you'll find: picnic areas, playground, toilets, trails and a boat ramp. You may find Hutton's Vireo and Red-breasted Sapsucker along with the usual riverine birds. You can rejoin the freeway at Exit 129 if you are traveling north.

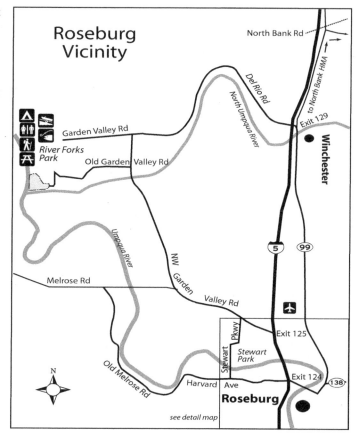

I-5 Exit 129. If you exit here heading east, you can turn south in 0.2 mile on OR 99 to an overlook at **Winchester Dam**. What you'll find: No facilities except a parking pullout. There's an underwater fish observation window at Winchester Dam across the North Fork of the Umpqua River. Steelhead and trout use this fish ladder. Canada Geese may be seen using the nest platform originally intended for Osprey. It's across the river from the overlook along the south bank. Check the river above the dam for Common Merganser, Belted Kingfisher, and possible wintering ducks including Hooded Merganser.

If you drive north on OR 99 from this exit, you can reach **North Bank Habitat Management Area.** Follow OR 99 (on the east side of I-5) north almost two miles, then turn right (east) onto North Bank Road. It's 5.3 miles from OR 99 to the west entrance to the North Bank Habitat Management Area, and another 1.3 miles to the eastern end of

177

this preserve. This is BLM land along the North Fork of the Umpqua River, set aside to help protect the Columbia white-tailed deer. This species is far less common than the larger black-tailed (mule) deer in this part of the West.

What you'll find: The east entrance gate is open Friday through Monday. Winter hours are 8 a.m. to 5 p.m., October through March. Summer hours are 8 a.m. to 8 p.m., April through September. The gate is closed Tuesday through Thursday, but pedestrian access is open 24 hours a day at both entrances. There are picnic tables and toilets at the east entrance. The preserve contains ten thousand acres and reaches 1,500 feet elevation on Round Timber Mountain. Dominant trees are white oak, madrone and Douglas-fir. There are bigleaf maple along the river. The old ranch roads make for good hiking. Hunting is allowed here in season.

Birds you might find include California Quail, Western Kingbird, Ash-throated Flycatcher, White and Red-breasted Nuthatch, Brown Creeper, Hutton's and Warbling Vireo, wintering Say's Phoebe, Lazuli Bunting, Western Bluebird, Red-breasted Sapsucker, Acorn and Lewis's Woodpecker, Western Tanager. Vesper Sparrow nest in grasslands here. Both eagles and Red-shouldered Hawk have been found here as well.

I-5 Exit 136. Exit here for **Sutherlin** (elevation 540 feet). West of I-5, there's interesting birding at **Ford's Pond** (see *Sutherlin Vicinity* map for details). Nearly a hundred species have been reported to eBird from these locations, including some twenty species of waterfowl. These are mostly wintering birds. Birds nesting here include Wood Duck, Pied-billed Grebe, Osprey, Black Phoebe, Western Kingbird, five species of swallow, Bullock's Oriole and even Tricolored Blackbird some years. Local birders report Vesper Sparrows nesting on the pond's north side.

About 4 miles from I-5 Exit 136 on the east side is **Cooper Creek Reservoir**. See *Sutherlin Vicinity* map. Here you may find Chestnut-backed Chickadee, Black-headed Grosbeak (spring), Wood Duck, Western Tanager (spring) and nesting Purple Martins. The best birding is usually at the shallow end of the lake.

Nearby, **Platr I Reservoir** is a couple of miles farther east. At the north end of the dam, Platr I Reservoir has a small park. What you'll find: There are picnic tables, toilets and a small playground. There

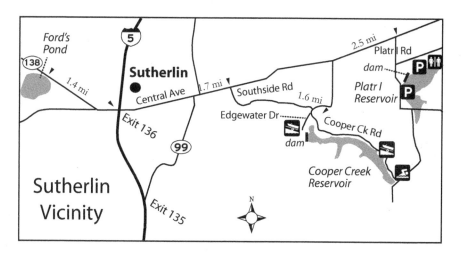

are two areas for viewing the lake (see map). Both offer clear vantage points, as the lake has no perimeter brush or willows. From either parking area you can walk along the grass-covered dam and have a clear view of the whole lake.

Platr I Reservoir is known to have a nesting colony of Purple Martins, a scarce bird in the Pacific states. Look for the white plastic nesting gourds hanging on the southeast edge of the reservoir near a grove of trees. Osprey, Red-shouldered Hawk and White-tailed Kite can be found here along with ducks and a variety of passing shorebirds in fall. By that season the water level is low, exposing extensive mudflats. White Pelicans and a large number of Great Egrets can be found here in autumn. Ebird shows over 70 species here including Black Phoebe and Violet-green swallow in summer.

I-5 Exit 138. Oakland. The oak woodlands around this small historic town have Wild Turkey, Scrub-Jay and White-breasted Nuthatch. If you want to bird **Mildred Kanipe Memorial Park,** continue through Oakland and take County Road 22 (Driver Valley Road) east, then turn north onto Elkhead Road. See *Oakland Vicinity* map. It's about 7 miles from Oakland, 8 miles from Exit 138 to the county park. What you'll find: picnic areas, toilets, nature trails and fishing. This park, open for day use only, has 1,100 acres of grasslands, oak woodland and scrub habitat where you can find White-tailed Kite, Grasshopper Sparrow and Western Meadowlark. The peacocks near the park entrance are not native, of course. There are no eBird records for this area yet.

I-5 Exit 140. If you're southbound, take this exit for **Oakland** and **Kanipe Park**. See above.

I-5 Mile 142. Cabin Creek Rest Areas. Hermit Thrush is likely here in winter. Check the deep shade for possible Varied Thrush on migration and in winter. The southbound rest stop has some mature forest and borders a grassy hillside. The woods are largely oak with heavy underbrush. Birds I've found here include Lazuli Bunting, Black-headed Grosbeak and numerous Spotted Towhee.

I-5 Mile 145. There's a farm pond here west of I-5. There's no good place to stop but I've noted in passing that Ring-necked Ducks and Hooded Mergansers are sometimes there in winter months.

I-5 Mile 150. You're passing through Pleasant Valley. Possible raptors here include Bald Eagle and Red-tailed Hawk.

I-5 Mile 168. This is the county line, with Lane County to the north and Douglas County to the south.

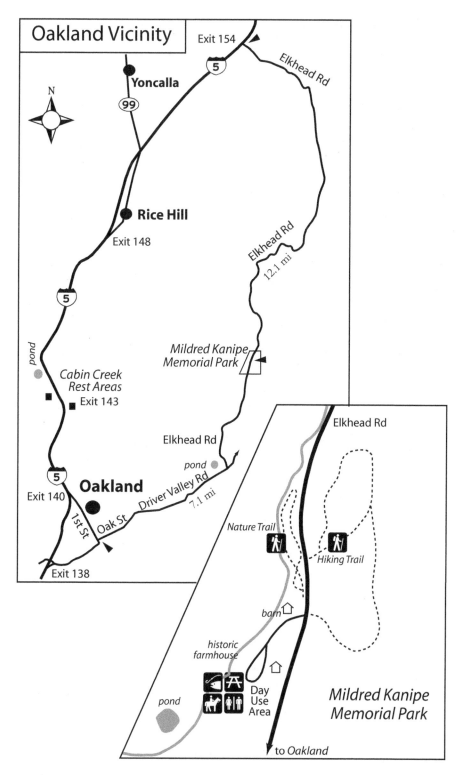

Oakland Vicinity

Exit 154

Elkhead Rd

Yoncalla

99

N

Rice Hill

Exit 148

Elkhead Rd

12.1 mi

5

pond

Cabin Creek
Rest Areas

Exit 143

Mildred Kanipe
Memorial Park

Elkhead Rd

pond

5

Oakland

Exit 140

1st St   Oak St   Driver Valley Rd   7.1 mi

Exit 138

Elkhead Rd

Nature Trail

Hiking Trail

barn

historic
farmhouse

Day
Use
Area

pond

Mildred Kanipe
Memorial Park

to Oakland

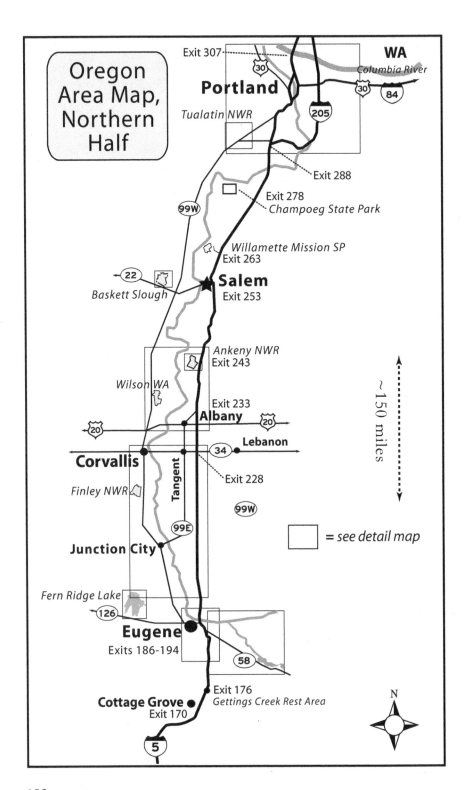

Oregon Area Map, Northern Half

WA

Exit 307

Portland

Columbia River

30

30

84

Tualatin NWR

205

Exit 288

99W

Exit 278
Champoeg State Park

Willamette Mission SP
Exit 263

22

Salem
Exit 253

Baskett Slough

Ankeny NWR
Exit 243

Wilson WA

Exit 233

Albany

20

20

Lebanon

34

Corvallis

Exit 228

Tangent

~150 miles

Finley NWR

99W

99E

= see detail map

Junction City

Fern Ridge Lake

126

Eugene
Exits 186-194

58

Exit 176
Gettings Creek Rest Area

Cottage Grove
Exit 170

N

5

Turkey Vulture

Chapter 9

Central Oregon

I-5, OR 99W and OR 99E
Lane, Linn and Benton Counties

Central Oregon is dominated by the Willamette River and Willamette Valley. The major cities are Eugene, Corvallis, Albany and Salem, which is the state capital.

I-5 Exit 176. Gettings Creek Rest Area is just north of Cottage Grove. One March visit yielded Robin, Golden-crowned Sparrow, Varied Thrush and Hermit Thrush. Check the surrounding pastures for Greater White-fronted Goose during fall migration. I have seen elk near the highway in this area in winter. The woods here are oak, ash, Douglas-fir and maple. The southbound rest area borders a small damp thicket that should be good for migratory songbirds and can be accessed around Mile 177.

I-5 Exit 182. Go east and just after crossing a small creek turn left (north) onto Emerald Parkway, then almost immediately turn left onto Melton, following signs that point toward the airport. After Melton rounds a corner and parallels the freeway you will see Creswell's Garden Lake Park entrance on your right. There are two small lakes and dense waterside forest. Pied-billed Grebe breed here, Belted Kingfisher, Hooded Merganser and humans fish here. The woods may have warblers on migration. Freeway noise prohibits birding by ear. There are toilets, covered picnic area, fishing and short trails.

I-5 Exit 186. Exit here if you're headed northbound and want to visit the **Cascades Raptor Center** at 33275 Fox Hollow Road, and **Spencer**

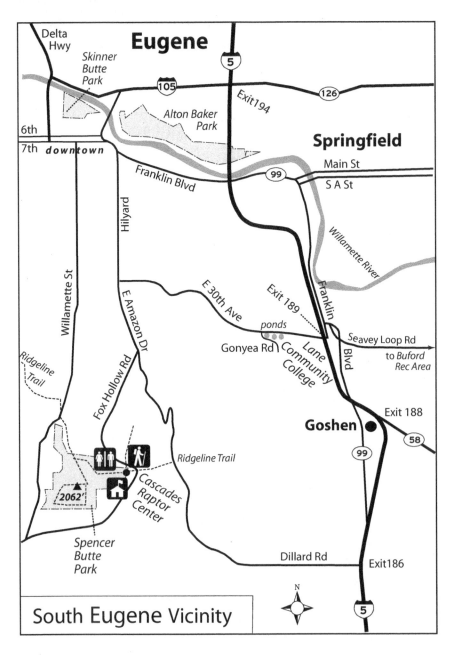

Butte Park in south Eugene. See *South Eugene Vicinity* map. What you'll find at the raptor center: toilets, trails, visitors center, and a bird feeding station; an entrance fee is charged. Check their website for hours and admission charge. There are usually a couple dozen species of rescued birds at the raptor center, including owls.

Across the road from the raptor center is the eastern trailhead of **Ridgeline Trail**, which meanders 14 miles through various habitats west of here, including the woods on Spencer Butte, adjacent to (just west of) the raptor center. The butte's elevation, 2,062 feet, makes it the highest peak in this part of the Willamette Valley. Spencer Butte Park is a city park, open for day use only with dogs allowed on leash. What you'll find: toilets, drinking water, trails, picnicing, and great views of Willamette Valley. Woodpeckers and warblers can be found in the trailside woodlands. Among the birds reported from Spencer Butte Park are Northern Pygmy and Saw-whet Owls in winter, summering Vaux's Swift; Mountain Quail; Rufous Hummingbird; Hutton's, Cassin's and Warbling Vireo; Violet-green Swallow; Bushtit; Chestnut-backed Chickadee along with the larger Black-capped; Pacific Wren; and nearly all the western warblers on migration including Townsend's, Hermit and Black-throated Gray. A flock of Gray Jays has been reported here in late September, a prime time for wandering resident birds. EBird shows over 90 species for the Spencer Butte woodlands, including Pileated Woodpecker and wintering Varied Thrush.

I-5 Exit 188, East. Dexter Reservoir and More. If you head eastward you will be on OR 58. This leads to a series of state parks, the farthest about 15 miles out. See *East Eugene Area Parks* map. The first reached is **Elijah Bristow State Park**. Bristow has almost 850 acres of woods, meadow and riverside lowlands. The forest here is oak, maple, ash, red cedar, Douglas-fir and western hemlock. Here you can find a wide range of forest and wetland birds: Cassin's, Hutton's and Warbling Vireo, as well as an occasional nesting Red-eyed Vireo. Other species to expect in warm months: Pacific-slope Flycatcher, Western Wood-Pewee, Yellow-breasted Chat and Lazuli Bunting.

Bristow is linked by 5 miles of trail, or a couple of miles of highway, to the Dexter State Recreation Area, the next park upstream. **Dexter Reservoir** is a good birding spot from September through May. It's at the base of the Cascades foothills and is formed by a dam on the Middle Fork of the Willamette. Though the dam is below 700 feet in elevation, the surrounding ridges rise to more than 2,000 feet.

Rarities occur here, like Yellow-billed Loon and Sabine's Gull. Also reported are Redhead; Long-tailed Duck; Horned, Red-necked and Clark's Grebe; Hutton's Vireo; Pacific Wren; Wrentit; and MacGillivray's Warbler in spring. Osprey nest in the area annually. California and Glaucous-winged Gulls may gather on the lake in winter.

Fall Creek Reservoir State Park is a short drive north of OR 58 and Dexter Reservoir, which will give you another chance at birds frequenting this area on migration and in winter. Turn north off OR 58 toward the town of Lowell and follow *East Eugene Parks* map.

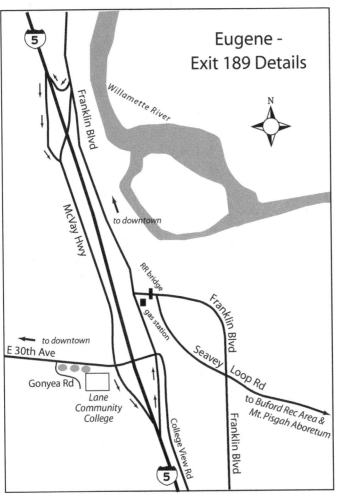

I-5 Exit 189, East. Exit here and head east about 2 miles to **Mount Pisgah**, which is largely contained within the **Howard Buford Recreation Area.** Buford is one of the IBAs in the Willamette Valley. What you'll find: toilets, horse trails, a visitors center at the arboretum, and a plant nursery. There is a fee for parking.

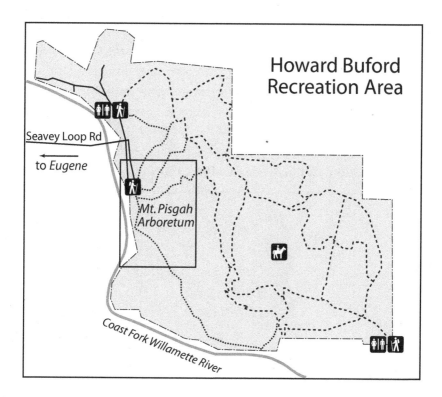

This I-5 freeway Exit (189) can be confusing. Consult the *Eugene-Exit 189 Details* map and the following instructions to reach Mount Piscah/Howard Buford:

From I-5, southbound: Exit the freeway at Exit 189. At the base of the off-ramp, turn right and continue driving south toward East 30th Avenue. At the stop light at East 30th Avenue, make a left turn and cross over the freeway. At the stop sign just past the overpass, turn left again. At the Shell Station, make a right turn onto Franklin Boulevard, cross under the railroad bridge, and follow Franklin around a curve. Turn left onto Seavey Loop Road and continue about 1.5 miles. After you cross a short bridge over the river, follow the right fork of the road into the arboretum parking lot.

From I-5, northbound: Exit the freeway at Exit 189. At the stop sign at the end of the off-ramp, go straight ahead. Make a right turn onto Franklin Boulevard and cross under the railroad bridge. Continue as above to the arboretum parking lot.

Birding here is best from April through October. This county park includes over 2,300 acres of habitat. It's east of central Eugene and the University of Oregon's main campus. Lane County maintains the recreation area, which includes more than 200 acres of forest in the Mount Pisgah Arboretum along the western side of the recreation area. At 1,516 feet, the peak of Mt. Pisgah stands a thousand feet higher than the surrounding river valley. There are over 17 miles of hiking trails in the park.

EBird data show this to be a rich site for woodland species during spring migration: Willow, Pacific-slope and Hammond's Flycatcher;

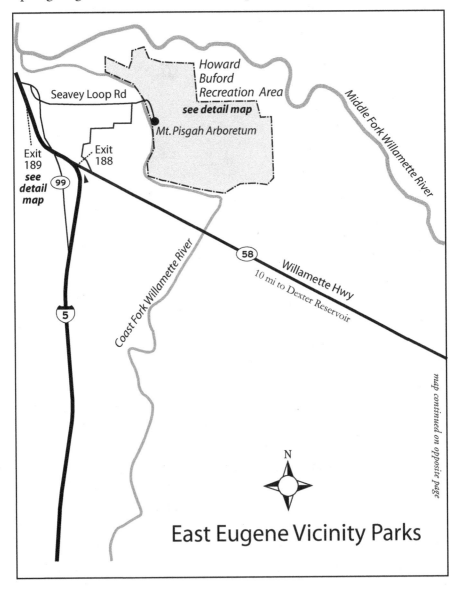

East Eugene Vicinity Parks

Cassin's Vireo; nine warbler species including MacGillivray's, Townsend's and Black-throated Gray; Lazuli Bunting; and Lesser Goldfinch have all been sighted here. Resident species include Western Meadowlark, Chestnut-backed Chickadee, Wrentit and Spotted Towhee. Breeding species include Olive-sided Flycatcher, Violet-green Swallow, Bushtit, Cedar Waxwing, Western Tanager, Lazuli Bunting and Black-headed Grosbeak. EBird shows 110 species have been reported for this site.

Volunteers at Mount Pisgah conduct tours of the Nature Conservancy's **Willamette Confluence Project**, which covers over 1,200 acres just north of Mount Pisgah. It's the riparian habitat where the Coast and Middle forks of the Willamette River converge. This area has a breeding population of Vesper Sparrow.

I-5 Exit 189, West. Lane Community College Sewer Ponds. These ponds can be found if you go west of I-5 at Exit 189, just off the interstate at the edge of the college campus. Take the Exit south to the campus entrance, Gonyea Road. The ponds are right along East 30th Avenue. See *Eugene - Exit 189 Details* map. There is no safe pullout near the ponds, so proceed uphill on Gonyea Road to the college parking

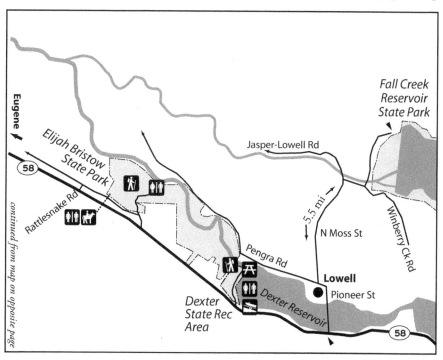

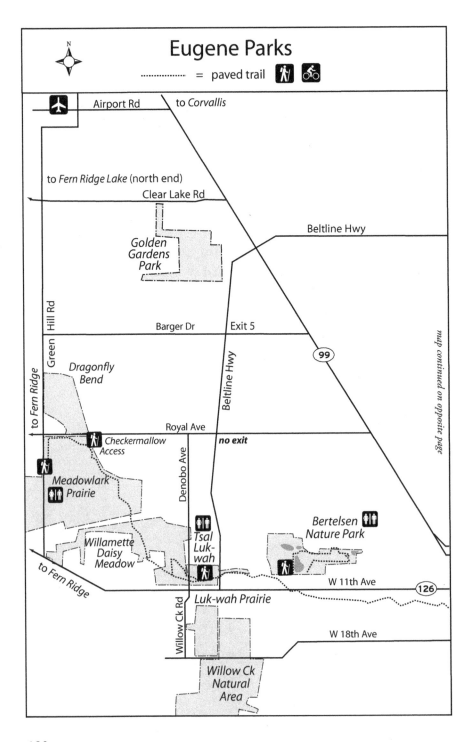

Eugene Parks

.... = paved trail

Airport Rd   to *Corvallis*

to *Fern Ridge Lake* (north end)

Clear Lake Rd

Beltline Hwy

Golden
Gardens
Park

Green Hill Rd

Barger Dr   Exit 5

Beltline Hwy

99

Dragonfly
Bend

to *Fern Ridge*

Royal Ave

Checkermallow
Access

no exit

Denobo Ave

Meadowlark
Prairie

Bertelsen
Nature Park

Willamette
Daisy
Meadow

Tsal
Luk-
wah

to *Fern Ridge*

W 11th Ave   126

Willow Ck Rd

Luk-wah Prairie

W 18th Ave

Willow Ck
Natural
Area

map continued on opposite page

area and make the short walk back downhill. The sewer ponds are good for waterfowl and shorebirds on migration. Hooded Merganser and Cackling Goose, Sharp-tailed and Solitary Sandpiper are among species reported here. One autumn day I found several hundred Cackling Geese crowded onto the largest of the three ponds here.

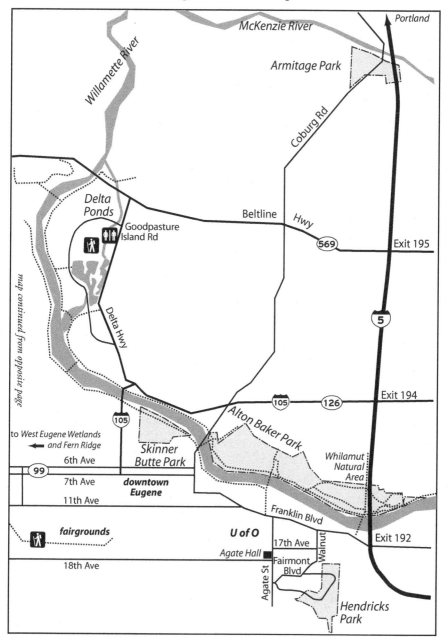

I-5 Exit 192. Eugene and Environs. Eugene is the largest city on I-5 between Portland and Sacramento. The city has several good birding sites and numerous parks. See *Eugene Parks* map. The farthest out, west of town on OR 126 about 12 miles, is Fern Ridge Reservoir, an IBA that has a colony of nesting Purple Martins, hard to find in the Pacific States. In open spaces at the airport, Northern Shrike, Merlin and other grassland hunters can be found in winter. Eugene's numerous walkways along the Willamette are actually the upper reaches of the Willamette Greenway Park System, which stretches from Eugene north to Portland. The Lane County Audubon website has information on free bird walks and recent sightings of interest.

Eugene's elevation next to the Willamette River is just over 400 feet. It has a moderate climate. The average high in July and August is under 82 degrees. In January and December the high is around 46, while the average low is 33. Eugene averages more than 50 inches of rain annually, with about 8 inches each month from November through January. July and August are generally dry. There are usually small amounts of snow each winter.

West Eugene Wetlands. This is a collection of open space parcels west of Eugene on both banks of the Willamette River. A coalition of landowners including City of Eugene, Corps of Engineers, BLM, Nature Conservancy and their conservation partners administer and continue to restore over a dozen sites for hiking and day use. One general rule across the wetlands: dogs on leash. The habitat is wet prairie and seasonal marsh including some riparian forest. The West Eugene Wetlands office is in the Tsal Luk-Wah parcel on Willow Creek Road a short distance north of OR126. There are restrooms at the Education Center, and a visitors center is planned for that location. Other tracts included within West Eugene Wetlands are the Willow Creek Natural Area, Dragonfly Bend and Luk-Wah Prairie. The two major parcels in the Wetlands are Bertelsen Nature Park and Meadowlark Prairie.

Stewart Pond. If you're heading west out of Eugene on OR 126 toward Fern Ridge, you'll pass near Stewart Pond. This pond, in the West Eugene Wetlands, is in **Bertelsen Nature Park,** which is administered by the BLM. What you'll find: toilets and trails. There are also three smaller ponds at Bertelsen. The area includes a large emergent wetland, small ponds and surrounding oak savannah. Eighty species are listed for this area in eBird, including Wood Duck, wintering Cinnamon and Blue-winged Teal, American Bittern, White-tailed Kite, wintering Rough-legged Hawk and Golden-crowned Sparrow. Wrentit and Marsh Wren nest here. This is one of the southernmost points in the Willamette Valley where Glaucous-winged Gulls are regular.

Further west of Eugene but still a few miles east of Fern Ridge Reservoir is **Meadowlark Prairie.** Look for Green Hill Road as you go west on OR 126. There are two access points here to the BLM's 380-acre Meadowlark Prairie. What you'll find: toilets, picnic areas and trails. This area has wet and upland prairies and riparian corridors along Amazon Creek and other streams flowing eastward to the Willamette. Old agricultural levees have been removed so the streams now are free to meander during high water in winter and spring. Encroaching woodland flora are managed to maintain the prairie that was originally maintained by fire. Here wintering raptors can be observed, including Rough-legged Hawk and White-tailed Kite. Wintering Short-eared Owls have been seen here and ducks often use the wetlands along Amazon Creek. May is an ideal time to bird this spot. Black-tailed deer and elk may also be seen here.

Willow Creek Natural Area. Take OR 126 west after leaving I-5 at Exit 192. This is the same route you would take to get to the south part of Fern Ridge Lake, but well before Fern Ridge turn south onto Willow Creek Road. This Natural Area is over 400 acres of Willamette Valley wet grasslands west of Eugene. It's a Nature Conservancy property. Numerous waterfowl sighted here include Eurasian Wigeon. Glaucous-winged Gull, Merlin, Prairie Falcon and Peregrine are all possible in winter as well. Golden-crowned Sparrow is abundant in the cold months. Species possible here in season: Vaux's Swift, Anna's Hummingbird, Willow Flycatcher, Hutton's Vireo, Swainson's Thrush with its upward fluting song in spring, Lazuli Bunting, and Black-beaded Grosbeak. EBird shows 120 species reported here. There are numerous rare plants here so it's especially important to stay on the marked trails.

At the northern access point to Meadowlark Prairie, called **Check-ermallow Access**, there's a trail to Amazon Creek and a small dam often attracts migrating shorebirds. The Fern Ridge Path passes through here and provides birding access to seasonal marshes. Western Meadowlark is a year-round resident and brilliant singer in winter and spring. It was this bird's fluting song that allowed J. J. Audubon to first distinguish this species from its nearly identical eastern cousin.

I-5 Exits 192, 194, 195. Fern Ridge Reservoir and Wildlife Area. For access, see *Eugene Parks* map, for details see *Fern Ridge* map. There are several ways to get there but Exit 195 takes you over the least congested route to Fern Ridge, ending up on the eastern shoreline. See entry for Fern Ridge Lake, East Area below. It is further to most of the other birding sites around Fern Ridge.

Fern Ridge Lake and the surrounding area offer a rewarding mix of birding habitats all year long and may be the most birded locale between Portland and the Sacramento Wildlife Refuge. It is a registered IBA. The lake is actually a flood-control reservoir built (in 1941) and maintained by the Corps of Engineers. The reservoir is kept full in summer, although average depth is only 11 feet with a maximum of 33 feet. Beginning in October the reservoir is drawn down, exposing mudflats that attract shorebirds, American Pipit and other species.

EBird has over 230 species reported from more than a dozen locations around Fern Ridge Reservoir. Because it's heavily birded, numerous rarities have been reported from Fern Ridge: Emperor Goose; Brant (far from the sea); Falcated Duck; Red-necked Grebe; White-faced Ibis (far north of its usual range); Pacific Golden-Plover; Solitary, Wood, Stilt, Buff-breasted and Sharp-tailed Sandpiper; Spotted Redshank in mid-summer on year; all three phalarope species; and a dozen gull species. The lake attracts wandering or lost ocean birds because when full it covers over 9,300 acres, or about 27 square miles. So far, two jaeger species have been recorded here in addition to Sabine's Gull.

Fern Ridge pulls in a variety of land birds as well: eight species of flycatcher, eight woodpeckers, seven swallow species including Purple Martin (nesting) that linger into August. All the likely western warblers have been seen here along with a vagrant Palm Warbler.

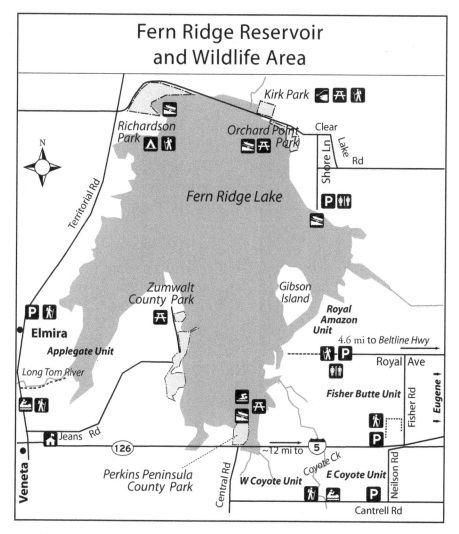

Fern Ridge Reservoir and Wildlife Area

Sixteen sparrow species have been reported including wintering Harris's, White-throated, Tree and Swamp. Other unusual sparrows seen here include Grasshopper, Brewer's and Vesper. Golden-crowned will be abundant every winter along with White-crowned and an occasional Lincoln's Sparrow hiding in the brush.

Lapland Longspur have turned up here. Other regional specialties seen here are Wrentit, Chestnut-backed Chickadee, Swainson's Thrush (more easily heard than seen) and Lazuli Bunting. How rich is the habitat mix? Well, both Evening Grosbeak and Great-tailed Grackle have been seen around Fern Ridge, and they prefer very different habitats. There are numerous birding spots, all shown on the map.

Around Fern Ridge are five developed county parks. At the north end of the reservoir are **Orchard Point Park, Richardson Park** and **Kirk Park.** At the south end you will find **Zumwalt Park** and **Perkins Peninsula Park.** What you'll find: toilets, hiking trails, fishing and picnic areas. Fees are charged at each park except Zumwalt and Kirk. There is an annual Lane County Park pass that is worthwhile to purchase if you are birding in the county regularly.

In addition to the county parks, around the perimeter of Fern Ridge Reservoir you'll find parking areas where you have access to good birding spots, the lake and places to launch a canoe, and to walks in wildlife areas.

Following is a list and descriptions of the best places for birding on the perimeter of Fern Ridge, arranged roughly by location: that is, which side of the lake they are on. Consult the *Fern Ridge* map. You could visit one or two birding spots, or you could take a circular tour around the lake. The distance would be at least 15-20 miles, depending on your side trips. The following descriptions go around the lake in a clockwise direction, starting at a midpoint on the eastern shore.

Fern Ridge Lake, East Area

Royal Amazon Unit. This area is about 13 miles from I-5, Exit 195. Take Beltline Highway, then after it takes a sharp turn south, turn west onto Royal Avenue and go the end. Along this route you pass Dragonfly Bend and Meadowlark Prairie open space. The latter has a viewing platform along Green Hill Road south of Royal Avenue. You can also get to Royal Avenue by turning north on Fisher Road after visiting the Fisher Butte Unit (see **Fern Ridge Lake, Southeast Area**).

At the end of Royal Avenue, there's a small parking lot and toilets. From there you can walk west on a gravel trail into the marsh on the eastern edge of Fern Ridge. In less than half a mile, you'll find a viewing platform just south of the trail. The platform overlooks the marsh and impounds of the Oregon Wildlife Area's Fisher Butte Unit (see below). Acorn Woodpeckers are in the large oaks east of the gate. This grassland is good for sparrows. West of the gate, the trail leads into canary grass and cattail marsh. During the winter and when the water level declines, one can walk beyond the vegetation area to the exposed mudflats.

Old gravel roads provide access to **Gibson Island** when the water is low. In the rainy season, boots are recommended for this hike. Gibson Island is about a mile west from the Royal Avenue parking lot. In fall and winter the mudflats and shallow water can be alive with shorebirds and waterfowl. One October, I saw two American Bittern in less than ten minutes. Northern Harrier and Peregrine can be expected and are easily watched in the flat, open terrain.

EBird shows nearly 200 species reported from Royal Avenue and its birding trails. Clark's Grebe, Virginia Rail, Sora, American Bittern, White-tailed Kite, Red-shouldered Hawk, Black and Caspian Tern in summer, Marsh Wren, wintering Short-eared Owl and Merlin can be seen here. Grasshopper Sparrows have been known to nest in these fields. Some uncommon birds have been seen: Emperor Goose, Brant, Eurasian Wigeon, Snowy Egret (north of its usual range), Sabine's Gull, Lapland Longspur. White-fronted Geese may number in the hundreds here in fall.

If shorebirds are your pleasure, Royal Avenue is your place: both American and Pacific Golden-Plover have appeared on migration. Other shorebirds to find: Black-necked Stilt breed here; Red Knot, Ruff, sandpiper species including Stilt, Sharp-tailed and Pectoral, both yellowlegs, Long-billed Curlew, both dowitchers, Marbled Godwit, American Avocet out of its normal range, Wilson's Snipe and Red-necked and Wilson's Phalarope in late summer. Ten shorebirds species on an August, September or October visit would be normal, despite the distance from the ocean. A first year Golden-Plover in 2011 sparked the usual American or Pacific debate.

Also reported from here: Peregrine, Horned Grebe, Bonaparte's Gull on migration, Northern Shrike, Evening Grosbeak in fall. Summer birds include: Purple Martin using nest boxes on poles in the marsh, Cedar Waxwing, Yellow-headed Blackbird, Lincoln's and Vesper Sparrow.

Fern Ridge Lake, Southeast Area

This area is most directly reached via I-5 Exit 192 and OR 126. If you have first gone to the Royal Avenue access, you can cut down to OR 126 on Fisher Road. Consult *Fern Ridge Lake* map.

Fisher Butte. Before reaching the reservoir's south end and just west of Fisher Road is a gated gravel road heading north from OR 126 (West 11th Avenue) towards Fisher Butte. A marked trail leads the hiker down the road through wet low prairie and seasonally flooded impoundment areas. The croplands are planted exclusively for wildlife food. Please be aware that this unit is frequented by waterfowl hunters in the fall, and winter closures may be in effect. The parking areas, though, provide viewing year-round.

During the winter one can see concentrations of waterfowl, shrikes, raptors, and large flocks of sparrows. Winter waterfowl viewing is best in the morning and evening. Canada Geese using the area from November through April include Duskies, a member of the Canada Goose complex. EBird shows over 140 species reported from this area. Twenty-three species of waterfowl have been sighted, including Ross's and Cackling Geese, breeding Redhead, Eurasian Wigeon and Canvasback. Over twenty species of shorebird have been reported, including Semipalmated Sandpiper, both yellowlegs, Wilson's and Red-necked Phalarope and Pectoral Sandpiper. August is the best time for shorebirds here. Tricolored Blackbird have also been seen in late summer.

The two **Coyote Units** of Fern Ridge Wildlife Area, East and West, are nearby, but on the opposite (south) side of OR 126. This area has grasslands and riparian trails. Along Cantrell Road (see *Fern Ridge* map) are two parking areas. Two parallel trails go north, one on each side of Coyote Creek, and there is also canoe access here. The cropland and moist soil units adjacent to the parking lots are excellent for all kinds of wintering waterfowl. Raptors, sparrows, shrikes, goldfinches, and blackbirds are also common. Late in the season, wintering flocks of waterfowl, including Tundra Swans, can often be found in the wet grass fields adjacent to the roads. Please note that waterfowl hunters may be present in the fall. Winter waterfowl and raptor viewing from the parking areas can be amazing, particularly near dusk. A bit west of here on Cantrell Road you will find the Wildlife Area headquarters.

Perkins Peninsula County Park is located near the south tip of the lake on OR 126 a little past the Coyote Units. What you'll find: a boat launch, picnic areas, swimming beach and fishing access. There's a parking fee. Perkins is on a small peninsula with excellent views of the reservoir in the summer, mudflats in the winter. There are large oaks, apple trees, willows, pines, and Douglas-fir, which are good places to find migrant passerines. A boardwalk leads out into a marshy bay on the west side of the park. The park is closed to motor vehicles during winter months but remains open year-round for foot traffic. It's a good place to observe nesting Osprey in spring.

West of Perkins Peninsula Park about 0.6 mile is a pullout on the north side of OR 126 overlooking the lake. Yellow-headed Blackbirds nest here. Purple Martins can be observed using the nest boxes on visible snags. Both species breed at other locations on the lake, but those areas generally are inaccessible except by boat. A variety of waterfowl is frequently visible from this site.

Fern Ridge Lake, Southwest Area

This area is reached by continuing west on OR126 to Territorial Road, which goes along the western edge of the lake. Territorial Road can also be reached from the north side of the lake via Clear Lake Road. See *Fern Ridge* map.

Zumwalt County Park. Zumwalt County Park is a largely undeveloped, natural park located along Jeans Road on Jeans Peninsula jutting into the southern portion of Fern Ridge. Zumwalt is open daily through the summer. In winter, while the reservoir is low, vehicle access is limited to the parking areas at the gates. Walking access is year-round. There is a parking fee. The south portion of Zumwalt has picnic facilities and relaxing open spaces while the northern section has a variety of habitat: marsh, grassland, lake shoreline, brush and willows, mixed hardwood, and Douglas-fir. Pileated Woodpeckers use the older trees at the north end of this park.

Birds here can include Red-shouldered Hawk, Virginia Rail, Hutton's Vireo, Wrentit, Brown Creeper, Bewick's and Marsh Wren, and Spotted Towhee. Migrating warblers include Black-throated Gray. In fall there can be flocks of Evening Grosbeak.

Applegate Unit— Long Tom River. The Long Tom River access in the Applegate Unit of the Fern Ridge Wildlife Area is in the southwest corner on Territorial Road, half-way between the towns of Veneta and Elmira. What you'll find: a parking lot on the east side of Territorial Road. Canoes can be put into the Long Tom River here, and there is a nature trail along the river, through the woods and open meadows. You can canoe or kayak down the Long Tom to the lake. The old river forks to the left and then, shortly downstream from the access point, meanders through a dense woodland understory. Log jams may present some difficulty on the channels. Wood Ducks, Osprey and Swainson's Thrush may be found in this area.

Applegate Unit— North Elmira Site. Immediately north of Elmira on the east side of Territorial Road is a parking area that provides access to wildlife lands. You'll find a wide area of open and woodland habitats here as well as hiking access to the Long Tom River delta where it empties into Fern Ridge. Great Blue Herons forage near the lake. Marsh Wren can be found in the cattail marshes during the summer. Wilson's Snipe winter here.

Fern Ridge Lake, Northwest Area

This area is most directly reached from the freeway by turning west off of OR 99 onto Clear Lake Road, which skirts the north side of the lake. You will leave I-5 at Exit 195 if this is your main destination. If coming from OR 126, you will turn north onto Territorial Road.

Richardson County Park. Richardson County Park is at the west end of the dam and at the northwest corner of Fern Ridge Lake. What you'll find: both traditional and RV campsites, a swimming beach, boat ramp, playground, hiking trails, toilets and picnic grounds. There's a parking fee. Richardson County Park contains 157 acres, much of it forested, so it's a good spot for songbirds, vireos and flycatchers. Warblers are common here during September migration, including Black-throated Gray. There are views of the lake and shore for waterbirds and shorebirds in fall. The park has a long, open waterfront beach and views of the western end of the dam.

Fern Ridge Lake, Northeast Area

This area is also most directly reached from the freeway by turning west off of OR 99 onto Clear Lake Road, which skirts the north side of the lake, having left I-5 at Exit 195.

Kirk Park. Kirk Park is the farthest west facility in this quadrant and is north of the dam along Clear Lake Road. What you'll find: toilets, picnic areas, fishing, and hiking trails. This county park has great towering oaks and a large year-round pond with a marshy border. Kirk Park is adjacent to the outflow from Fern Ridge Reservoir. Though it's just across the road from the dam, you cannot get onto the dam directly from Kirk Park. Waterfowl, Belted Kingfisher and gulls frequent Kirk Pond.

Nearby, **Orchard Point County Park** is at the northeast corner of Fern Ridge Lake at the east end of the dam. It is about 14 miles from I-5 Exit 195. What you'll find: There are two sections to the park: the recreation and picnic area have a separate entrance from the marina. Orchard Point covers 49 acres. The park is open dawn to dusk, with picnic areas, marina and boat ramp, concession stand and playground. Dogs are allowed on leash in all Lane County Parks. There's a parking fee.

In fall and winter the boat docks and ramp are landlocked, but you can scope the mudflats and lake along the dam face for shorebirds and waterbirds. The parking area at the marina offers a good vantage point for viewing grebes and other lake birds. The marina also offers access to the dam, which is about 1.2 miles long. In fall and winter this is a good place to find shorebirds, grebes and diving ducks.

EBird shows over 150 species recorded from Orchard Point, Kirk Park and the Fern Ridge Dam, which is accessible from the Orchard Point Marina parking lot. This large boulder dam is walkable all the way to the outlet near the western end. Some prizes reported from this north end of Fern Ridge: Falcated Duck, Eurasian Wigeon, Redhead, Red-necked Grebe, Franklin's Gull, Bank Swallow, White-throated Sparrow, Evening Grosbeak. Blown or flown in from the ocean: Black-legged Kittiwake, Sabine's Gull, Mew Gull, Parasitic and Long-Tailed Jaegers.

Shore Lane. On the east side of Fern Ridge, at the south end of Shore Lane is a parking lot, toilets and a boat ramp. It's a half-mile from Clear Lake Road by either approach (see *Fern Ridge Lake* map). Ducks, grebes and marsh-loving songbirds may be found here, including Marsh Wren and Swainson's Thrush (summer). Starting in October the lake will be quite a distance from dry land, but with a scope, numerous shorebirds and waterfowl can be visible. With care you may be able to walk a few dozen yards onto the mudflats for closer scoping of the waterfront and lake birds. There's a woodland adjacent to the parking area that can be birded. EBird shows almost 60 species reported from this single location at Fern Ridge, including Blue-winged Teal. A Snowy Owl was here for some time during a recent irruption of that species.

For further information on facilities contact Fern Ridge Wildlife Area, 26969 Cantrell Road, Eugene, OR 97402. (541) 935-2591. This is an agency of the State of Oregon, open Monday through Friday, regular business hours. EBird shows nearly 100 species just from the area surrounding the headquarters.

Other Eugene Area Locales. There are many fine and active birders in the Eugene area, so rarities are often sighted in unusual places. One winter a Red-naped Sapsucker settled into pines next to a Safeway grocery parking lot in town. But there are some spots that are less chancy – even dependable – for rewarding birding.

Consult the *Eugene Parks* map for the various locations. Eugene has three I-5 exits (192, 194 and 195) and any of them will eventually get you to these listings, all of which are west of the freeway. They are grouped below by the closest interchange.

I-5 Exit 192. Agate Hall, at 1791 Agate Street (which connects to Franklin Boulevard), is a Mission-style building constructed in 1924 for use as a junior high school. Now it houses offices of the University of Oregon. Each September the chimney is used by thousands of migrating Vaux's Swifts, who are watched by dozens of birders every evening. Sometimes a Kestrel or Sharp-shinned Hawk will be waiting to snatch a swift as it comes down to roost. A second autumn roost of Vaux's Swifts is the chimney of a store at Fifth and Willamette in downtown Eugene.

Hendricks Park. Hendricks Park, reached just off of Agate Street in the same neighborhood, is the oldest city park in Eugene. Its 78 acres include a mature Douglas-fir forest with many oaks and broadleaf maples beneath the canopy. What you'll find: parking, toilets, trails and information. EBird data is sparse, but this park is a good place for woodpeckers, including Acorn, and other forest birds like wintering kinglets of both flavors, nuthatches and Brown Creepers. Besides the rhododendron garden, here the star of the show is the Pileated Wood-pecker that may be seen.

For **Whilamut Natural Area** within **Alton Baker Park,** located right along the north bank of the Willamette River just east of Coburg Road near downtown Eugene, eBird shows 115 species. Wintering waterfowl may include Greater White-fronted Goose, Cackling Goose, Eurasian Wigeon, both scaup, and Hooded and Common Merganser. Merlin and Peregrine are possible in autumn. Seven gull species have been recorded, including Glaucous-winged and Mew. Vaux's Swift breed here. Anna's Hummingbird is resident. This is a hotspot for fall and spring migrants as well. Birds of passage may include Rufous Hum-mingbird, Red-breasted Sapsucker, Western Wood-Pewee (also breeding here), and Lazuli Bunting. Bushtit and Black-capped Chickadee can be abundant every autumn. Whilamut Natural Area has no facilities, but Alton Baker Park is equipped with toilets, play and picnic areas, off-leash dog park, trails, information, and gardens. Note that the east end of Alton Baker Park is adjacent to the University of Oregon football stadium (Autzen Stadium) which means parking and streets will be congested on autumn days when there are home football games.

Skinner Butte Park sits across the Willamette River from Whilamut Natural Area (see above) and is connected by foot and bike bridge. Feeders in the public gardens here may attract Black-headed Grosbeaks, finches and other species. What you'll find: parking, toilets, paved paths, trails and picnic areas. Skinner Butte's 110 acres are a favorite spot for local birders seeking spring migrants. The north end of the park runs along the south side of the Willamette River. The butte rises above the river valley and the surrounding city offering a green oasis to northward bound birds. Skinner Butte is steep-sided, but you can drive to the top, 682 feet in elevation. The woods on the butte are mixed ponderosa, red cedar, oak and maple.

EBird shows over 90 species recorded here, including eight flycatchers and ten warblers. From April through September, Vaux's Swift can be seen over the butte. Together Skinner Butte and Alton Baker parks are prime spring birding spots. Some years Bald Eagles nest on this stretch of river. A September or late August migrant flock can yield Wilson's, Black-throated Gray, Orange-crowned and Townsend's Warbler; Warbling and Cassin's Vireo; Hammond's and Pacific-slope Flycatcher; Western Tanager; and Black-headed Grosbeak. Other birds found here include Brown Creeper and Bushtit, often in numbers.

I-5 Exit 194. Delta Ponds City Park in Eugene is about 3.5 miles from Exit 194 off I-5. Take I-105 west. After reaching the Willamette River, turn north onto Delta Highway as it follows the river. The park is right off Delta Highway on the west (river) side. Delta Ponds is on an island in the Willamette River and contains 125 acres. See *Eugene Parks* map. What you'll find: toilets, trail and viewing platforms. There's a parking lot at the northwest corner of the park along Green Pasture Island Road. A gravel trail curls around much of the eastern set of ponds. Most Oregon riparian species can be found here in season.

Breeding birds here include Wood Duck, Green Heron, Willow Flycatcher and Black-headed Grosbeak. A score of waterfowl have been sighted here, including Eurasian Wigeon in winter. River otters are also possible. Common Nighthawk has been found here in warm months. During autumn migration, the partially dry ponds provide habitat for shorebirds, sometimes including Pectoral Sandpiper. Wintering sparrows may include Lincoln's and White-throated. EBird shows over 110 species recorded here.

I-5 Exit 195. Armitage Park. From Exit 195 go west a mile on Beltline Highway, turn north onto Coburg Road. Armitage Park, a Lane County park on the McKenzie River is on Coburg Road in about 2 miles. This river flows west from the Cascades and flows into the Willamette north of Eugene. What you'll find: 57 acres of riparian forest, toilets, picnic grounds and a dog park. There's a parking fee. Birds you could find here include Osprey, Bald Eagle, Great Blue Heron, Belted Kingfisher, American Dipper, Spotted Sandpiper and Common Merganser. The forest here has Western Screech-Owl, Spotted Towhee, Downy Woodpecker, Black-capped Chickadee, Northern Flicker, Brown Creeper, Chestnut-backed Chickadee, Fox Sparrow, Hermit Thrush, House and Purple Finch, Hutton's Vireo, Red-breasted Nuthatch, Bushtit, Lesser and American Goldfinch and Steller's Jay. Migrants or wintering birds can include Townsend's Warbler, Varied Thrush and Red-breasted Sapsucker.

Golden Gardens City Park. If you are coming from or going to the north side of Fern Ridge Lake (see entry for Fern Ridge) you will already be in the neighborhood. Consult *Eugene Parks* map. Golden Gardens City Park, covering 147 acres, is just off of Clear Lake Road, on the way to the lake. It includes former gravel pits, now ponds that attract wildlife. It also has brush and cottonwoods that attract songbirds. Surrounding farmland yields grassland birds like Savannah Sparrow and Western Meadowlark.

Eugene Airport. The airport is also in the vicinity of Clear Creek Road, the northernmost access road to Fern Ridge Lake. From OR 99, turn west onto Airport Road, which is about a mile north of Clear Creek Road (the route to the lake). Like many airports, Eugene's is surrounded by grassland, and that attracts certain species. Rough-legged Hawk, Prairie Falcon and Harrier may be seen here in winter.

North of Eugene

Note: *There is no bridge crossing the Willamette River between Junction City and Corvallis. Winter ground fog can be dense on the Willamette Valley.*

I-5 Exit 205. Oak Grove Rest Area. From both directions, the rest areas provide a chance to bird oak woodland. Along the Willamette Valley expect Canada Geese, Red-tailed Hawk, American Kestrel, Brewer's and Red-winged Blackbirds, Turkey Vultures, Blue Heron, Great Egret,

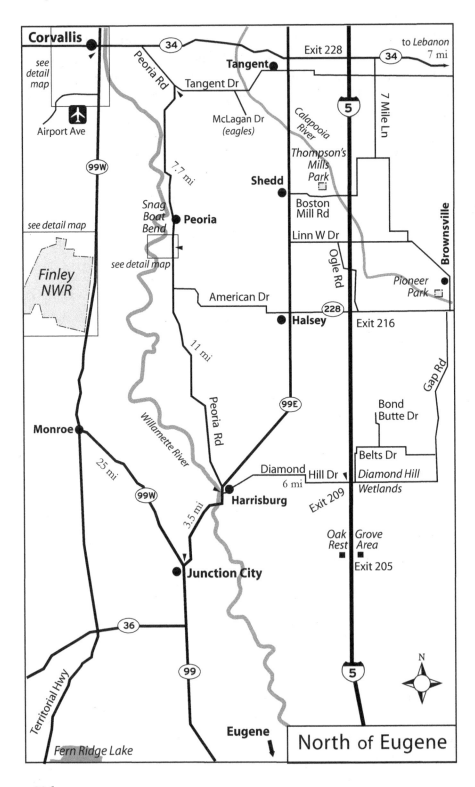

North of Eugene

both eagles, Tundra Swans, Glaucous-winged Gulls, Rough-legged Hawk and Prairie Falcon. Kestrel and Great Blue Heron are year-round residents. The southbound rest area here has a stand of mature oak and deciduous trees plus a small seasonal slough on its western border. Birds I've found here in warm months include Western Wood-Pewee, Lesser Goldfinch and Brewer's Blackbird.

I-5 Exit 209. Diamond Hill Wetlands. Exit here onto Diamond Hill Road (see *North of Eugene* map.) There are wetlands in both directions. Nearest to I-5 is the privately owned, restored Diamond Hill Wetlands, which includes 130 acres of marsh and 300 acres of prairie. It's located 1 mile east of the freeway on the north side of Diamond Hill Road. In winter large flocks of Dunlin and numerous waterfowl species may be found here. Both eagles and Peregrine are occasionally seen, along with Northern Harrier and an occasional Rough-legged Hawk in winter. Short-eared Owls may hunt the fields on winter evenings. Some winter days these fields fill with gulls, which can include California, Ring-billed, Thayer's and Glaucous-winged.

Also in this area are **Gap Road, Bond Butte Drive** and **Belts Drive**, south of Brownsville and east of I-5. See *North of Eugene* map. If you are heading north, you can continue north on Gap Road and return to I-5 via Exit 216, west of Brownsville. See below. This area is especially good for grassland sparrows. Spotted Towhee; Chipping, Brewer's, Vesper, Lark, Savannah, Grasshopper, Fox, Song, Lincoln's, White-throated, White-crowned and Golden-crowned Sparrows; and Junco have all been reported in this area. Loggerhead Shrike is possible in warm months, Northern Shrike in winter. Turkey Vultures gather in the grass fields after mowing, feasting on the chopped up mammals and snakes. Bald Eagles also may hunt carrion in the pastures here in winter. There's little eBird data for this section of Linn County.

I-5 Exit 216. Ogle Wetlands and **Pioneer City Park.** See *North of Eugene* map. Heading east on OR 228, in a short distance you will see Ogle Road on your left. Turn north to bird Ogle Wetlands. Returning to OR 228, continue east looking for possible winter birds in the farmland. Prospects are good for Cackling Geese, Bald Eagles, Great

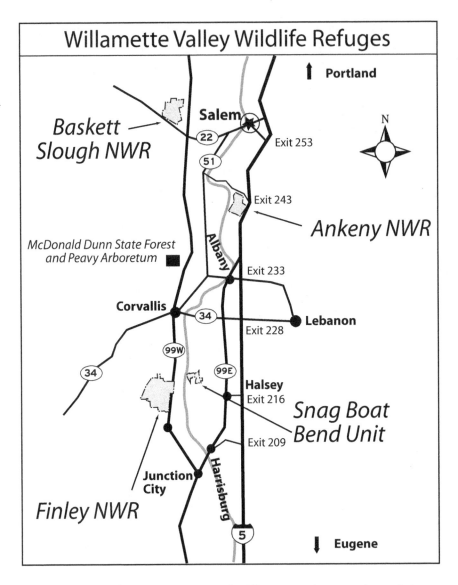

Willamette Valley Wildlife Refuges

Blue Herons and American Kestrels. If you continue on into the town of Brownsville about 4 miles from the freeway, you can bird Pioneer City Park on the Calapooia River. EBird holds no data for these sites. Rarities from past seasons include Pectoral and Stilt Sandpiper, Tufted Duck, White-faced Ibis (north of its usual range), Blue-winged Teal (not expected this far west) and Red-breasted Merganser (far from the nearest ocean). Pioneer Park produces warblers on migration and woodpeckers year-round, including Red-breasted Sapsucker.

West of I-5. I-5 Exits 209, 216, and 228. There are a number of birding spots west of I-5 between Eugene to the south and Corvallis (which is on not on I-5 but is on 99W) to the north. All can be reached via these I-5 exits, via OR 99E or OR 99W (which go up either side of the Willamette River) or from Corvallis. Check the *North of Eugene* map to see what will work best for you.

William L. Finley National Wildlife Refuge (NWR). This is a minimum three-hour detour, but birding can be especially rewarding during the wet months of fall and winter. Once you cross the Willamette River, you have left Linn County and entered Benton County. The refuge is about 10 miles south of Corvallis or 7.5 miles north of Monroe on OR 99W. Watch for Milepost 93 near the National Wildlife Refuge entrance sign. If you have time for only one stop, drive 2.8 miles west from OR 99 on Finley Road to Cabell Marsh. It's a short walk downhill from the parking lot to overlook the marsh.

The Finley National Wildlife Refuge covers over 5,300 acres. It's the southernmost unit of the Willamette Valley NWR. Other units are Ankeny and Baskett Slough. A small, separate portion of the Finley refuge, **Snag Boat Bend,** is further south. See the next entry for details. This large main section of Finley on OR 99W includes creeks, ponds, marsh, woodland and grassland. Wooded areas have mature oaks, maple and Douglas-fir. There are 12 miles of hiking trails, an auto tour route and wildlife viewing platforms. There's a visitors center with limited hours, and there are toilets, but only three in the entire refuge. If you hike the trail to Pigeon Butte in the southeast quarter of the refuge, you'll get panoramic views of the Willamette Valley. There is also a photo blind on McFadden Marsh. The Willamette itself is several miles east of the Finley NWR.

Almost 250 species of birds have been reported at the Finley Refuge. In addition, there are numerous mule deer and elk. In winter, resident Canada Geese are joined by Cackling Geese and Dusky subspecies. Twenty-nine species of waterfowl have been recorded at Finley NWR, including Tundra and, rarely, Trumpeter Swans; Brant; Eurasian Wigeon; Redhead; both scaup; and all three mergansers. Over two dozen shorebirds have been reported to eBird and eleven species of flycatcher.

The elusive American Bittern nests here in small numbers. Nesting raptors include Osprey (gone in winter), White-tailed Kite, Bald Eagle, Northern Harrier and Cooper's Hawk. Both Virginia Rail and Sora breed here, along with five species of owl, including Long-eared. Northern Shrike is a winter regular.

Breeding birds include Vaux's Swift, Rufous Hummingbird, Pacific-slope Flycatcher, Cassin's and Hutton's Vireo, Horned Lark, Violet-green Swallow, Chestnut-backed Chickadee, Bushtit, four species of wren, Swainson's Thrush, Black-throated Gray Warbler, MacGillivray's and Wilson's Warbler, Spotted Towhee and Lesser Goldfinch. Gyrfalcon have

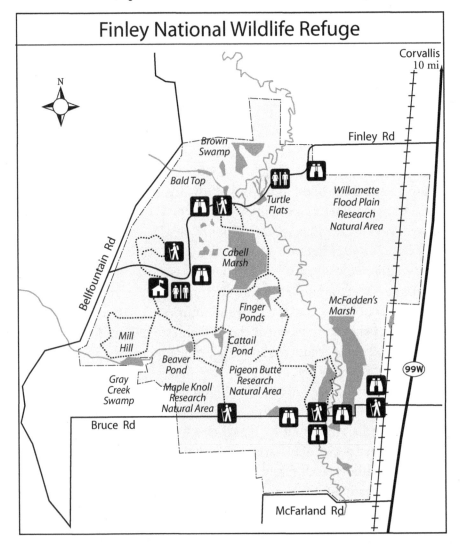

been found here in late winter. Other unexpected birds spotted here include Ruffed Grouse, Mountain Quail, White-faced Ibis, wintering Goshawk, Swainson's Hawk on migration, Burrowing and Saw-Whet Owl and Hammond's Flycatcher on migration. Black Phoebe and Lewis's Woodpecker have also been seen here in winter.

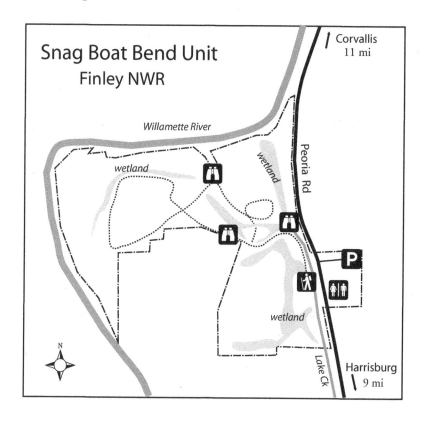

Snag Boat Bend. Elevation 275 feet. This unit of the William L. Finley National Wildlife Refuge is separate from the main part described above. It is not too far as the bird flies but is a roundabout trip by car (consult the *North of Eugene* map). This is also the only part of the extensive Willamette Valley National Wildlife Refuges that actually borders on the Willamette River itself.

What you'll find: toilets, a hiking trail and a photo blind. This unit is over 375 acres of riparian habitat with seasonal wetlands. There is a boardwalk and overlook at Beaver Pond. In the winter, nearby fields can have Tundra Swan flocks, Prairie and Peregrine Falcon, Rough-legged Hawk and Burrowing Owl. There's little data on birding here, but

Marsh Wren and Spotted Towhee are resident. The Golden-crowned Sparrow is an abundant winter bird. Nesting birds include Black Phoebe, Western Wood-Pewee, Willow Flycatcher, Yellow-breasted Chat, Swainson's Thrush and Wilson's Warbler. Listen for Pileated Woodpecker drumming and calling in the cottonwood gallery forest.

I-5 Exit 228, East. Lebanon. If you go east on OR 34 from Exit 228 you will be heading toward Lebanon. There are several good birding places in this direction. Lebanon is about 7 miles from I-5. Four miles north of Lebanon are **Griggs Mill Ponds** (on Brewster Road) where ducks and even a Swamp Sparrow may be found in winter. The ponds can also be reached from Exit 233 at Albany (see below). Grassland birds like Harrier, Western Meadowlark and Horned Lark can be expected. Wintering sparrows in the thickets may include Lincoln's and White-throated among the many White-crowned and Golden-crowned.

I-5 Exit 228, West. If you're southbound, this is your I-5 exit for **William L. Finley National Wildlife Refuge,** both the main unit and Snag Boat Bend (see details above). From Exit 228 take OR 34 west towards Corvallis, which has several good birding sites. But before you get there, if looking for grassland birds you may need to go on a tangent. Actually you need to go to Tangent, west of I-5 on OR 99E, elevation 246 feet. Tangent is near two interesting birding locations, one east and one west of town.

    Thompson's Mill State Heritage Area. About a mile west of I-5 turn south off OR 34 onto OR 99E. Go through the town of Tangent and on to the burg of Shedd, then turn east on Boston Mill Road. What you'll find: The Thompson's Mill State Heritage Area on the Calapooia River features a historic flour mill. A toilet is available. Birds possible in the pastures include wintering Prairie Falcon and Rough-legged Hawk. Other wintering birds: American Pipit, Dunlin and occasional Golden-Plover (both Pacific and American). One recent winter a Mountain Plover and Pacific Golden-Plover were sharing the same fields near Tangent. Other rarities occasionally found here include Snow Bunting and Lapland Longspur. Savannah Sparrow, Western Meadowlark and

Horned Lark breed in this area. An occasional Burrowing Owl may be seen in this general area in fall or winter.

There is a wintering Bald Eagle roost southwest of Tangent along the Calapooia River, a tributary of the Willamette, which flows down from the Cascades. From OR99W at Tangent, turn west onto North Lake Creek Drive, which soon turns into SW Tangent Drive. After crossing the Calapooia River turn south onto McLagan Road. About a mile south on McLagan you will cross Seward Road which runs east-west. Park near this intersection, as the east end of Seward is a private road. It is at that end where the eagles roost in trees near the river. Bald Eagles of all ages can be found here into early spring. The eagles are attracted to the area by the dense population of wintering waterfowl at nearby Finley NWR and across this low-lying river valley.

If you continue west on Tangent Drive you will reach Peoria Road. Turn south for the riverside village of **Peoria**, about 9 miles by road from Tangent. If you're in Corvallis or coming across from I-5 Exit 228 on the way to Corvallis, take Peoria Road south from OR 34 east of town. There are numerous feeders in town to attract wintering birds to private yards and gardens. You can park at the church on the south end of town and walk the two main roads. Peoria is a good birding spot in cold months, attracting vagrants that huddle along the river: Pyrrhuloxia, White-throated Sparrow, Palm Warbler and more regular western birds have been reported here.

Just south of Peoria on Peoria Road you will find the Snag Boat Bend unit of the Finley NWA. See Finley NWR entry above.

I-5 Exit 228, West. Corvallis is on OR 99W about 10 miles west of the freeway exit. The climate here is mild. Corvallis gets just over 40 inches of precipitation in an average year. August is the hottest month, with an average high over 81. January and December are the coolest months with an average high above 45, while the average low stays just above freezing. Over half the precipitation here occurs from November through February, with July and August being the driest months. Snow is rare. The elevation at this point in the Willamette Valley is only 235 feet, though it's more than 40 miles west to the Pacific Ocean. The Coastal Range separates this valley from the coastal weather. Marys

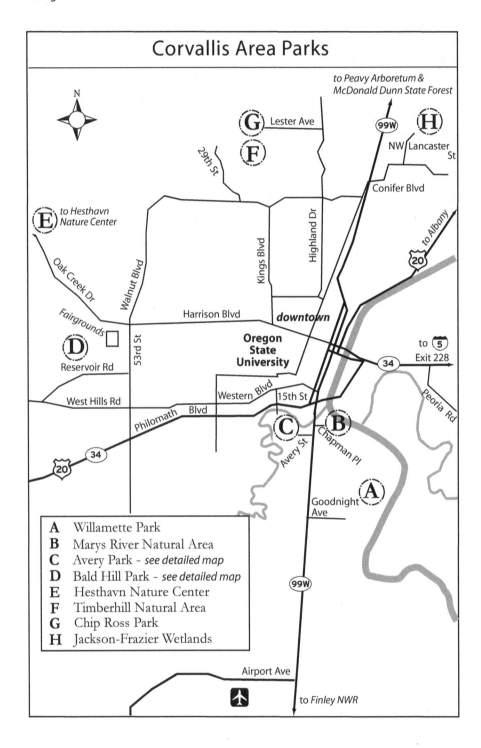

Corvallis Area Parks

to Peavy Arboretum &
McDonald Dunn State Forest

G Lester Ave
F

29th St

99W

H

NW Lancaster St

Conifer Blvd

E to Hesthavn Nature Center

Oak Creek Dr

Walnut Blvd

Kings Blvd

Highland Dr

to Albany

20

Fairgrounds

Harrison Blvd

downtown

D

53rd St

Reservoir Rd

Oregon State University

to 5 Exit 228

34

West Hills Rd

Western Blvd

15th St

Philomath Blvd

34

20

C

B

Avery St

Chapman Pl

Peoria Rd

A

Goodnight Ave

99W

A	Willamette Park
B	Marys River Natural Area
C	Avery Park - *see detailed map*
D	Bald Hill Park - *see detailed map*
E	Hesthavn Nature Center
F	Timberhill Natural Area
G	Chip Ross Park
H	Jackson-Frazier Wetlands

Airport Ave

to *Finley NWR*

Peak, west of Corvallis, is over 4000 feet high and gets winter snow. Some areas of the nearby Coastal Range receive about 100 inches of precipitation annually.

Corvallis Area Birding Spots

Corvallis is birded heavily by locals, and that means numerous rarities have been cited in recent decades: Snowy Owl, Red-naped Sapsucker, Allen's Hummingbird (a coastal species), Sooty Grouse (normally a montane bird), Gray Flycatcher, Indigo Bunting, Blue Grosbeak, Harris's Sparrow and Cassin's Finch (another mountain species).

Corvallis sites are listed south to north. See *Corvallis Area Parks* map.

Corvallis Airport. The airport is 5 miles south of Corvallis on OR99W, then west on Airport Avenue. You pass this way en route to Finley NWR from Corvallis. EBird shows over a hundred species for this area including 18 waterfowl and 11 raptors. It's worth birding in winter months. One year a Gyrfalcon was found here. Rough-legged Hawks may winter in this vicinity. More likely are Merlin and Short-eared Owls.

Willamette Park and Natural Area. This is Corvallis's largest city park. It is well down in southeast Corvallis, at the end of Goodnight Avenue off of OR 99W. What you'll find: picnic facilities, toilet, recreational facilities (Frisbee golf), paths, trails, and a boat ramp. The park contains over 280 acres, mostly undeveloped woodland, and it also offers open meadows and seasonal wetlands. Much of it is off-leash for dogs. The riparian forest includes huge oaks and maples and the park has nearly 1.5 miles of riverbank along the Willamette.

EBird shows over 130 species reported from this area, including seven species of wintering gull, Townsend's Warbler in spring and Swainson's Thrush in summer. Other resident birds include Western Screech-Owl, Hairy and Pileated Woodpeckers and Brown Creeper. Across the Willamette is a Great Blue Heron rookery.

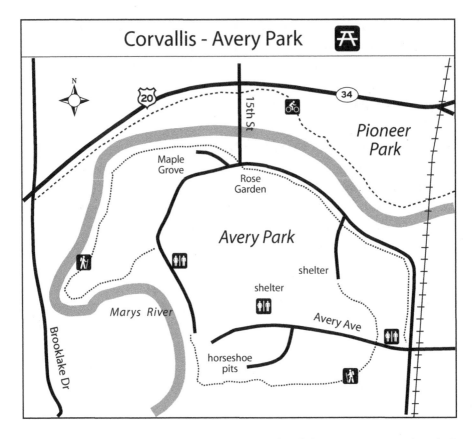

Avery Park and Natural Area is south of downtown. See detailed *Avery Park* map. From Philomath Boulevard (US 20/OR 34 bypass), exit at the 15th Street stoplight and cross the bridge south into the park. Or, from 99W South, turn west onto Avery Avenue, which dead-ends at the park. What you'll find: picnic areas, toilets, trails, nature center, sports fields and a bike trail. Avery Park is a riparian forest right along the Marys River and its bottomland. The park is over 75 acres. Trees here include oaks, bigleaf maple and Douglas-fir.

EBird records for Avery are sparse, but among birds found here are Pileated Woodpecker, Great Horned Owl, Belted Kingfisher, California Quail, accipiters, wintering Varied Thrush and Townsend's Warbler, Brown Creeper and Rufous Hummingbird. Spring warblers pass through on migration. Wrentits here are near the northern end of their inland range.

Marys River Natural Area. This 74-acre city park may be closed by winter flooding. It is situated where Marys River flows down from the Coastal Range into the Willamette River, south of downtown just west of OR 99W on Chapman Place. What you'll find: toilets, a wheelchair accessible boardwalk and a hiking trail. This area is mainly riparian forest and native prairie along the seasonal wetlands. In addition to expected marsh and riparian bird species, you may find Vaux's Swift overhead. Nesting species include Lazuli Bunting, White-crowned Sparrow, Common Yellowthroat and Western Bluebird. Ebird records are sparse for this park as well.

Bald Hill Natural Area is near Benton County Fairgrounds in west Corvallis. See *Corvallis Area Parks* map for how to get there and *Bald Hill Park* map for details. What you'll find: trails, horseback riding, bike path, off-leash dog area. The multi-modal path leading into the natural area may be accessed from three locations: a path next to the Benton County Fairgrounds, behind the gate off of Oak Creek Road to the north, and at an entrance off of Reservoir Road. This park has

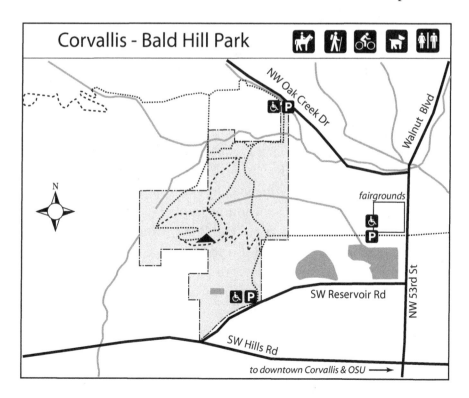

over 280 acres and protects some significant mature oak savannah, once a dominant habitat type in the Willamette Valley. There are also native grasslands and wetlands. The summit of Bald Hill affords a panoramic view of the nearby portion of the Willamette Valley.

Barn Owls have roosted in the old barn, while Great Horned Owls can sometimes be found in the woods. EBird shows 80 species reported from Bald Hill, almost entirely land birds, ranging from Red-shouldered Hawk to Rufous Hummingbird, from Northern Harrier to Red-breasted Sapsucker. Other birds likely here are Spotted Towhee, Swainson's Thrush (spring), Western Bluebird and Lazuli Bunting (summer). One winter, a vagrant Blue Jay was found here. During migration you could find Wilson's and Black-throated Gray among the warblers. Golden-crowned Sparrows winter here.

Hesthavn Nature Center is located on the western edge of Corvallis in oak savannah. From downtown Corvallis, take Harrison Boulevard west and keep going after it crosses Walnut and turns into Oak Creek Drive. Covering a little more than 5 acres, this small nature reserve is the property of the Audubon Society of Corvallis. What you'll find: a visitors center where you can find out about the many programs and field trips offered, picnic areas, toilets, display cases and a nature trail. A book on the birds of Hesthavn shows over a hundred species in the area.

Northwest of central Corvallis via OR 99W (See *Corvallis Area Parks* map for how to get there) is **Chip Ross Park** and the adjacent **Timberhill Natural Area.** Chip Ross Park, owned by the city, is on a hill with forested slopes, mostly oak and Douglas-fir. It has over 125 acres of open space, and that's enhanced by the 47 acres in adjacent **Timberhill Natural Area** just to the south, another Corvallis city property.

McDonald Dunn State Forest and **Peavy Arboretum**, which belong to Oregon State University, are also adjacent to Chip Ross Park on the north, although the main entrance to this extensive property is further up OR 99W, 6 miles from downtown Corvallis. You turn left (west) onto Arboretum Drive to reach the entrance.

The McDonald Dunn State Forest, which serves as a training ground for University forestry students, is a huge 11,250 acres. The State Forest, and the Peavy Arboretum within it (see *Peavy Arboretum* detail map),

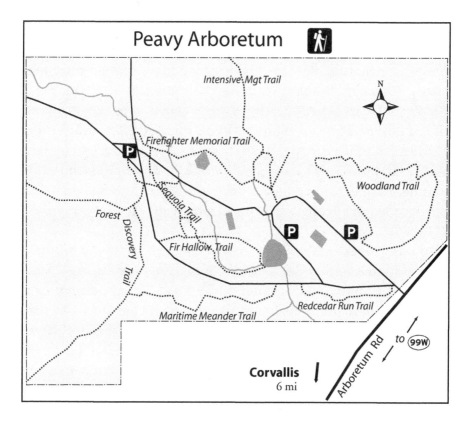

Peavy Arboretum

Intensive Mgt Trail

Firefighter Memorial Trail

Sequoia Trail

Forest Discovery Trail

Fir Hallow Trail

Woodland Trail

Maritime Meander Trail

Redcedar Run Trail

Arboretum Rd to 99W

Corvallis
6 mi

cover several ridges in the rugged terrain on the western edge of the Willamette Valley and the eastern slopes of the Coastal Range. In this vicinity are Dimple Hill at 1,495 feet, and Price Peak at 1,875 feet. Within the state forest are protected stands of old-growth forest, areas believed to be Spotted Owl habitat. Other parts of the state forest are managed as commercial timber, with regular harvesting and replanting. Habitats in this large area include oak woodland, evergreen dominated forest, grasslands, mountain meadows, and riparian corridors. There are some stands of western hemlock and red cedar as well as bigleaf maple (in wet areas). In drier locations poison oak is abundant here.

Birds to be found include Pileated Woodpecker, Olive-sided Flycatcher (spring and summer), Purple Martin (spring and summer), Brown Creeper, Hutton's Vireo and Nashville Warbler. Brushy areas around the park may have Wrentit, Western Bluebird and Lazuli Bunting (in warm months). Rarities that have turned up here include: Ruffed Grouse and Red-naped Sapsucker. This is a rich spot for land birds, and eBird shows 70 species from Peavy Arboretum and Chip Ross Park combined. These include Band-tailed Pigeon, Vaux's Swift, Anna's and Rufous Hummingbird, Red-breasted Sapsucker, Pileated Woodpecker, Olive-sided and Pacific-slope Flycatcher (both in spring), three local vireos (Cassin's, Hutton's, Warbling), Chestnut-backed Chickadee, Blue-gray Gnatcatcher (a spring vagrant north of its range), Wren-tit, Swainson's Thrush (summer), Black-throated Gray and Wilson's Warblers (possible nesters), Western Tanager, Black-headed Grosbeak and Lazuli Bunting. That list should make for a nice spring morning's birding. Rarities spotted here in the past: Ruffed and Sooty Grouse, Spotted Owl and Red-naped Sapsucker (normally east of the Cascades).

Jackson-Frazier Wetlands. This is a 144-acre preserve in northeast Corvallis at the north end of Lancaster Street. You get to Lancaster Street by way of Conifer Boulevard, off of OR 99W. This is north of Chip Ross Park but south of the Peavy Arboretum (see *Corvallis Area Parks* map). Much of the wetland is administered by Benton County Natural Areas & Parks Department, with the assistance of the Jackson-Frazier Wetland Advisory Committee. You can walk a two-thirds-mile-long wooden boardwalk in the southeast corner of the park.

Jackson-Frazier Wetlands is an important refuge and stopover for birds. More than 90 species have been identified here. Among them are Virginia Rail, Sora and Marsh Wren, as well as Great Blue and Green Heron, Killdeer, Wilson's Snipe and various ducks. The shrubs harbor sparrows, Bewick's Wren, Wrentit, Common Yellowthroat and Spotted Towhee. In the trees one can find finches, winter and summer warblers, Cedar Waxwing, Western Tanager and thrushes. Northern Harriers patrol the open areas, and Sharp-shinned and Cooper's Hawk hunt in the trees for small birds. This could be an exciting stop during the spring migration.

North along OR 99W. Six miles from Corvallis you will reach the entrance to McDonald Dunn State Forest and Peavy Arboretum (see details above). If you continue driving north along OR 99W from McDonald Dunn rather than returning to I-5, you will come to several other good birding areas west of Albany, such as E.E. Wilson Wildlife Area and Luckiamute State Natural Area. The Wilson Wildlife Area is about 10 miles from the Peavy Arboretum. These spots are detailed under the Albany listing below and on the *Albany Vicinity* map.

I-5 Exits 233 and 234. Albany Area Birding Spots. See *Albany* map for exact locations. Elevation here is 212 feet.

South Albany. Grand Prairie Park, with its expanse of 10 acres in southeast Albany, is a winter specialty area, good for a quick stop. What you'll find: toilets, picnic tables, a playground, a creek forming a small lake, and pathways. In addition to gulls and ducks, species you might find include Eurasian Wigeon, Thayer's, Western, California, Glaucous and Glaucous-winged Gulls. Varied Thrush have wintered here some years. Bald Eagle and Osprey fish here.

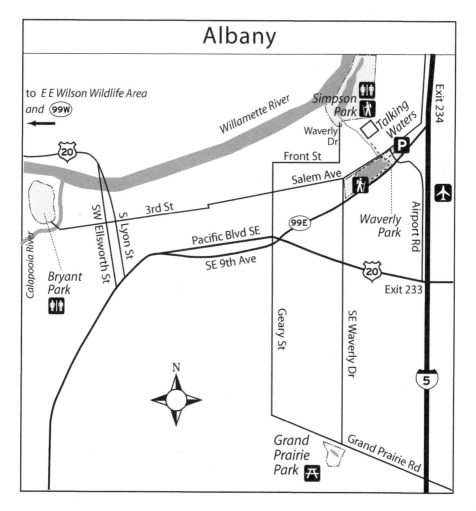

West Albany. At the confluence of the Calapooia and Willamette Rivers, **Bryant Park** covers 73 acres. What you'll find: toilets, recreational and picnic areas, access to river, stream and lake, bike path and trail access. There is usually an Osprey nest here each spring.

North Albany. Simpson Park, an Albany city park on the banks of the Willamette, is a good place for migrant or wintering waterfowl and shorebirds. What you'll find: toilets and a nature trail. The trail runs along the river and old logging ponds. The riparian forest of Douglas-fir and deciduous trees has Red-breasted Sapsucker and abundant songbirds, especially during migration. Wintering ducks could include Eurasian Wigeon. Bewick's and Pacific Wren, Hutton's Vireo and Spotted Towhee can also be found here. Ebird lists almost 100 species for this park.

Right off OR 99E, **Waverly Park** has a small lake, toilets, paved trail, paddleboats in summer. This is a good place to stretch your legs and have a short walk. The trail goes around the lake, then crosses over Salem Avenue on the north edge of the park and continues along Cox Creek, which drains Waverly Lake into the nearby Willamette River. There may be several species of wintering ducks, California and Ring-billed Gulls and a few songbirds in the bordering trees.

Between Simpson and Waverly Parks you can find **Talking Waters Gardens**, a wastewater bioremediation area. There is a trail around the 10-acre site, which attracts waterbirds, shorebirds and landbirds. Talking Waters was first opened to public access in June, 2012, so bird records are scant.

I-5 Exit 233. Rural Roads East of Albany. If you take time to explore some of the rural roads east of Albany you'll find extensive farmland and patches of oak woodland. Birds you can encounter in the wooded areas include California Quail, Bewick's Wren, winter sparrow flocks including Golden-crowned and White-crowned, nesting Orange-crowned Warblers, Black-headed Grosbeak, Northern Orioles, and Western Wood-Pewees, Year-round birds include Black-capped Chickadee, Western Scrub-Jay and Spotted Towhee.

One eastside option is **Griggs**. From Albany I-5 Exit 233, head east on US 20. Continue going straight onto OR 220 as US 20 veers southeast, then turn south on Brewster Road to reach the town of Griggs. This is about 9 miles from I-5. Former mill ponds here can be rich birding, especially in fall and winter: waterfowl, Black Phoebe and even American Bittern have been found here.

I-5 Exit 233. West of Albany and north of US 20 you will find more promising birding habitat, especially in winter.

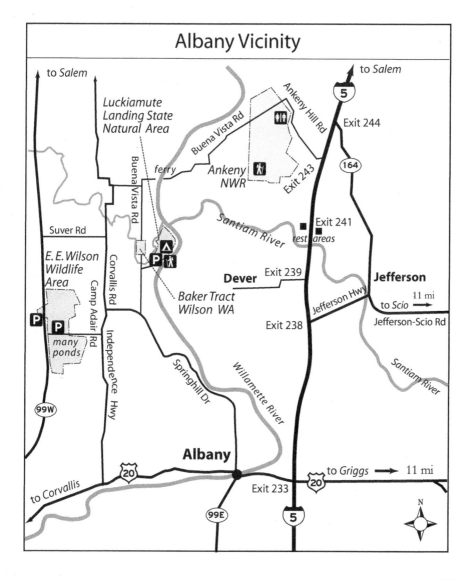

Albany Vicinity

E.E. Wilson Wildlife Area and **Baker Tract** is reached from I-5 Exit 233 at Albany, then west on US20 and north on OR 99W. The **E.E. Wilson Wildlife Area** includes much of what was once the Adair military base. What you'll find: picnic areas, toilets, wheelchair accessible path, trails, horseback riding, fishing and hunting. The parking areas are along Camp Adair Road east of OR 99W and west of Independence Road. Independence Road comes north from US 20 about 4 miles west of Albany. The habitat includes grassland, brush and forested wetlands. There are some surviving stands of white oak as well. This wildlife area covers over 1,700 acres, with numerous ponds and small streams.

There is a small widely separated unit called **Baker Tract** northeast of the main wildlife area. Baker Tract has 55 acres on the east bank of the Luckiamute River (see *Albany Vicinity* map) situated very near the Luckiamute Landing State Natural Area (see next entry). Nearly 160 birds have been recorded on eBird from this location. Among the sixteen species of wildfowl are wintering Tundra Swans and all three species of teal. Wood Ducks are abundant and Cinnamon Teal are regular breeders. California Quail are also abundant. Ten species of raptor have been found at Wilson Wildlife Area, including Merlin, Harrier and Rough-legged Hawks. A variety of shorebirds have been found, including Solitary Sandpiper and both yellowlegs species. In winter, a Long-eared Owl has been found, while Northern Shrike and Varied Thrush are more likely in the right habitat: thrush in deep woods, shrike in windy grasslands. Rufous Hummingbird is a summer breeder here.

A vagrant Yellow-bellied Sapsucker wintered here and the usual lowland woodpeckers are around in the winter, with Flicker and Downy Woodpecker the common breeding species. Most of the usual migrant western songbirds turn up here in season, while some like Violet-green swallow, Wilson's Warbler, Yellow-breasted Chat and Swainson's Thrush stay around to breed in the riparian thickets. Common Nighthawks have been seen and may also be regular breeders here.

Mammals at Wilson Wildlife Area include mule deer, beaver, brush rabbit, bobcat, California ground squirrel, camas pocket gopher, nutria (introduced), muskrat, river otter, mink, opossum, raccoon, striped skunk and Townsend's mole. Ringneck and gopher snakes are abundant.

The side roads around the Wilson Wildlife Area and northward can provide rich winter birding. Cackling Geese, Northern Harrier and even Trumpeter Swans are seen here. Songbirds may include Wrentit, Bushtit, Bewick's Wren and Spotted Towhee.

Northeast of the main unit of the Wilson Wildlife Area is **Luckiamute Landing State Natural** Area in Polk County, which you will enter if you drive north from Wilson on OR 99W. Luckiamute is about 5 miles from the 99W intersection with Suver Road (see *Albany Vicinity* map). Turn right onto Suver Road, follow it to Corvallis Road/NW Independence Highway and turn right. Turn left onto Spring Hill Drive, left onto Buena Vista for about a third of a mile and look for the park sign.

The Luckiamute River meanders through the 615-acre north tract of the State Natural Area. The Luckiamute is named for the local Indian tribe, driven from the area in the 19th century. It enters the Willamette River from the west, just a stone's throw from the Santiam River confluence from the east. Travelers paddling the Willamette Water Trail can camp at the boat-only access site. If you don't have a canoe or kayak, the North Trailhead opens nearly 3 miles of hiking trails along a meadow and through a riparian hardwood forest of Oregon ash and bigleaf maple.

The 300-acre south parcel of the State Natural Area is a great place for wildlife viewing and fishing (although the pond isn't stocked). Park at the South Trailhead and make the half-mile trek to the West Pond. See if you can catch a glimpse of western pond turtles at the north end of the old gravel pit. An Oregon native, the turtle is dark green or brown with cream and brown flecks on its neck and head. These turtles are included on Oregon's Sensitive Species List. The State Natural Area has the expected mix of riparian species, including breeding Black-headed Grosbeak, Wrentit and Song Sparrow. Unexpected Trumpeter and Tundra Swans have been seen here in winter.

I-5 Exit 238. Scio. Exit here and go east on OR 99E toward Jefferson, then turn right on Jefferson-Scio Road to get to Scio. See *Albany Vicinity* map. A rich list of rarities has been reported from this small valley town, including all three species of phalarope and Mountain Quail below 400 feet elevation. Local ponds are the richest birding spots in Scio. Also check along city streets for feeders. Regular birds here include Vaux's Swift (warm months) and Lesser Goldfinch.

I-5 Exit 239. Exit here onto Dever Connor Road and drive through the flat farmland west of I-5. There are reports of resident Burrowing Owl along the 4 miles of this road. American Pipits feed here on migration. Red-tailed Hawks and Savannah Sparrows should be expected as well.

I-5 Mile 241. Exit to the rest stop at Santiam River Bridge. This river is a major tributary flowing down from the Cascades into the Willamette. Cliff Swallows nest beneath the highway overpass. Kestrel hunt here. Parking lot birds are Brewer's Blackbird and American Robin. You'll find ample picnic grounds on both sides of the freeway and an underpass that connects the northbound and southbound rest stops. There is river access here. Linn County is south of the river, Marion County is north. Both rest stops are on the Marion County side of the Santiam River. The best spring birding here is in the riparian woods on the west side of I-5. Northbound travelers can walk or drive beneath I-5 to reach the west (southbound) rest area.

I-5 Exit 243. Ankeny National Wildlife Refuge. Roadside signage is almost nonexistent here, so you'll need to follow the *Albany Vicinity* map for how to get here and the *Ankeny NWR* map for details. There is no sign for Ankeny in either direction on I-5, yet this is the only unit of the Willamette Valley National Wildlife Refuge close to the interstate. Take Exit 243 onto Ankeny Hill Road and proceed in a roughly northwesterly direction to Ankeny National Wildlife Refuge (NWR). About 2 miles from I-5 you will come to an overlook with a dirt parking lot, a short trail to a viewing platform and a toilet building.

What you'll find: toilets, nature trails, a boardwalk and photo blinds. There are also brochures available here. Ankeny, an IBA, offers numerous viewing pullouts. The four best viewpoints are shown on the map. In addition to many waterfowl in season, this spot can offer great views of the abundant resident muskrats. Ankeny NWR encompasses over 1,700 acres, including 600 acres of riparian forest and 500 acres of seasonal wetlands. None of the refuge rises above 300 feet in elevation. The

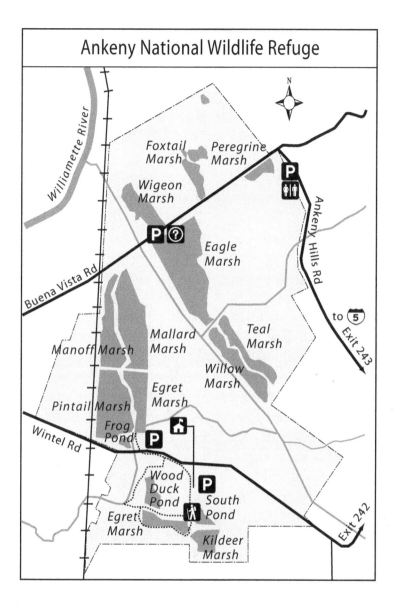

woods are largely deciduous trees: ash, oak, maple, willow.

Further along Ankeny Hill Road, turn left (or roughly southwest) onto Buena Vista Road. There are pullouts on both sides of the road before you come to the driveway to the parking lot at Eagle Marsh. Here's a covered viewing platform and an information kiosk. Further down Buena Vista you will come to Wintel Road in the hamlet of Sidney. Turn left onto Wintel, and proceed roughly easterly cutting back across the refuge to the south of your first crossing.

There are two short trails along Wintel Road on the refuge's southern end. On the north side of Wintel is a parking lot and boardwalk through woodland into Pintail Marsh. It's called that because the Northern Pintail has been reported here in every month of the calendar.

Further east and on the south side of Wintel is a sign to Rail Boardwalk and a parking lot. This longer trail takes you through bottomland forest and fields, past some small ponds.

EBird shows more than 185 species reported from Ankeny. The Dusky Canada Goose is especially abundant here in winter. I often see them right along the freeway on the approach to Exit 252. In winter you should find thousands of White-fronted Geese; some Snow Geese are also possible. The most abundant birds may be Cackling Geese in winter. Winter ducks include Shoveler, Green-winged Teal, Ruddy Duck and Bufflehead.

Breeding ducks at Ankeny include all three teal species, Pintail, Gadwall, Shoveler, Ring-necked Duck, Hooded Merganser, Bufflehead and Ruddy Duck. Though often shy, the Cinnamon Teal is abundant here. Among the grebes, the Red-necked has been spotted occasionally. Wilson's Snipe and Phalarope are both uncommon breeders as well. Migrant shorebirds such as Solitary and Pectoral Sandpiper may show as early as the last days of July. Both yellowlegs can be found here in late summer.

Eight species of gull have been seen here in winter. Also possible: Kestrel, Coot, Bewick's Wren, Song Sparrow, Western Meadowlark, Spotted Towhee and Golden-crowned Kinglet. Other birds that winter here include Harrier, Merlin, Rough-legged Hawk, Bald Eagle, American Pipit, Horned Lark and Savannah Sparrow. The Pileated Woodpecker and Rufous Hummingbird both breed here, as do Cassin's, Hutton's and Warbling Vireo. Most of the lowland western species are here: Lazuli Bunting, Black-headed Grosbeak, Black-throated Gray Warbler, Wilson's Warbler, Lesser Goldfinch, Yellow-headed Blackbird, and occasionally Tricolored Blackbirds will breed here.

Northern Spotted Owl

The Northern Spotted Owl, Strix ocidentalis caurina, is a medium-sized, highly nocturnal and secretive forest owl. It has long been at the center of political controversy. No final recovery plan has yet been approved at the federal level, partly due to the owl's status as a flashpoint in discussions of national policies on public and privately owned forest land. This owl was first listed as "threatened" in 1990 under the provisions of the Endangered Species Act, which was signed into law by President Nixon in 1973 , but arguments over its status and importance have never stopped. The last published census data are from 2004, before the Barred Owl invasion really got up to full speed in the western United States. Nothing has been published since that date. There are two Spotted Owl subspecies found southeast of this guide's focus, and those are not listed as threatened.

The Northern Spotted Owl is native to some forests within easy reach of Interstate 5. It is also one of two species on the Endangered Species List regularly seen in the region included in this guide. The other is the Bald Eagle in the Lower 48 States. Both are labeled "threatened" by the United States Fish and Wildlife Service.

The Spotted Owl is known to still be breeding in the Coastal Ranges, Cascades and Siskiyous. Also, it's on Washington's Olympic Peninsula. The invasion of the Barred Owl from the northeast may make the Spotted Owl's already threatened future even bleaker. The more aggressive and adaptable Barred Owl has spread across many western forests and replaces or interbreeds with Spotted Owls, thus giving rise to "Sparred" Owl offspring. If you want to spend nights looking, or more likely listening, for the Spotted Owl, it is best to check with local experts for possible locations.

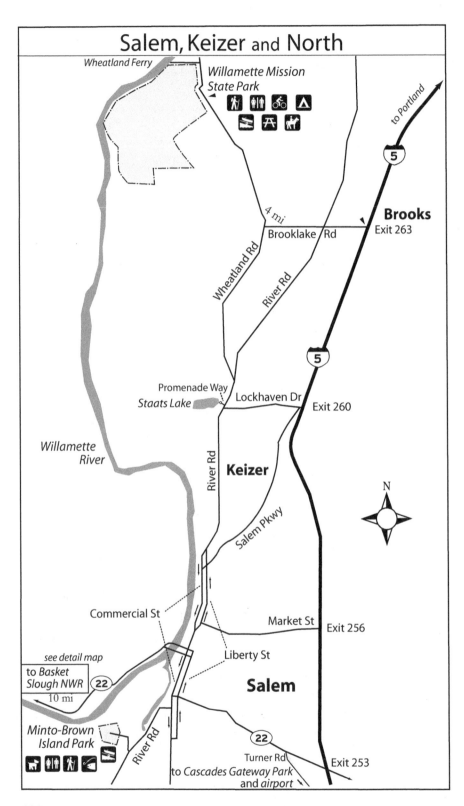

Salem, Keizer and North

Wheatland Ferry

Willamette Mission
State Park

Willamette River

to Portland

5

4 mi

Brooklake Rd

Brooks
Exit 263

Wheatland Rd

River Rd

5

Promenade Way

Staats Lake

Lockhaven Dr

Exit 260

River Rd

Keizer

Salem Pkwy

N

Commercial St

Market St

Exit 256

Liberty St

see detail map

to *Basket
Slough NWR* **22**

10 mi

Salem

Minto-Brown
Island Park

River Rd

22

Turner Rd

Exit 253

to *Cascades Gateway Park*
and *airport*

Canada Goose

Chapter 10

Northern Oregon

I-5, I-205, and I-405, Salem to Portland
Marion, Clackamas and Washington Counties

I-5 Exit 253. Salem. Elevation: 135 feet. Exit here onto OR 22, which will take you west about 2 miles into central Salem. This is the capital of Oregon. Rough-legged Hawks occasionally winter along the rural roads in the flat portion of the Willamette Valley around Salem. A variety of gulls may gather in winter at Cascade Gateway Park near the airport. Among them can be Thayer's and other species usually found in coastal locations. See the *Salem, Keizer and North* map.

Minto-Brown Island Park is on the southwest side of downtown Salem off River Road; follow the map. What you'll find: toilets, picnic areas and nature trails across almost 900 acres of open space. Habitats include riparian forest, ponds, backwater sloughs and open grassland. The best birding is along the Willamette River and around parking area #3.

EBird shows nearly 150 species reported from this urban park. Wintering waterfowl include Cackling Goose, all three teal species, Lesser Scaup, and Hooded and Common Merganser. Resident birds include California Quail, Anna's Hummingbird, Pileated Woodpecker, Steller's Jay, Scrub-Jay, Bushtit, Wrentit, Spotted Towhee and White-crowned Sparrow. Among the breeding birds here are Olive-sided Flycatcher,

Warbling Vireo, five species of swallow, Cedar Waxwing, Swainson's Thrush, Western Tanager and Black-headed Grosbeak. Wintering birds can include Hutton's Vireo, Varied Thrush in the deepest forest, Pacific Wren, Townsend's Warbler and Golden-crowned Sparrow. A Northern Saw-whet Owl was found here one recent winter.

If you continue west on OR 22 beyond Salem, you can get to **Baskett Slough National Wildlife Refuge (NWR)**, part of the Willamette Valley NWR complex. As you cross the Willamette River on the west side of Salem, you leave Marion County and enter Polk County. What you'll find at Baskett Slough: parking, toilets and trails – but the trails are closed October 1-March 31 annually. Dogs and bicycles are not allowed on the trails.

Baskett Slough has 2,500 acres of open space. On the NWR are 1,173 acres of cropland, which provide forage for wintering geese; 300 acres of forests; 550 acres of grasslands; 500 acres of shallow water seasonal wetlands; and 35 acres of permanent open water. The *Baskett Slough* detail map shows several good birding spots at Baskett Slough. Colville Road is especially good because it transects the refuge between the east and west boundaries. This unit of the NWR is especially focused on providing wintering habitat for Dusky Canada Geese.

Baskett Slough is one of the richest birding spots along the section of Interstate 5 covered by this book. EBird shows over 200 species for this location. Over two dozen waterfowl have been seen here, including Tundra and Trumpeter Swans, Emperor Goose, Black Duck, Eurasian Wigeon and both scaup. Pied-billed Grebe, Gadwall, Cinnamon Teal and Ruddy Duck are among the breeding species here. White Pelicans are common in late summer only. Other occasional sightings include Snowy Egret, White-faced Ibis, White-tailed Kite, Rough-legged Hawk (winter), Ferruginous Hawk, and once a Gyrfalcon.

More than 20 species of shorebird have been recorded here, including all three phalaropes (in autumn); Ruff, Solitary, Baird's and Pectoral Sandpiper; and Pacific Golden-Plover. Black, Caspian, Common and Forster's Tern have all appeared as birds of passage. Other wintering birds have included Snowy, Short-eared and Burrowing Owl. Some year-round songbirds are Horned Lark, Bewick's and Marsh Wren, Spotted Towhee, White-crowned Sparrow, Brewer's Blackbird and Western

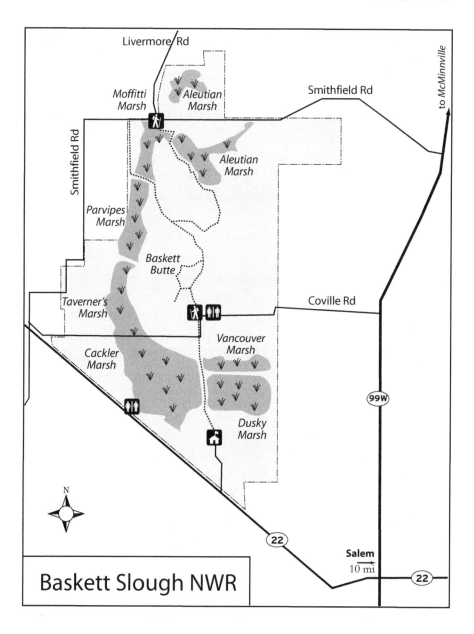

Baskett Slough NWR

Meadowlark. Some surprises here have included Indigo Bunting (an "eastern" species), Common Grackle, Red Crossbill, American Tree Sparrow, Harris's Sparrow, Snow Bunting and Gray Jay.

I-5 Mile 259. At this point Interstate 5 crosses the 45th Parallel. That is halfway between the North Pole and the Equator.

233

I-5 Exit 260. Statts Lake. You'll find this former mill pond in downtown Keizer. If you're southbound on I-5 take Exit 260. If you're northbound, take exit 260B. The only public access to view the lake is at the Promenade Street traffic circle, at the east end of the lake where it meets the west side of the traffic circle. There is no public parking at that exact location.

This is an excellent spot for viewing wintering waterbirds from November through March. Ducks, Cackling Geese, possibly loons and grebes, along with gulls, may be seen here.

I-5 Exit 263. Willamette Mission State Park. This park is 4 miles northwest of I-5 from Exit 263. To get there go west on Brooklake Road then north on Wheatland Road. There is a day-use fee. Fees are also levied for special facilities. What you'll find: toilets, picnic area, nature trail, boat access and a horse camp. There are eight miles of hiking trails through grassland and forests along the Willamette River. Some of the black cottonwoods here are the largest in United States. The park covers nearly 1,700 acres, including some walnut and filbert orchards.

This is a good spot for waterfowl in winter. Songbirds and woodpeckers are here year-round. Neotropical migrants breed or pass through every spring and late summer. Among birds you may find here are Anna's and Rufous Hummingbird, Swainson's Thrush, Cedar Waxwing, Lazuli Bunting, Spotted Towhee and Black-headed Grosbeak. There's little eBird data for this site so far.

I-5 Exit 271. Exit here for the town of Woodburn on OR 99E, where the winter of 2012 saw a Brambling settle in at a backyard feeder bird.

I-5 Exit 278. Champoeg State Park. Pronounced "sham-poo-ee," this state park is on the south bank of the Willamette River about 8 miles west of Exit 278. Exit west onto Ehlen Road. When you get to Case Road, turn north to reach the park and the river. A day-use fee is charged. What you'll find: a visitors center, toilets, a museum, trails, picnic areas, camping sites including ones for RVs, a boat launch, fishing and a historic garden. Pets are allowed. Champoeg State Park is on the site where the original vote was taken to form Oregon's first provisional territorial government in 1843. The park encompasses 617 acres of woodlands, riverfront, wetlands and prairie.

Among the birds you can find here are Bald Eagle along the Willamette, Band-tailed Pigeon, Western Wood-Pewee in summer, Steller's and Western Scrub-Jay, Chestnut-backed Chickadee, Swainson's Thrush (summer), Varied Thrush (winter), Pacific Wren (winter), Spotted Towhee, and Golden-crowned Sparrow (winter). Great Horned Owls and Barred Owls are seen in the park. Ebird records nearly 100 species here.

In the winter there can be good roadside birding around the town of **Lafayette**, about 15 miles west of here on OR 99W. In addition to hundreds of Cackling Geese in the farm fields, an Emperor Goose (Siberian vagrant) has been known to winter in this part of Yamhill County.

I-5 Mile 282. Baldoch Rest Areas. The northbound rest area is spacious and forested with mature Douglas-fir. Dogwoods bloom in the understory in April. OK place for common forest birds like Robin, Junco and Red-breasted Nuthatch. Will attract some migrants in spring and fall.

I-5 Mile 286. This is the line between Washington County, to the north, and Marion County, to the south.

I-5 Exit 288. I-205. This exit puts you on I-205 heading east to a number of birding sites and the east side of Portland. Details follow in the I-205 portion of this chapter.

Portland, Oregon and Its Suburbs

Portland sits astride two large rivers at their confluence: the Columbia and its great tributary, the Willamette. Both rivers are subject to tidal effects, though the Pacific is more than a hundred river miles away. Portland's climate is mild and humid. July and August are the warm months, with an average high just under 80 degrees; summer lows average less than 60. In January and December the average high is about 45, the overnight low about 35. Snow is rare, but any significant amount of it can bring Portland to a halt. Normally, they don't need snowplows, so when they do, they have to bring them down from the mountains. Mount Hood, a Cascade volcano, is south-southeast of Portland and rises over 11,000 feet. Infamous Mount Saint Helens, the most recently erupting Cascade volcano, is about 60 miles north of downtown Portland in the state of Washington.

The Willamette and Columbia were once bordered by marshy forests interlaced with side channels and seasonal sloughs. Many miles of levees, lots of tree removal and industrial development have destroyed much of that former habitat. Yet today Portland and its suburbs are blessed with many restored wetland and prairie areas. Also, Portland has expansive re-grown forests in and near the city. In fact, Portland can boast both America's largest forest and largest protected wetlands within city limits. There are three national wildlife refuges easily reached from downtown Portland. Tualatin River is southwest, while Steigerwald and Bridgeport are north across the Columbia River in Washington. If you're around the area in late March or early April, check the wooded parks for the blossoming trillium. Forest Park, Mary S. Young State Park and Tryon Creek State Natural Area are good bets. The latter has an annual trillium festival in late March.

Portland's official bird is the Great Blue Heron, which can be seen often along its rivers, streams and lakes. In winter, less than half an hour from central Portland, you can be watching Sandhill Cranes and Trumpeter Swans on Sauvie Island. The relatively mild winters here mean wintering birds like Townsend's Warbler, White-throated Sparrow and Varied Thrush are possible every year. More open areas can attract Short-eared Owls, Snowy Owls during irruptions, and Northern Shrike.

If you're staying in Portland for an extended period of time or making repeated birding visits, you might get a copy of *Birding Portland and Multnomah County* by John Fitchin. You can find it at the Portland Audubon Society Nature Store. Another useful reference is *Wild in the City* by Michael C. Houck and M. J. Cody. It will help you find birding sites farther afield than the I-5 corridor. In 2003 Fitchin and a birding partner got over 220 species in Multnomah County during a Big Year effort. Portland Audubon Society is very active throughout the region, with a busy schedule of field trips ranging from local and regional to statewide and international. It also co-hosts an annual Festival of the Birds to coincide with International Migratory Bird Day each May.

There are three more-or-less parallel interstate highways traversing the Portland Metro area: Interstate 5 stays close to the Willamette River until it joins the Columbia. Interstate 205 loops through the southern portion of Portland then turns north to skirt east Portland before it crosses the Columbia and enters Washington. Interstate 405, just a few miles long, circles around the western edge of Portland's commercial and cultural center (downtown). So we will divide our birding areas by the interstate that is nearest each one.

Consult *Greater Portland West* and *Greater Portland East* maps to get "the lay of the land" and find the various birding sites.

Interstate 205 Corridor.

I-5 Exit 288. This is the southern terminus of the Interstate 205 Corridor. At this point you are in Washington County. If you head east on I-205, in the first mile you pass out of Washington and into Clackamas County. I-205 is a beltline-type highway that first skirts the southern part of greater Portland, then turns sharply north to skirt the east side of the city all the way to the Columbia River, and across it into Washington State. It passes just east of the Portland Airport.

I-205 Exit 6. If you exit here you can enter West Linn's Old Town, and then a few blocks south, find Willamette Park at the confluence of the Tualatin and Willamette Rivers. What you'll find: toilets, picnic areas, a playground, playing fields, a boat ramp and trails. The park is over 22 acres and includes some mature riparian forest.

This is a good spot for wintering ducks and gulls, which often loaf on the dock near shore. Double-crested Cormorant, Great Blue Heron, Osprey, Belted Kingfisher and other riverine species can be seen passing by or fishing along the rivers here. Swallows and Vaux's Swift hawk insects here in the warm months. Among the songbirds here are Bewick's Wren. There is little eBird data, but the park offers a good chance to scope the broad Willamette for waterfowl, gulls and Double-crested Cormorant.

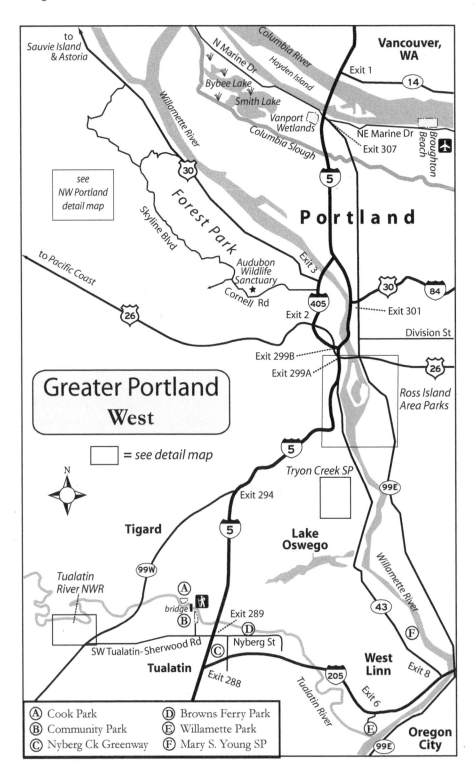

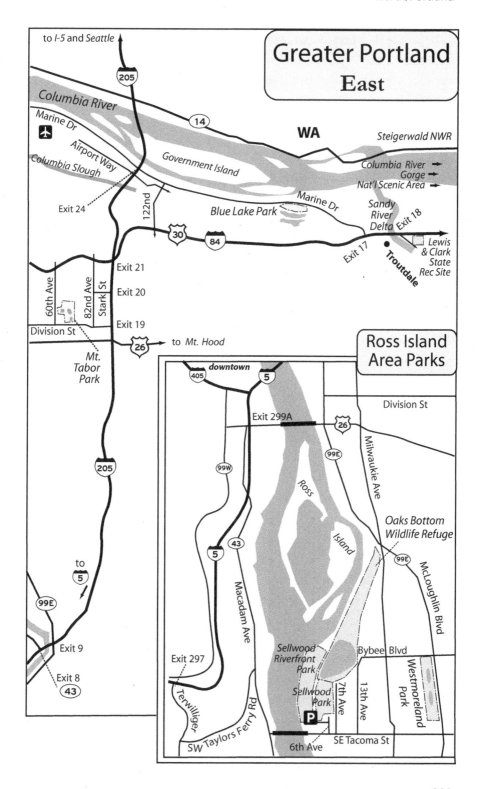

Greater Portland
East

to *I-5* and *Seattle*

205

Columbia River

14

Marine Dr

WA

Airport Way

Government Island

Steigerwald NWR

Columbia Slough

Columbia River →
Gorge →
Nat'l Scenic Area →

Exit 24

122nd

Marine Dr

Blue Lake Park

Sandy
River
Delta

Exit 18

30

84

Exit 17

Lewis
& Clark
State
Rec Site

Troutdale

Exit 21

60th Ave

82nd Ave

Stark St

Exit 20

Division St

Exit 19

26

to *Mt. Hood*

Mt.
Tabor
Park

205

Ross Island
Area Parks

405

downtown

5

Exit 299A

Division St

26

99W

99E

Milwaukie Ave

to

5

5

43

Ross

Island

Oaks Bottom
Wildlife Refuge

99E

McLoughlin Blvd

99E

Exit 9

Macadam Ave

Exit 8

43

Exit 297

Sellwood
Riverfront
Park

Bybee Blvd

Westmoreland
Park

Terwilliger

Sellwood
Park

7th Ave

13th Ave

P

SW Taylors Ferry Rd

6th Ave

SE Tacoma St

I-205 Exit 8. Mary S. Young State Park. This exit is just west of the bridge over the Willamette River. From this exit go north about 2 miles on OR 43 paralleling the river. Turn right on Mary S. Young Drive, which goes into the park of the same name. What you'll find: toilets, trails, picnic areas, playing fields and an off-leash dog area. There are over 100 acres of playing fields and riparian forest, with 8 miles of trails, including one trail that goes north along the Willamette to Cedar Island Park. A 0.6-mile trail takes you down to the Willamette riverbank and back to the parking lot. This is a good place to get a quick taste of the northwestern rain forest. Ferns and mosses grow on every inch of space along tree trunks; undergrowth is dense and lush.

Birds here, as you might expect, are those that like dense, shady forests: Song Sparrow, Pacific Wren, Northern Flicker, Golden-crowned Kinglet, Hermit Thrush and American Robin. Varied Thrush are likely in the winter. Along the river you may find ducks, Canada Geese, Double-crested Cormorants, and Glaucous-winged and other gulls. Tree-loving songbirds will move through here on spring migration, including warblers, vireos and flycatchers. EBird contains little data from this site.

I-205 Mile 16. This is the county line, with Clackamas County on the south, Multnomah on the north.

I-205 Exit 19 (northbound) and Exit 20 (southbound). Mount Tabor City Park. Northbound, take Exit 19 from I-205, go west on Division, north on SE 60th Avenue, then right, into the park, on Salmon Street. Southbound, take Exit 20, take Stark Street west, the south on SE 92nd Avenue to Division and continue as above. Mount Tabor Park is about 1.5 miles from I-205 using either exit. What you'll find: picnic areas, trails, toilets, playgrounds and an off-leash dog area. See *Greater Portland, East* map.

Many local birders find this forested, steep-sided hill to be a superb place to see migrant warblers and flycatchers in spring and again in autumn. It is a welcoming green island in a dense city, and if it's tasty insects you crave, this place is magnetic. Birds you may find here include Olive-sided, Hammond's and Dusky Flycatcher; American Pipit; and MacGillivray's, Black-throated Gray, Hermit, Wilson's, and

Townsend's Warblers. Some birds regularly found in the right habitat include Chestnut-backed Chickadee, Brown Creeper, Band-tailed Pigeon, Western Tanager and Fox Sparrow. Western Wood-Pewee and Pacific-slope Flycatcher breed here.

Mount Tabor is heavily birded in season, and the birders here are likely to note the occasional "eastern" warbler, like Canada, Blackpoll or Tennessee. All three of the "Pacific" vireos can be found here: Warbling, Cassin's and Hutton's. Varied Thrush are around nearly every winter, and sporadic sightings of Evening Grosbeak have been reported. Swainson's Thrush, Townsend's Solitaire, Hammond's Flycatcher, Calliope Hummingbird and Gray Flycatcher are among those birds that have turned up here during migration. Almost any good sighting here is sure to be reported to Oregon Birds Online and the local rare bird alert. Ebird shows 130 recorded species, good for alakeless urban park. As a bonus Mount Tabor offers excellent views over much of Portland.

I-205 Exit 21. This exit puts you onto I-84, the Columbia River Highway, and is the quickest way to the Sandy River Delta (see next entry) and the Columbia River Gorge.

I-205 Exit 24. Columbia River, South Bank. The Columbia here is so large it seems like a bay not a river. From Exit 24 there are a series of birding opportunities to the east and west.

To the east, you will exit onto **NE Airport Way.** If you are southbound, go east of I-205, under the Interstate. The first street on your left is **NE Glenn Widing Drive.** Turn left (north) and park near the small pond there. You may find Hooded Merganser in winter. There should also be other ducks, Pied-billed Grebe, etc. It is a nice place to get your land legs if you've just escaped an airplane and rented a car in a city that is new to you.

As you continue east on Airport Way you will come to NE122nd Avenue. Turn left here and go north to **Marine Drive.** Then turn right (east). You are now driving along a steep levee with the river visible on your left. In fall and winter there are likely to be large floats of scaup in the river, mostly Greater. At any safe pullout scope the broad river if you can. Expect various grebes, possible Common Loon, and any of the likely wintering gulls.

About three miles east of I-205 on Marine Drive you will see Blue Lake Road going into **Blue Lake Park**. What you'll find: toilets, picnic areas, playground, trails and trout fishing. In summer there are boat rentals and a "sprayground" of gushing water for cooling off. This park's 64 acres are mostly landscaped or in lawn, but at the west end of the park there is a wetland with a nature trail.

At Blue Lake you'll find Common Merganser, and you'll have another chance for grebes and wintering ducks. South of Blue Lake is **Fairview Lake**, from which a canoe trail winds westerly down the Columbia Slough to Kelly Point where the Columbia and Willamette come together. You can get more information from the Columbia Slough Watershed Council.

Nearby, a choice destination for birding is the **Sandy River Delta**. The Sandy River drains the eastern slope of the Cascades and then runs northwest to the Columbia. The delta is roughly 11 miles east of I-205. For the *west* side of the Sandy River Delta, continue east on NE Marine Drive to Sundial Road (the first street after crossing NE 223rd Avenue), then turn north and follow Sundial to its end. From here it's a short walk to the Columbia River. The cottonwoods here are full of migrants on some spring days. Among them can be an occasional Red-eyed Vireo—pretty ordinary if you're from New Jersey but scarce on the Pacific Slope.

If you are coming to the west side of the Sandy River Delta directly from I-205 and skipping the Marine Drive/Columbia River area, you will need to merge onto I-84 at I-205 Exit 22 and leave I-84 at Exit 17.

To get to the *east* side of the **Sandy River Delta**, use **I-84 Exit 18**. But if you have already been birding along Marine Drive, continue going east and eventually you will merge onto I-84 at Exit 17 and then exit in only a mile, at Exit 18.

Go north under the freeway after exiting I-84 at Exit 18. There are free dirt parking lots with access to the trails here. The Columbia itself is 2.5 miles by foot to the north. This area is the westernmost section of the enormous Columbia River Gorge National Scenic Area. This Scenic Area extends 85 miles eastward, up the Columbia River in both Oregon and Washington, to where the north-flowing Deschutes

River enters the Columbia. Here on the Oregon side of the river, the scenic area encompasses 77 waterfalls as streams come down from the plateau and fall onto the Columbia's floodplain.

EBird lists over 150 species for the Sandy River Delta. The habitat is a rich mix of riverside beach, riparian forest, seasonal ponds and floodplain grassland. Waterfowl and denizens of the riparian forest abound here. Regulars include Great Horned Owl in the towering cottonwoods, Yellow Warbler, Western Wood-Pewee, Willow Flycatcher, Swainson's Thrush, Yellow-breasted Chat, Back-headed Grosbeak and Bullock's Oriole in breeding season. Lazuli Bunting may be found in the open brushy areas. Less commonly reported are Western and even Eastern Kingbirds nesting, Red-eyed Vireo in warm months, Solitary Sandpiper on migration, Harris's Sparrow in winter, and once even a wintering Snow Bunting in the grasslands. A Yellow-billed Cuckoo has been reported here in July. This species is not a regular breeding bird anywhere in Oregon. Another "eastern" species that's been found here in summer is Indigo Bunting.

Along the river Bald Eagles are seen year-round, Ospreys spring and summer, Peregrine any time and Merlin in winter. On the water Surf Scoters sometimes ride the tide in this far from the Pacific. An occasional Red-breasted Merganser may appear in spring, and in cold months there can be a rich mix of grebes and gulls on or near the river. There are over 160 species reported for the Sandy River Delta.

South of **I-84 Exit 18** is **Lewis & Clark State Recreation Site** which offers birding access to the Sandy River and its neighboring forest as well. Eastbound you are within the boundary of the site as soon as you leave the interstate. Westbound you will exit onto Crown Point Highway, which curves underneath the interstate to the south, and then you are inside the recreation site. From the riverside you can hike up the steep face of Broughton Bluff, which affords great views of the Sandy River Delta on the south bank of the Columbia River a few miles north. Lewis and Clark Recreation Site is over 60 acres.

What you will find: toilets, boat ramp, swimming beach, picnicking, fishing, trails. Day use, no fee. Birding here should give you access to riparian species.

I-5 Corridor North of the I-205 Intersection

I-5 Exit 289. Tualatin. Elevation 123 feet. This area is shown on the *Greater Portland West* map, bottom half. If you're northbound you'll notice on your right (east of the freeway) a small wetland downhill from the gas stations and shopping areas. It is a portion of the **Nyberg Creek Greenway**, a 13-acre wetlands surrounded by suburban development. You can bird from the parking lot behind one of the gas stations along SW Nyberg Street. Here I've seen numerous wintering birds: Hooded Merganser, American Wigeon, Bufflehead, Shoveler, Green-winged Teal, American Coot, Pied-billed Grebe, Great Egret and Great Blue Heron. In summer the local swallows feed in large numbers. If you continue east on Nyberg Street, you will reach **Browns Ferry Park** on the Tualatin River, which here flows eastward toward the Willamette.

Tualatin Trail, Browns Ferry Park, Tualatin Community Park, Cook Park. A trail system along the Tualatin River connects these parks, including a bridge across the river that connects Tualatin Community Park on the south with Tigard's Cook Park on the north. What you'll find: toilets, a nature trail, picnic areas, boat access, public transit, and a visitors center in Tualatin Community Park.

River birds such as Common Merganser, Green and Great Blue Heron, Bald Eagle and Belted Kingfisher are here. Shorebirds stop here on migration. Land birds that have been seen here include Pileated Woodpecker, Hutton's Vireo, Violet-green Swallow, Bushtit, Spotted Towhee and Lesser Goldfinch.

If you want to drive a bit further, go west on Tualatin-Sherwood Road from I-5 Exit 289 to intersect with OR 99W (Pacific Highway). Go north a short distance to **Tualatin River National Wildlife Refuge (NWR)**. It is the northernmost unit of the Willamette River Valley NWR complex. The distance to this NWR from I-5 is about 6 miles. What you'll find: a visitors center, toilets, picnic tables, a nature trail, and two overlooks, one on the Tualatin River, the other along a wetland. You can reserve a photo blind. Dogs are not allowed, and the refuge closes at dusk. Some hunting and fishing are allowed on the refuge. See *Tualatin River NWA* detail map.

The visitors center, on a small rise, has great views south across marshy grasslands. The refuge is based in Washington County with one unit in neighboring Yamhill County. Some units of the NWR are viewable only from adjacent roads. Tualatin River NWR includes over 5,000 acres of permanent and seasonal wetlands and forest along the Tualatin River, which flows eastward from the rainy Coastal Range and empties into the Willamette River near Oregon City east of I-5.

Trees here include white oak, cottonwood, broadleaf maple, willow, ponderosa pine, Douglas-fir and western red cedar. There is a small patch of oak savannah as well. The forest understory includes dense stands of sword fern and some head-high bracken. There's a bird festival at Tualatin NWR every May. The nearby town of Tualatin gets about 41 inches of rainfall per year and has a mild climate, with temperatures mostly between freezing and 80 degrees. As in much of the Pacific Coast area, the dry months are June through September.

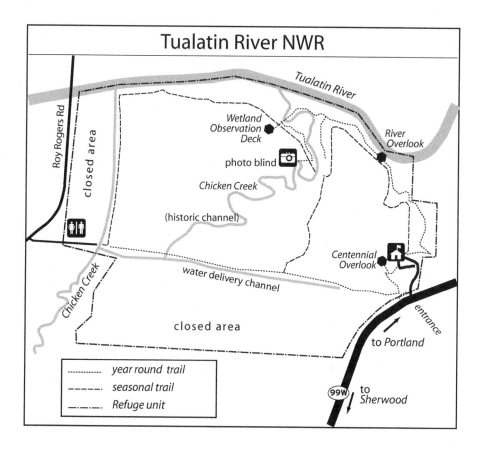

Tualatin River NWR

Tualatin River

Roy Rogers Rd

closed area

Wetland
Observation
Deck

photo blind

Chicken Creek

(historic channel)

River
Overlook

Centennial
Overlook

Chicken Creek

water delivery channel

closed area

entrance

to Portland

99W to
Sherwood

.... *year round trail*
------ *seasonal trail*
-..-..- *Refuge unit*

This place is an IBA. EBird shows over 180 species at Tualatin: 26 species of waterfowl, wintering Screech-Owl, Osprey in summer, Bald Eagle year-round. Heavy waterfowl migrations occur in spring and fall with many ducks wintering here. In October I've seen thousands of Taverner's Canada Geese in the air over Tualatin River NWR. One recent winter, an Asian vagrant Emperor Goose drew birders from afar. Shorebirds use the mudflats during fall migration. Cedar Waxwings and Robins feed in the riparian forest. Some winter days the refuge has 50,000 waterbirds. Breeding birds include Cinnamon Teal, California Quail, Virginia Rail, Sora, and Wilson's Snipe, which winnow and display in spring. Also, Vaux's Swift, Red-breasted Sapsucker and Pileated Woodpecker, Pacific-slope Flycatcher in the forested areas, Cassin's Vireo, Bank Swallow (a scarce bird in much of the western U.S.), Bushtit, Pacific Wren and Spotted Towhee breed here. Mammals you might encounter include coyote, bobcat, elk, river otter and red fox.

I-5 Mile 290. Just north of Exit 290 you cross another county line, with Washington County to the south, Clackamas to the north.

I-5 Mile 293. This is yet another county line: Multnomah County is to the north, Clackamas to the south.

I-5 Exit 297 (northbound) or 299A (southbound). Oaks Bottom Wildlife Refuge and **Sellwood Riverfront Park.** What you'll find at Sellwood Riverfront Park: dog off-leash area, picnic area, toilets, boat ramp and bicycle trail. If you are southbound take Exit 299A, go east on US 26, then south on OR 99E. If you're northbound, take Exit 297, go south on Terwilliger for half a mile, go left onto Taylor's Ferry Road, then follow the *Ross Island Area Parks* map. This area is in the flood plain on the east side of the Willamette River.

Oaks Bottom is a 140-acre refuge and part of the Portland city park system. It has forest, pond, marsh and grasslands. What you'll find: trails but no services, and the park is closed overnight. Oaks Bottom is a short walk north of the Sellwood Parks below. Go north from the Sellwood Riverfront parking lot along the street that heads toward the Oaks Bottom Amusement Park. Across from the amusement park entrance there is a pedestrian underpass that will take you under the railroad tracks to the trails of the wildlife refuge. Oaks Bottom is also accessible from the Springwater Corridor Bicycle Trail which parallels the Willamette River on its eastern bank.

Among the 160 species EBird records for this location are: Tundra Swan, Eurasian Wigeon, Canvasback, Pintail, Redhead, both scaup, seventeen species of shorebirds, Varied Thrush (winter), both kinglets(winter), Evening Grosbeak (on migration). Birds that are possible year-round: Western Scrub-Jay, Spotted Towhee, Bewick's Wren, Bushtit, Black-capped Chickadee, Anna's Hummingbird, Wood Duck. Breeding birds in the vicinity include these species spotted at Oak Bottom: Violet-green and Tree Swallows, Osprey and Bald Eagle, Cooper's Hawk, Belted Kingfisher, Common Yellowthroat and Wilson's Warbler. There's a large Blue Heron Rookery on nearby Ross Island in the Willamette and the big birds often hunt around the pond at Oaks Bottom.

Sellwood Riverfront Park and adjacent **Sellwood Park** comprise 20 acres of heavily used urban open space. Yet there's a small nature trail, good views of the open river, boat docks where you can see both directions along the Willamette, and some nice riverfront forest dominated by black cottonwoods. What you'll find: toilets, picnicing, dog play area, boat docks, playground, sports fields. It is a half-mile walk from Sellwood Riverfront Park north along the railroad tracks to a pedestrian underpass into Oaks Bottom. This underpass is opposite one of the main gates into the Oaks Park Amusement Park with its carnival rides and skating rink.

Being in central Portland, this area is birded heavily and well. There is an online checklist available. Over 180 species have been seen here. Some unexpected ones: Red-necked Grebe, Marbled Godwit, Common Redpoll, Snowy Egret, Pileated Woodpecker, Say's Phoebe, Blue Grosbeak and Blackpoll Warbler. More likely birds include American Pipit and Semipalmated Sandpiper on fall migration, numerous wintering ducks including all three teal species, breeding Wood Duck, and large numbers of Pintail, Shoveler, Gadwall and Ring-necked Duck in winter. In addition to Great Blue Heron, Osprey fish here in warm months. Great Egret also visit.

Nine species of gull have been reported, Glaucous-winged always. In winter, others could include California, Ring-billed, Herring, Mew, Western and the difficult to detect Thayer's. Red-breasted Sapsucker, Western Wood-Pewee, Willow Flycatcher and Hutton's Vireo nest in the forest. For westerners this is a good area for Purple Martin; there's a nesting colony here. Bewick's is the nesting wren species. Common Yellowthroat is the nesting warbler, but his kinfolk may show up after breeding season, including Black-throated Gray, Wilson's and Townsend's.

Sellwood Park on its wooded bluff is the site of Portland's annual Festival of the Birds every May. All of this is just a short bike ride from downtown Portland.

If you're at Oaks Bottom or Sellwood in late fall or winter, you might venture about ten blocks east to **Westmoreland Park.** Go via SE Bybee Boulevard (see *Ross Island Area Parks* map). In summer Westmoreland has an impressive concentration of Canada Geese, while in winter the park is home to a variety of gulls. I have seen the ball field at the south end of the park covered with Cackling Geese in autumn. The lakes are narrow so you can often get close to study the Mew, Thayer's, California, Western and other gulls that mingle here. There have even been sightings of an Oregon rarity, an Asian native, the Slaty-backed Gull, looking like a Western Gull on steroids. Occasionally an unusual duck will join the usual Mallards, wintering Wigeon and Hooded Mergansers. One October I photographed a Surf Scoter here, far from its usual ocean habitat.

Tryon Creek State Natural Area. What you'll find: a nature center, picnic areas, toilets, trails, including some paved bike trails. If you take Exit 297 and go south on Terwilliger Boulevard for 2.5 miles, you will reach the entrance to Tryon Creek State Natural Area on your right (west side of road). The park can also be reached from I-5 Exit 290. See *Tryon Creek State Park* detail map. It is a heavily forested park where trails wind through the Tryon Creek watershed. There are bird feeders at the Nature Center. Much of Tryon is heavily wooded with second- or third-growth timber. Most of the common forest bird species are regular here, including Pileated Woodpecker. The Pileated and Northern Flicker are resident, and a Red-naped Sapsucker was found

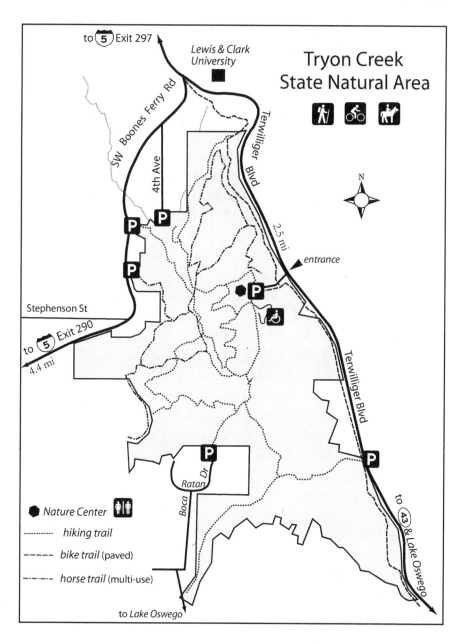

here in the fall. Owls reported here include Barred, Northern Pygmy and Northern Saw-whet. The Pacific-slope Flycatcher is a likely breeder near the creek. There you may also find breeding Swainson's Thrush, Vaux's Swift and Pacific Wren. Listen for the wren's rapid, energetic singing in early spring. Some winters Varied Thrush are abundant. The park's official checklist names over 70 species.

I-5 Exit 302. Northwest Portland. Exit and follow signs for US 30 westbound for **Sauvie Island.** (An alternate route would leave I-405 at Exit 3. See I-405 section of this chapter). It is 8 miles along US 30 from I-5 Exit 302 to the Sauvie Island Bridge, which takes you onto the island. This low-lying island is made of river sediment deposited over eons where the Willamette flows into the Columbia River. The island is home to many farms, wildlife management areas and patches of riparian forest. On the south it is bordered by the narrow and sluggish Multnomah Channel. On the north side of the island you look onto the broad expanse of the mighty Columbia's main channel and across to Washington State. See *Sauvie Island* and *Northwest Portland* maps. On clear days you get great views of explosive Mt. St. Helens.

Sauvie Island. What you'll find: toilets, parking, picnic areas, trails, wildlife viewing blind. Parking permits are required, available at the grocery store next to the east end of the Sauvie Island Bridge. Be sure to pick up an island map as well. Most roads here are narrow with no shoulders. Drive cautiously. There is no gasoline sold on the island and a full circuit of all roads is more than 35 miles. Ebird has records from a dozen specific birding areas on the island. In winter you can spend two full days of enjoyable birding just on this island.

Sauvie Island, an IBA, affords good birding in any season, but fall and winter can be spectacular. In a total of 24,000 acres there are over 12,000 acres of wetlands, savannah, cottonwood bottomlands, and upland Oregon white oak forest managed by Oregon Department of Fish and Wildlife as Sauvie Island Wildlife Area. The conditions at a particular spot or farm field can change from year to year, season to season. One January it may be a marsh or a grassy field, but in July, a plowed field. The northern end of the island is in Columbia County, while most of Sauvie is in Multnomah. There's a sign on Reeder Road where you cross the county line.

One of the northernmost wintering populations of Sandhill Cranes can be found on this island from September through April. Many more cranes stop here on their migration north each spring. Most winters, a handful of Trumpeter Swans can be found on Pope Lake or Sturgeon Lake. White-fronted and Snow Geese may be joined by Cackling Geese and various races of Canada Geese, including Dusky. Bald Eagles are plentiful in winter as are duck species. Eurasian Wigeon can be found on quieter waters, and I've also found Eurasian (Common) Teal, which European authorities recognize as separate species from our Green-winged Teal. Redhead are regular here. Both Emperor and Ross's Goose have been recorded here.

About 210 species have been reported on eBird for various locations on Sauvie Island, headlined by 29 species of waterfowl. A Christmas Count can turn up 120 species. Northern Harrier, Red-tailed Hawk and Kestrel are year-round raptors. In winter you may find Prairie Falcon, Peregrine, Rough-legged Hawk, Merlin, Golden Eagle and small accipiters in the wooded areas. Barn Owls are regular in some of the island's barns. Shorebirds and gulls are mostly birds of passage. In autumn shorebirds arrive in great variety, including Stilt, Semipalmated, Baird's and Pectoral Sandpiper, Mew, Slaty-backed and Franklin's Gulls. Glaucous-winged are common in colder months. In addition to occasional late summer Caspian Terns, Common Terns have been found here on fall migration. Sora and Virginia Rail are hard-to-find summer birds. Small numbers of Wilson's Snipe breed in the wetlands here. Northern Shrike may pass through in spring, sticking to the open fields or forest edges. Among rarities that have turned up: Common Ground-dove, Emperor Goose, Long-eared Owl.

Breeding birds include Rufous Hummingbird, Western Wood-Pewee, Purple Martin (scarce on the Pacific Coast), Violet-green Swallow, Bushtit, Pacific and Bewick's Wren, Swainson's Thrush, Cedar Waxwing, Spotted Towhee, Black-headed Grosbeak and Bullock's Oriole. Wintering sparrows include White-throated, White-crowned, Golden-crowned, Fox and Lincoln's, and even an occasional Swamp or Harris's. Spring transients have included Harris's and Clay-colored Sparrows. Among migrant swallows in fall you may find some Bank and Black Swifts as well. Gray Flycatcher, normally further east, has been seen among migrants in September. The island is regularly birded by Portland area experts, and rarities are reported to Oregon Birds On-line and the local rare bird alert. Portland Audubon organizes various birding events on the island, so check their website.

Sauvie Island Road System

There are several roads you can explore on Sauvie Island. See *Sauvie Island* Map. On crossing Sauvie Island Bridge from US 30 (NW Saint Helens Road), you will reach Sauvie Island Road: turn left. **Reeder Road** intersects Sauvie Island Road about 1.5 miles north of the bridge, then it angles across the island. Much of the first three miles of Reeder Road (heading roughly northeast) are bordered by farmland.

At about 1.5 miles, **Oak Island Road** intersects and heads north. Oak Island Road, a dead end road, can offer great opportunities to see waterfowl and raptors. Barns along here may have Barn Owls. Great Horned Owls may be nesting in late winter along the slough that parallels the road on its western side. The hedges harbor wintering sparrows. Often you can see or hear Sandhill Cranes in the flooded fields in fall and winter. Some mixed flocks of geese can be near the roadway. At the end of the road is a patch of woods that may have wintering songbirds and accipiters. Migrating warbler flocks may include vagrants such as Palm Warbler in fall. A nature trail from the final parking area is open only in late spring and summer. The open areas along this road may be the best spots on Sauvie Island for Rough-legged Hawk, Merlin, Peregrine, and uncommonly, Prairie Falcon. Even a Ferruginous Hawk has been reported here in winter. The hedges often harbor coveys of California Quail.

Continuing across the island on Reeder Road, just past Milepost 3 is **Coon Point**. What you'll find: a gravel parking lot, toilets, and a paved pedestrian ramp to the top of the levee. The view from here is good in all directions, and a scope is especially useful. In fall you can find large flocks of White Pelicans and Great Egrets on Sturgeon Lake, to your west. In winter expect Sandhill Cranes, Bald Eagles, various geese and many species of ducks on this lake. Uncommon geese seen here in the past include Ross's, Brant and Emperor. Red-breasted Sapsuckers and raptors may perch in the large oak trees along the road. This may be the best spot to look for Tundra and Trumpeter Swans. In summer you can walk down off the dike and bird along Sturgeon Lake's marshy margins. Most or all of the lake may be dried up by then. The small pond east of Sturgeon Lake is called Phalarope Pond. In warm months there may be White Pelicans here if there's enough water.

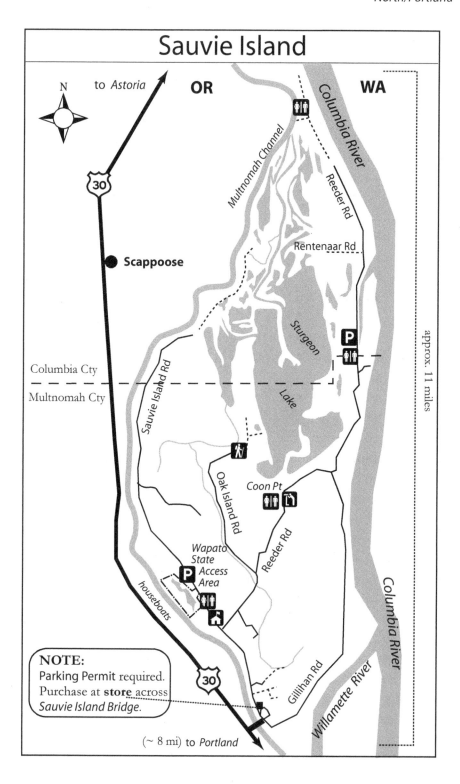

Sauvie Island

to *Astoria*   **OR**   **WA**

N

US 30

Scappoose

Multnomah Channel

Columbia River

Reeder Rd

Rentenaar Rd

Columbia Cty

Multnomah Cty

Sturgeon

Lake

Sauvie Island Rd

Oak Island Rd

Coon Pt

Wapato State Access Area

houseboats

Reeder Rd

Gillihan Rd

Willamette River

Columbia River

approx. 11 miles

NOTE:
Parking Permit required. Purchase at **store** across *Sauvie Island Bridge.*

US 30

(~ 8 mi) to *Portland*

At about 4.5 miles, Reeder Road elbows toward the north. Here it intersects with **Gillihan Road,** which runs south through mostly private farmland to the south end of the island. That part of Sauvie is usually the least productive bird-wise but may have large gatherings of Pintail in flooded fields and some Sandhill Cranes in winter. Roaming shorebird or icterid flocks may also be found in the fields.

Just before Milepost 7 on Reeder Road there is a dirt road heading east. It ends at a parking lot in the riparian woods with walking access to long sandy beaches along the Columbia River on the island's east shore. This area is good for accipiter, possible Pileated Woodpecker and Red-breasted Sapsucker, and sparrows in winter. The river can be checked for gulls, ducks, loons and Bald Eagles.

At about 7.4 miles, between two farmsteads on the west side of Reeder Road, there's a dirt parking area, a good-sized raised viewing platform, and toilets.

This platform overlooks a wetland that is often crowded with ducks and geese in cold months. It can make for some exciting birding, with plenty of birds to slowly pick through for the unusual or rare. Here is the best place to look for Redhead, Canvasback and other diving ducks. There can be thousands of waterfowl here, including swans and Cackling Geese. Bald Eagles may come in to hunt. Here I once watched a Bald Eagle pluck a Cackling Goose out of the water, then lose it when the eagle perched on a piling in the lake. Among fall shorebirds Stilt, Pectoral and Solitary Sandpiper have been found here. Dowitchers, Western and Least Sandpipers can be abundant.

At Milepost 10 you can turn left (west) onto **Rentenaar Road** (see below). But continuing on Reeder Road, you will see numerous pull-offs and access to the levee along the Columbia River. Here you can bird more wetlands and riparian forest, and climb the levee to check for shorebirds on the beach, as well as waterfowl, Bald Eagles and Osprey along the Columbia. Reeder Road terminates around Milepost 12.

Rentenaar Road is a short, dead-end road, yet nearly 120 species have been reported to eBird from this location. There are several pull-offs and a wildlife viewing platform on a levee at the west end of the road. There's rich marshland on both sides of Rentenaar. In addition to cranes and waterfowl, this is good habitat for wintering sparrows and Marsh Wren. Both Sora and Virginia Rail are possible. From the viewing platform one winter I counted over 3,000 Cackling Geese in a dense flock right below where I stood. Other possible wintering birds include Redhead, Cinnamon Teal, Eurasian Wigeon, Canvasback and Merlin. Bewick's Wren, Spotted Towhee and Savannah Sparrow are year-round. Migrant flocks here will include western warblers and vireo, even an occasional Red-eyed Vireo in September. A Harris's Sparrow wintered here recently.

Sauvie Island Road runs along the west shore of the island, paralleling Multnomah Channel and US 30 on the far side of the channel. Here expect Bald Eagle in winter, gulls, ducks, Great Blue Heron and Belted Kingfisher. At the end of the public access, check further west along the channel for more eagles. In the open areas check the wintering *icterid* flocks carefully for possible Tricolored or Yellow-headed Blackbirds and even the Pacific rarity, Rusty Blackbird. In summer you might spot Purple Martins in nest boxes across the channel near the houseboats.

Sauvie Island Wildlife Area Headquarters is on the east side of Sauvie Island Road just past the intersection with Reeder Road. What you'll find: toilets and information. About a mile past the headquarters and 2.5 miles north from the Sauvie Island Bridge, you will come to **Wapato Greenway Access State Park** on the west side of the road. What you'll find: There's a small dirt parking lot, a picnic pavilion, trails, and a viewing platform. Dogs are ok on leash.

The trail here leads through riparian forest to a viewing platform on Virginia Lake. Ducks are abundant in winter, mostly dabblers with possible Eurasian Wigeon and Common Teal. Pintail and Ring-necked Ducks are regular. There is usually a Great Horned Owl somewhere near the parking area. Sparrows may fill the bushes in winter. Red-breasted Sapsucker and both kinglets (winter) are possible here. September migration brings passing warblers, including Black-throated Gray. The passing birds often flock with the resident Black-capped Chickadees. Steller's Jay, Spotted Towhee and Brown Creeper are forest residents here.

I-5 Exit 307, West. Northwest Portland. Exit here for **Marine Drive**, which parallels the Columbia River both east and west of I-5. See *Northwest Portland* map. West of this intersection it is called North Marine Drive.

To visit **Vanport Wetlands**, head west on North Marine Drive. Take the first possible left-hand turn, North Force Avenue, on the western edge of the Portland Convention Center property. In about 100 yards Force Avenue takes you to Vanport Wetlands, a marsh administered by the Port of Portland. Right along Force Avenue is Force Lake, administered by Portland Parks & Recreation. The lake is now being cleaned and de-trashed by a local volunteer group. Access is limited but there is some good viewing from the perimeter. There are often waterfowl on Force Lake as well as Green and Great Blue Herons. Blue-winged Teal and Redhead can be expected here, along with other more common western ducks. Cinnamon Teal are regular. Snow Geese may be among the Canada Geese. If the water level is low enough in fall you can expect a variety of shorebirds here as well. Pectoral Sandpiper may stay briefly in autumn. Both yellowlegs, Western Sandpiper and Wilson's Snipe are among the expected shorebirds here. Up to five species of swallows can be abundant in spring and summer, feeding just over the water or skimming the surface. Purple Martin and Yellow-headed Blackbird are possible September birds.

South of Force Lake and the golf course entrance on the right, Force Avenue is often closed to cars but you can walk the road alongside the marsh and in a quarter mile you approach a slough and some lawn area of a city park. This walk can be good for warblers, sparrows and other songbirds (and you, too).

2.5 miles west of I-5 Exit 307 off North Marine Drive you will find **Smith and Bybee Lakes Wildlife Area.** It encompasses over 1,900 acres, and is managed by the Metro regional government council. The Smith and Bybee Lakes area is the largest protected wetland area within city limits in the United States and is a designated IBA. Turn left (south) off of Marine Drive into the parking lot next to paved trails. What you'll find: toilets, parking lot, information displays, bus stop, canoe launch, paved trail and bicycle path. The paved Interlaken Trail begins about a quarter mile west of the parking lot. The trail runs generally south between the two main lakes and includes covered viewing platforms and an overlook near a marsh. The trail is just over a mile round trip. It floods during wet periods.

Here a mix of bottomland, wetland, and forest provide fine birding. Cottonwood, Oregon ash, alder, bigleaf maple and willows grow in the riparian forest here. Some of the ash trees are more than a century old. Marsh thickets include willows, red-osier dogwoods and spiraea. Sedges, rushes, beggars tick, rice cutgrass and reed canary grass grow in open meadows. Aquatic plants flourish in the sloughs and ponds.

This is a rich area for forest and marsh species, with many waterfowl wintering here. Visitors may be surprised to see river otter, beaver, Bald Eagle, Pileated Woodpecker, western painted turtle and black-tailed (mule) deer all inhabiting this site surrounded by industrial sprawl. It is a remnant of the once extensive floodplain at the confluence of the Willamette with the Columbia. Floods are prevented now by levees, but the lowlands still collect water and attract birds and birders. Part of the year the city opens a channel that once again allows tidal water in and out of the lakes from the nearby estuary of the Columbia.

The only known breeding population of Streaked Horned Larks in Multnomah County is in this area, and the birds show up at Smith and Bybee Lakes Wildlife Area, especially in winter. Peregrine Falcon and Northern Harrier hunt the marshes and meadows. In fall, large flocks of 300 or more White Pelicans may gather here. Tens of thousands of waterfowl winter in the wildlife area including Green-winged Teal, Pintail Duck, Northern Shoveler, Common Merganser, Bufflehead, Lesser Scaup, Ring-necked Duck, American Wigeon, Gadwall, Ruddy Duck, Wood Duck and Pied-billed Grebe. There are also occasional sightings of Brant, Canvasback, Redhead, Blue-winged Teal, and Tundra Swan. Gulls here may include California as well as the large pale Glaucous-winged. Fall rarities have included Franklin's and Sabine's far from the Pacific. Some winters a few hardy Tree Swallows may be found overhead.

The lakes recede or disappear completely each summer, leaving plenty of inviting mudflats for autumn migrations. Fall shorebirds reported here include Semipalmated Plover; Red-necked Phalarope; and Semipalmated, Stilt and Pectoral Sandpiper. Shorebird populations can reach several hundred on an autumn day. Overhead you may see two swift species in September along with many Vaux's and a few Black. Also watch for Purple Martin among the swallows in fall, and the uncommon Bank Swallow may pass by. Nesting species: Great Blue Heron, Bald Eagle, Osprey, Willow Flycatcher, Swainson's Thrush, Marsh Wren and Savannah Sparrow. Bushtit, Brown Creeper, Bewick's Wren, Marsh Wren, Pacific Wren and both kinglets are found here. Spotted Towhee is resident. EBird shows 180 species at Smith and Bybee. Resident mammals include river otters, beavers and coyotes.

I-5 Exit 307, East. Northeast Portland. See *Greater Portland* maps. Exit here for **Marine Drive** (called NE Marine Drive on this side of I-5) and head east and you'll parallel the south bank of the Columbia River on your left. The Portland Airport will be on your right. In winter you can expect grebes, ducks and gulls along the river. Many Great Blue Herons and Red-tailed Hawks hunt the open space around the airport runways. In winter there are often huge rafts of Greater Scaup on this section of river. On the airport property or on nearby open land you may find an occasional wintering Rough-legged Hawk, a species more common east of the Cascades. At **Broughton Beach** a Snow Bunting wintered recently. Tufted Duck have occurred there as well.

For more information on birding the eastern end of Marine Drive beyond the airport, see the I-205 section earlier in this chapter.

Interstate 405 Corridor

I-405 Exit 2. A Quartet of Birding Spots in the Hills of West Portland. See *Greater Portland, West* and *Northwest Portland* maps. Every September in northwestern Portland thousands of Vaux's Swifts roost at **Chapman Elementary School**. It's one of the most highly populated known swift roosts in the western United States. After sunset, the swifts pour into the school's large chimney. Some counts number several thousand swifts in a single night. Hundreds of swift watchers gather most evenings during the season and more congregate at Wallace Park across the street. If you want to see some swifts, here's some useful advice from the Portland Audubon Society website:

Parking for several blocks around the school is usually full by 6 p.m. Plan to park further away and walk 4-6 blocks. Pettygrove Street is a DEAD END! DO NOT drive up Pettygrove Street. It creates a congested and potentially dangerous situation. Blocked driveways and double-parked cars are illegal and impact the safety of children and pets and access for emergency vehicles.

Park in one of the Courtesy Parking Areas: Montgomery Park, 2701 NW Vaughn offers free off-street parking. Travel west on Vaughn Street past the traffic light at NW 27th. Take the second right to enter the parking lot. To get to the school from here walk back to the traffic light and then four blocks south on 27th Ave to Raleigh Street. Allow an extra 10 minutes and forget about the stress of looking for parking!

You can use Public Transportation: The Portland Street Car and bus lines 15 and 17 travel within two blocks of Wallace Park. For planning your route visit TriMet's Trip Planner and enter NW Pettygrove and NW 25th Ave in the "To:" field.

Ride your Bike: But be thoughtful and courteous about where you choose to leave your bike. Use the school bike racks. Group your bikes together and lock them out of the way of prime swift watching seats. Ask permission before parking bikes on private property. Don't be offended if permission is not given, you may be the 100th person to have asked. Do not block the street with bikes.

Walk: Plan your evening, meet your friends somewhere nearby and then walk over. The phenomenon of Vaux's Swifts is happening ALL OVER Northwest Portland in the hour leading up to sunset. Even a half-mile away, just look up and you'll see hundreds of swifts making their way towards the school.

Forest Park and **Portland Audubon Wildlife Sanctuary.** These two birding locations are adjacent to each other two miles from I-405 Exit 2. What you'll find: Forest Park has no facilities per se, but does offer more than 70 miles of forested trails. Audubon Wildlife Sanctuary has toilets and a visitors center. The Audubon Nature Store and Interpretive

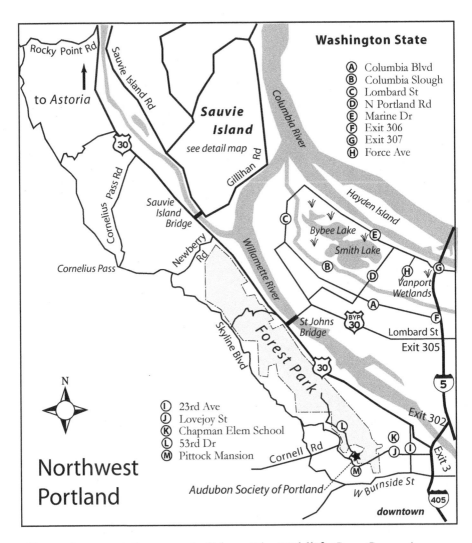

Washington State

(A) Columbia Blvd
(B) Columbia Slough
(C) Lombard St
(D) N Portland Rd
(E) Marine Dr
(F) Exit 306
(G) Exit 307
(H) Force Ave

(I) 23rd Ave
(J) Lovejoy St
(K) Chapman Elem School
(L) 53rd Dr
(M) Pittock Mansion

Northwest Portland

Center is open daily except holidays. The Wildlife Care Center is open every day of the year. Some trails in Forest Park are open to bicycles.

To get here, from Exit 2, take 14th or 17th Avenue north to NW Lovejoy and turn left (west). Lovejoy becomes Cornell, which leads to the Audubon Sanctuary after you go through two highway tunnels. It's then another few hundred yards to NW 53rd Drive, which provides access to some of the many trailheads in Forest Park. See *Northwest Portland* map.

This aptly named park comprises over 5,100 acres; it's the largest forested park within city limits in the United States. It contains miles of trails but no other facilities. The forest runs parallel to the ridge of the Tualatin Mountains and drops down toward the Columbia River to the north. While Forest Park and the three Audubon tracts are all steep, most of the area is only a few hundred feet above sea level. The Portland Audubon Society has three nearby refuge properties contiguous to Forest Park. Together they total 150 acres.

Forest Park itself has grown over the decades and now includes two formerly separate parks that are still named on highway signs: Macleay and Holman. The locale gets about 40 inches of rain in a normal year and no freezing temperatures, so the forest is both dense and lush, with much of the ground overgrown by ferns and other shade-tolerant plants. The forest is composed of a wide variety of trees including Douglas-fir, western red cedar, western hemlock, western yew, bigleaf maple, red alder, grand fir and black cottonwood along streams. Much of the forest is second growth in what has been protected parkland since 1948, so the trees are large by now. Altogether this park provides a huge swath of open space on the edge of a modern city.

The **Audubon Sanctuary** maintains feeders at the visitors center, just outside the large windows. Here you may see Anna's Hummingbird any day, Chestnut-backed and Black-capped Chickadees, Bushtits, nuthatches, Hairy and Pileated Woodpeckers on the suet, and an occasional hungry Cooper's or Sharp-shinned Hawk. Some other birds you may see in warm months are Black-headed Grosbeak, Wilson's Warbler, Warbling Vireo, Pacific-slope Flycatcher in the low brush. Hermit Thrush nest and thus serenade here in spring, Varied Thrush may show up in winter. Band-tailed Pigeons are regulars at the feeding station, but skittish. Brown Creeper may feed on the nearby tree trunks. Spotted Towhee are also resident here. Over 100 birds have been identified in this forest including Screech-Owl, the invasive Barred Owl, Northern Pygmy and Northern Saw-whet Owls. Vaux's Swift nest in this forest. Woodpeckers here are: Red-breasted Sapsucker, Downy, Hairy, Pileated and Northernand Northern Flicker. The most likely flycatchers are Olive-sided in the canopy, and Pacific-slope in damp brushy areas. Other birds to expect: Hutton's and Cassin's Vireo with Hutton's being non-migratory, Steller's Jay, Violet-green Swallow, Pacific Wren (resident), Black-throated Gray and Townsend's Warbler in spring and late summer, and Western Tanager. The forest also attracts wandering flocks of Evening Grosbeaks, cheeping like baby chickens during April-May and August-September. They will appear at feeders.

There's an active wildlife care center that you can visit next to the Audubon Nature Store. On a recent visit I met a resident Great Horned Owl and watched a handsome pair of American Kestrels who watched me in turn. The care center often rescues Black-headed Grosbeaks and other local songbirds. The sanctuary is open dawn to dusk for hiking and birding. If you continue west past the Audubon center you will intersect Skyline Boulevard.

Pittock Mansion is an attraction in itself, a century-old architectural wonder, and can be toured. To reach it take West Burnside and then follow the signs. It sits in a small city park surrounded by land owned by the Audubon Society. Some birds seen here regularly include wintering Varied Thrush, Red Crossbill, Hutton's Vireo, Red-breasted Sapsucker (look for trees with the parallel lines of drill holes), Anna's and Rufous Hummingbirds, Vaux's Swift in summer, Chestnut-backed Chickadee, Pacific and Bewick's Wren, Black-throated Gray Warbler on migration, and an occasional wandering Evening Grosbeak.

Skyline Boulevard. Follow the *Northwest Portland* map to Skyline Boulevard. This road runs several miles through the wooded hills and offers some tempting potential birds. At this time there's no eBird data for this road, but it passes through the southern edge of Forest Park and has been the location of many sightings unusual for Multnomah County: Cassin's Vireo, Western Bluebird, Mountain Quail, Red-breasted Merganser, and wintering Short-eared Owl near Skyline School. More expected birds here include Raven, Red Crossbill, Band-tailed Pigeon, Swainson's Thrush, Orange-crowned and MacGillivray's Warbler.

From Skyline Boulevard there are various routes north to US 30 and the bridge to **Sauvie Island.**

I-405 Exit 3. For **Sauvie Island** take Exit 3 onto US 30 westbound. See **I-5 Exit 307** in this chapter for details on birding Sauvie Island, one of the richest birding areas on this entire I-5 corridor.

Lewis and Clark Expeditionary Force

President Thomas Jefferson sent the Lewis and Clark Expedition to the Pacific Coast in 1803. This was the first overland trek from the east coast of the United States to what would become the west coast of the United States. In May of 1803, the men left Saint Louis, Missouri, traveling by foot and boat across the newly acquired Louisiana Territory. They moved west and north on the Missouri River, over the Rockies and along the Snake River in present-day Idaho. On reaching the Pacific Northwest, they entered a mostly unknown territory variously claimed by Britain, Russia, Spain and the United States. They canoed down the Columbia River to its mouth, just west of where Astoria, Oregon now stands, reaching the Pacific Ocean in November 1805. They spent the winter at nearby Fort Clatsop and left in late March 1806 for their return trek.

Meriwether Lewis and William Clark were the first ones to collect and describe many plants and animals of the American West that were unknown to science at the time. Among them were a woodpecker and a nutcracker. These two birds were later described and named Lewis's Woodpecker and Clark's Nutcracker by ornithologist Alexander Wilson, based on specimens collected by Lewis and Clark. The explorers were also the first to collect specimens of the colorful Western Tanager, Pronghorn and the Prairie Dog, two among many "new" species. The tanager is an abundant bird in the Columbia River Valley during spring migration.

On the lower Columbia River, the men observed what they called "buzzards of the large kind" flying overhead and feeding on a dead whale that would prove to be California Condors. Lewis sketched and wrote a detailed description of a condor that the group's hunters had shot.

In addition to their namesake woodpecker and nutcracker, Lewis and Clark are widely commemorated in place names in the Northwestern United States. In Oregon, there's a Lewis and Clark National Wildlife Refuge downstream from Portland consisting of 27 islands in the Columbia River. In Northwestern Oregon is the Lewis and Clark National Historic Park, which includes a reconstruction of their winter camp at Fort Clatsop, near Astoria, about 2 hours west from I-5 in Portland. The fort sits along the Lewis and Clark River estuary. The Lewis and Clark Recreation Site is at the western gateway to the Columbia Gorge.

Washington State has a Lewis River, a Lewis County, a Clark County, a town named Clarkston on the Snake River (Lewiston, Idaho is on the other side), and a Lewis and Clark State Park. The Judith River in Idaho is named after Clark's sweetheart, whom he later married. There is a Lewis and Clark Caverns State Park in Montana. The Lewis and Clark National Trail follows the expedition's route from Saint Louis to the mouth of the Columbia River. The trail headquarters is in Omaha on the Missouri River.

In addition to the birds and all the placenames, Lewis and Clark each have a namesake plant genus. *Clarkia* is a widespread group of western grassland wildflowers. *Lewisia* is the genus of the bitteroot plant.

Chapter 11
Washington South of Puget Sound

I-5 / I-205 / WA 14
Clark, Cowlitz, Lewis and Thurston Counties

There are two parallel freeway corridors through southern Clark County continuing into the state from Oregon. Both Interstate 5 and the more easterly Interstate 205 enter Washington across parallel bridges over the Columbia River. Each interstate allows close access to different birding spots. I-205 is only about 10 miles long in Washington and it merges with I-5 at I-5 Exit 7 in Washington.

Interstate 205 in Washington

The I-205 bridge across the Columbia River carries traffic over Government Island, which is not accessible by car.

I-205 Exit 27. Washougal. Exit here and go east on WA 14, which parallels the Columbia on the north bank. About 10 miles east of I-205 you will be in central Washougal, elevation 165 feet. At 15th Street turn right for **Steamboat Landing State Park**. What you'll find: This tiny park has a floating fishing pier extending well into the river. It's open 7 a.m. until dusk and has toilets. A trail runs east along the levee all the way to Steigerwald Lake National Wildlife Refuge (see below). In winter, scan the river for diving ducks, loons and grebes.

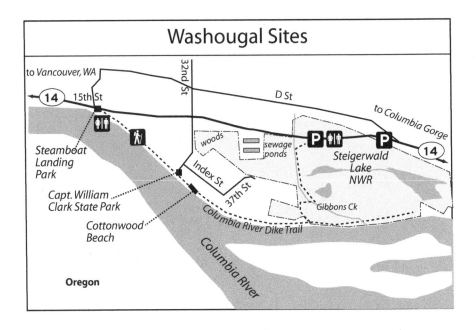

Near the east end of Washougal, you will see 32nd Street. You can turn right (south) here to reach **Captain William Clark Park** on the bank of the Columbia River. There are no facilities. This stretch of riverbank is rightly called Cottonwood Beach. A short trail takes you over the levee, through a dense band of cottonwoods and down to the riverside. Riparian birds are at home here. One winter there was a Red-naped Sapsucker down from Cascades.

Nearby, at the far end of 37th Street, there is some open land that overlooks the north end of **Steigerwald Lake National Wildlife Refuge**, but you will want to return to WA 14 and continue a bit east to access the refuge. Just before you reach it there is a pullout on WA 14 at the entrance to the Washougal Sewer Ponds (just south of the highway) where you can check for birds.

Steigerwald is an IBA. This reserve encompasses grasslands, oak uplands, cottonwood-topped riparian forest along Gibbons Creek, and seasonal wetlands. There are nearly a thousand acres in this NWR, with a 2.75-mile trail that takes you away from WA 14 into the refuge's interior. The trail heads south along Gibbons Creek from the parking lot at the first pullout on the south side of WA 14. Further east there is another pullout where D Street culminates at WA 14. Nearly three dozen waterfowl species have been reported at Steigerwald, most in fall and winter when a dozen species are usually abundant. Tundra and Trumpeter Swan have been seen, along with all three mergansers, both goldeneyes, a few Greater Scaup among the many Lessers, Eurasian Wigeon, Blue-winged Teal among the many Cinnamon and Green-winged in winter, and rarely a Surf Scoter, Long-tailed Duck or Tufted Duck. In winter, Horned Larks may be found along the levee and near the parking lot. Osprey and Harrier can be expected in warm months. All northern American falcons have been seen here, including Gyrfalcon.

This is not a rich spot for shorebirds. Summering birds here include Purple Martin; Vaux's Swift; Violet-green Swallow; Bewick's, Marsh and House Wren; Swainson's Thrush; Cedar Waxwing; Black-headed Grosbeak; and Bullock's Oriole. Wintering land birds include Western Meadowlark, both kinglets, Mountain Bluebirds seeking some warmth, and Golden-crowned Sparrows. About 140 species have been recorded here according to eBird.

I-205 / I-5 Junction. The junction of I-205 with I-5, north of the town of Salmon Creek, is about 10.5 miles north of the I-205 Columbia Rover crossing, at I-5 Mile 7.

Interstate 5 in Washington

I-5 enters Washington State from Portland over the Interstate Bridge that passes over Hayden Island, which is on the Oregon side of the border. During one winter irruption of Snowy Owls a single bird was seen hunting from a light post in the I-5 median strip in Vancouver, WA.

I-5 Exit 1B. WA 14. You can head east here on WA 14, Lewis and Clark Highway, to reach **Steigerwald Lake National Wildlife Refuge (NWR)**. It's about 17 miles east on the north bank of the Columbia River. (See I-205 section above for details.)

Closer in, you can leave WA 14 at Exit 1 for **Marine Park** on the north bank of the Columbia River. What you'll find: toilets (in warm months), boat ramp, trails, picnic area and ball field. This is a 26-acre park on the riverfront. Greater Scaup may gather offshore in winter. Sometimes a vagrant Tufted Duck will join them. You may spot a Common Loon here in winter and various gull species occur, including

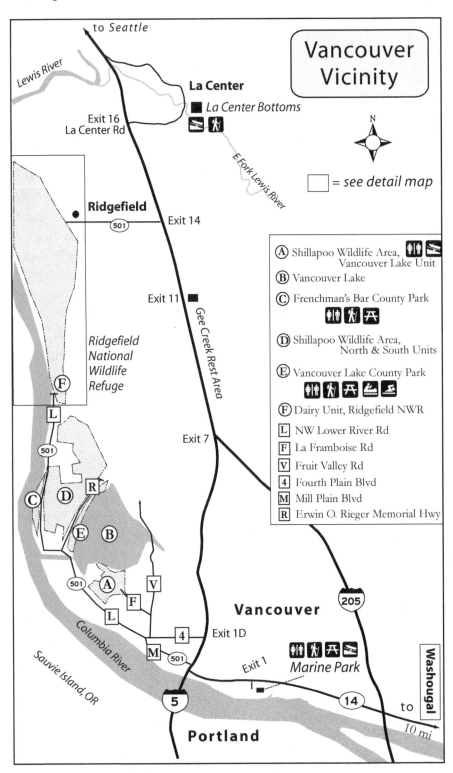

to *Seattle*

Lewis River

La Center

■ *La Center Bottoms*

Exit 16
La Center Rd

E. Fork Lewis River

Vancouver Vicinity

N

☐ = *see detail map*

● **Ridgefield**

501   Exit 14

Exit 11 ■

Gee Creek Rest Area

*Ridgefield
National
Wildlife
Refuge*

(F)

L

501

Exit 7

R

(C) (D)

(E) (B)

501

(A)   V

F

L

4   Exit 1D

M   501

(A) Shillapoo Wildlife Area,
      Vancouver Lake Unit

(B) Vancouver Lake

(C) Frenchman's Bar County Park

(D) Shillapoo Wildlife Area,
      North & South Units

(E) Vancouver Lake County Park

(F) Dairy Unit, Ridgefield NWR

L NW Lower River Rd

F La Framboise Rd

V Fruit Valley Rd

4 Fourth Plain Blvd

M Mill Plain Blvd

R Erwin O. Rieger Memorial Hwy

Vancouver

205

Columbia River

Sauvie Island, OR

Exit 1

Marine Park

5

14

Washougal

to

10 mi

Portland

Mew and Glaucous-winged. Likely songbirds in winter include both kinglet species and Pacific Wren. Bushtit and Spotted Towhee are here year-round.

I-5 Exit 1D. Various Lakes and Parks. Exit here and take Fourth Plain Boulevard west to reach several adjacent birding spots: **Vancouver Lake, Frenchman's Bar County Park, Shillapoo Wildlife Area** and the **Dairy Unit** of the **Ridgefield National Wildlife Refuge (NWR)**. This part of Washington State is on the Columbia's east bank directly across the river from Sauvie Island, northwest of Portland Oregon (see previous chapter). Through here, the Columbia River has a north-south orientation. See *Vancouver Vicinity* map.

    Shillapoo Wildlife Area. Overall, the three units of the Shillapoo Wildlife Area encompass 2,370 acres of riparian lowlands in the Columbia River floodplain. The whole is managed by Washington State. The intention is to turn the farmland within Shillapoo back into wetlands and natural grasslands and try to eradicate exotic, invasive plants.

    To reach Shillapoo's closest unit, the **Vancouver Lake Unit**, from I-5 Exit 1D take Fourth Plain Boulevard west about 1.5 miles to Fruit Valley Road. Turn north onto Fruit Valley Road, go half a mile and then west onto La Framboise Road. Go 1.7 mile on La Framboise Road and the Vancouver Lake unit will be on the west side of the road. La Framboise Road will dead-end at Vancouver Lake. What you'll find: toilets, a boat ramp. Fruit Valley Road continues north, intersecting many rural roads that will take you back to I-5 or to the main Ridgefield NWR entrance (see below).

    For the **Shillapoo North and South Units** and the other nearby parks, stay on Fourth Plain Boulevard, bypassing Fruit Valley Road. The street curves right and becomes NW Lower River Road (County Road 501). This road takes you west toward the Columbia River and then north. The lowlands around Vancouver Lake and nearby Columbia River shore are an IBA. Frenchman's Bar (see below) has access to the Columbia River. This complex of parks and open space are rich with riverside habitat: cottonwoods, permanent and seasonal wetlands, marsh and meadow.

It is about 5 miles from I-5 to the intersection of NW Lower River Road and Erwin O. Rieger Memorial Highway. From that point it's a short distance north on Rieger Memorial Highway to the entrance of **Vancouver Lake County Park**'s western unit. What you'll find: picnic areas, toilets, trails, fishing, "no-wake" boating (kayaks and canoes, with permit) and swimming. An entrance fee is charged. Dogs are allowed on leash in some areas. The park covers over 200 acres, much of it undeveloped, and includes 2.5 miles of lake shoreline. This road also dead-ends.

Back on Lower River Road, from the Rieger Memorial Highway intersection it is 5.7 miles to the road's terminus at the south end of the **Dairy Unit, Ridgefield NWR**. There are no open trails there or in Shillapoo Wildlife Area, but they can be birded from the road. The North and South Units of Shillapoo NWA are situated between these two roads (Lower River Road and Reiger Memorial Highway).

Before Lower River Road dead ends where it washed out many years ago, you will pass **Frenchman's Bar County Park,** a narrow strip between the road and the river, on your left. What you'll find: toilets, picnic areas, a playground, ball diamond, and trails. An entrance fee is charged, and the park is open for day use only. Frenchman's Bar consists of 120 acres on the east bank of the Columbia.

EBird shows over 150 bird species for this entire region around Vancouver Lake comprised of the various parks and wildlife preserves. Twenty-eight wintering waterfowl are recorded here, including Greater White-fronted Goose, Snow Goose, Ross's Goose (rarely), Brant, both scaup, both Goldeneye, all three mergansers, Cinnamon Teal, Wood Duck, Eurasian Wigeon, an occasional wayward Surf Scoter. An Emperor Goose has been seen here as well. Many of the Canada Geese that winter here are Duskies from Canada.

Other wetland birds found from Vancouver to the Columbia include Great Egret, American Bittern, Horned and Eared Grebe, Red-necked Grebe, Great Egret and Belted Kingfisher. Both Pacific and Red-throated Loon have been seen in the river at the end of SE Columbia Way. Wintering raptors include Harrier, Bald Eagle, Merlin, and Cooper's and Sharp-shinned Hawk. Osprey are here in spring and summer. Bonaparte's Gulls may rest on Vancouver Lake during migration.

Sandhill Cranes can be found wintering in this area along the Columbia River. In late winter and spring, other migrating cranes stop over, sometimes numbering in the hundreds before the next leg of their migration northward. There's usually a large Great Blue Heron rookery in the Shillapoo South Unit.

Land birds of interest here include the Pileated Woodpecker, wintering Northern Shrike, Bushtit, Violet-green Swallow, Pacific Wren (winter), Bewick's Wren, American Pipit (winter), a selection of western warblers in fall including Townsend's and Wilson's. Wintering sparrows may include Harris's and White-throated in addition to White-crowned and Golden-crowned.

I-5 Mile 7 (north terminus of I-205). If you are southbound and want to bird **Steigerwald Lake National Wildlife Refuge**, this is a shortcut, so exit onto I-205 southbound here.

I-5 Exit 11. Gee Creek Rest Areas. Both the northbound and southbound Gee Creek rest areas are spacious, forested, and give a little respite from the interstate. If you're northbound, take the exit for WA 502. Birds you might find include Steller's Jays, Juncos, Robins and migrant thrushes.

I-5 Exit 14. Exit here and take WA 501 west to reach the town of Ridgefield and the nearby northern units of **Ridgefield National Wildlife Refuge**. Ridgefield is an IBA (see *Ridgefield NWR* map). What you'll find: toilets, trails, information; an entrance fee is charged. Ridgefield NWR hosts the Birdfest and Bluegrass Festival in October. The Sandhill Crane is the logo bird for this event. The festival offers kayak and canoe tours of the refuge. Ridgefield NWR contains a mix of habitat including open water, marsh, seasonal wetlands, grasslands, riparian forest of Douglas-fir, western red cedar, bigleaf maple, cottonwood, red alder and willow.

It is 4.2 miles from I-5 Exit 14 to the office on the **Carty Unit**, the northernmost unit of Ridgefield NWR. I once encountered a Pileated Woodpecker right next to the parking lot at the Refuge headquarters. There are two short walking trails at the Carty Unit. The Oaks-to-Wetland Trail passes through a forest of Oregon ash trees and large, stately

Garry oaks. The dead trees in the woods here are perforated with large Pileated excavations.

In passing through the town of Ridgefield you will see small signs for motorboat and kayak launch ramps. The ramps offer a chance to bird along the narrow channel of Lake River. Gulls, Belted Kingfisher, heron and egret are possible, along with swallows in season.

South of town, look for the **River S Unit** of **Ridgefield National Wildlife Ref-**

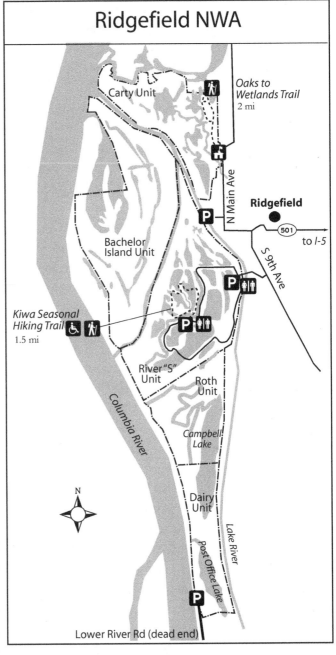

Ridgefield NWA

Carty Unit

Oaks to Wetlands Trail 2 mi

N Main Ave

Ridgefield

501

to I-5

S 9th Ave

Bachelor Island Unit

Kiwa Seasonal Hiking Trail 1.5 mi

River "S" Unit

Roth Unit

Campbell Lake

Columbia River

N

Dairy Unit

Lake River

Post Office Lake

Lower River Rd (dead end)

uge. What you'll find: a 4.5 mile auto trail and viewing blind, toilets, a 1.2-mile hiking trail; an entrance fee is charged. To reach River S Unit, turn onto South 9th Avenue at the east edge of Ridgefield. It is 1.2 miles from that turn to the entry station and information kiosk for this part of Ridgefield NWR. I once got to see a Harrier, a Peregrine and a Bald Eagle compete for the same Green-winged Teal here. Of course, the eagle carried the day and the dead duck.

EBird shows almost 200 species in the northern units of the Ridgefield NWR. Over 30 species of waterfowl reported include Brant, Trumpeter and Tundra Swan, Eurasian Wigeon, White-winged Scoter, Harlequin, both goldeneyes and all three merganser species. Some notable winter birds spotted here: Red-necked Grebe, White-tailed Kite, Red-shouldered Hawk, Merlin, Mew Gull, Northern Shrike, and Swamp and White-throated Sparrow. Migrating shorebirds you might encounter in fall: Pectoral, Solitary and Baird's Sandpiper. Sandhill Cranes are regular at Ridgefield in fall and winter as they cross the river from Sauvie Island in Oregon. Being so close to Portland and Vancouver, Washington, the NWR is frequently birded and rarities are found, including a Vermilion Flycatcher one autumn.

Year-round species include American Bittern, Northern Harrier, Virginia Rail, Sora, Wilson's Snipe, Great Horned Owl, Belted Kingfisher, Pileated Woodpecker, Bushtit, Chestnut-backed Chickadee, Bewick's and Pacific Wren and Spotted Towhee. Summer breeding birds: Vaux's Swift, Pacific-slope and Willow Flycatcher, Western Wood-Pewee, Swainson's Thrush, Black-headed Grosbeak, Bullock's Oriole and Yellow-headed Blackbird. Violet-green Swallows are here from late winter through August. Lewis's Woodpecker and White-faced Ibis have been unexpected winter visitors on occasion.

I-5 Exit 16. La Center Bottoms. Exit here onto NW La Center Road to reach the town of La Center. See *Vancouver Vicinity* map. Drive east almost 2 miles, then cross the bridge over the East Fork of the Lewis River. Turn right almost immediately after crossing the bridge and curve around the water treatment plant to a small parking area. From here follow the paved path into the **La Center Bottoms**, a county park. What you'll find: Good walking trails, viewing blinds, boat launch and information. One branch of the trail goes uphill along a wooded ridge to the back of the La Center School. The other branch of the trail goes down to the riverside levee and follows it for a couple miles. This affords views of birds along the river as well as in the marshy grassland east of the river. Birds you can expect here are Great Blue Heron, Great

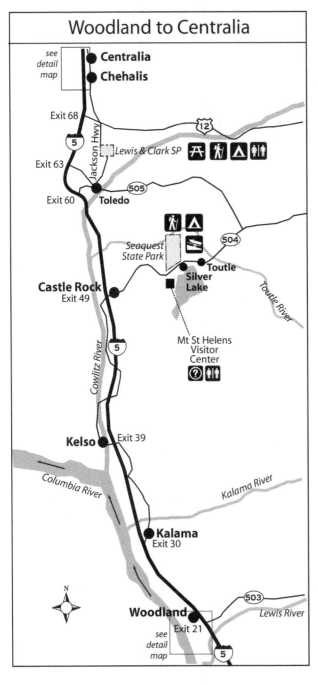

Woodland to Centralia

see detail map

● **Centralia**
● **Chehalis**

Exit 68

(5)
Exit 63

Jackson Hwy

Lewis & Clark SP

(12)

Exit 60 ● **Toledo** (505)

(504)

Seaquest State Park

● **Toutle**
■ **Silver Lake**

Castle Rock
Exit 49

Toutle River

(5)

Mt St Helens Visitor Center

Cowlitz River

Kelso ● Exit 39

Columbia River

Kalama River

● **Kalama**
Exit 30

N

(503)

Woodland
see detail map Exit 21

Lewis River

(5)

Egret, Belted King-fisher, Black-capped Chickadee and warblers in migration. Wintering sparrows will include Gold-en-crowned. Otters and Coho Salmon are regular on the river itself. On the downriver side of the bridge there is a rough boat ramp if you want to get onto the river. It is the only place in the park to get onto the river.

I-5 Mile 20. County Line. The bridge over Lewis River crosses the county line: Clark County is to the south, Cowlitz to the north.

I-5 Exit 21. Exit here for access to **Woodland Bottoms** loop (see map). This former floodplain is largely a drive-through, now protected by dikes for farm use. Birding here can be especially rewarding during migration seasons. March at the mouth of the Lewis River is usually a busy time. Waterbirds gather for the feast: loons, grebes, diving ducks and gulls. In winter, raptors hunt the bottomlands.

EBird shows nearly 140 species reported here, including almost two dozen waterfowl. Among raptors there may be White-tailed Kite and Rough-legged Hawk in winter. A dozen shorebird species have

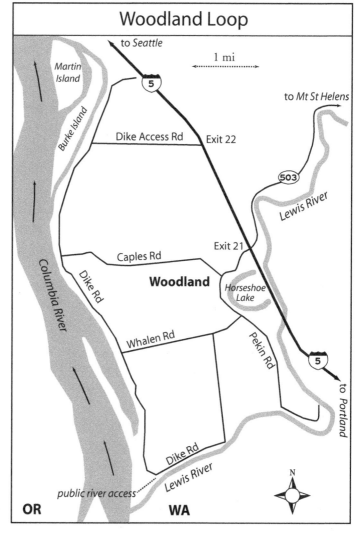

been noted, including Baird's and Solitary Sandpiper. Also, nine species of gull, including a Glaucous one winter, far from its usual northerly range. Short-eared Owl and Varied Thrush are other possible winter birds. Autumn sightings here have included Northern Shrike, Clark's Grebe, Rusty Blackbird and Red-necked Phalarope. Red-shouldered Hawk may be seen here on occasion.

I-5 Exit 27. Port of Kalama. Exit and go north on western access road which goes along the narrow strip of port and industrial land on the eastern bank of the Columbia River. Louis Rasmussen Park is 1.5 miles north of the exit and provides clear views up and down the river as well as access to thickets along the river. Possible birds include Bald Eagle, Osprey (spring and summer), Sandhill Cranes in the air (winter), numerous waterfowl, Double-crested Cormorant, gull species which may include Glacous-winged, Western, Mew, Thayer's, California and Ring-billed (mostly in winter).

I-5 Exit 39. Exit for **Kelso**, Washington. The climate in this area is cool and damp. Average rainfall is over 48 inches, and average high temperatures are under 80 degrees even in July and August. July is the driest month, with an average of 1 inch of rain. November and December each average over 7 inches. November through March the average overnight low is between freezing and 40 degrees. Yet in every month except July and August, subfreezing overnight temperatures have been recorded at least once. The elevation is only 80 feet, so snow is unusual.

I-5 Exit 49. Exit here on WA 504. Go east about 5.2 miles to **Mount Saint Helens Visitors Center,** elevation 500 feet. What you'll find: campsites, hiking trails, and picnic areas. An entrance fee is charged. **Seaquest State Park** is just across WA 504 from the visitors center. They're connected by trail and road. This is a good stop for geology as well as birding. At the visitors center you can take a half-mile hiking trail, on a boardwalk through the marsh, along the west shore of Silver Lake. Dogs are allowed on leash. The woodland here is dominated by red cedar and Douglas-fir. The three areas–Mount Saint Helens Visitor Center, Seaquest State Park and Silver Lake–have over 115 species reported to eBird.

Redhead Duck and Barrow's Goldeneye are among more than a dozen waterfowl reported at this inland site. Five grebe species have been found, including Red-necked. Great Blue Heron, Belted Kingfisher, Red-breasted Sapsucker, Steller's Jay, Western Wood-Pewee (spring and summer), Pacific Wren and Wilson's Warbler (summer) can be expected. One year an Eastern Kingbird was resident, far west of its usual range limit in eastern Oregon. Spotted Towhee and Marsh Wren are resident year-round.

I-5 Exit 53. Toutle River Rest Area. Dense rainforest trimmed back to make room for parking, toilets and picnic tables. Good place to make a quick check in winter for Hermit and Varied Thrush, Pacific Wren and other lurkers in dense shade.

I-5 Exit 68. Exit here and go east on US 12, then south on Jackson Highway to **Lewis and Clark State Park.** En route you will pass the small park at the John R. Jackson House Historic Site. What you'll find: Both state facilities have picnic areas and charge entrance fees. The state park has hiking trails, toilets and campsites as well. Caverns were formed under the park and surrounding area by cooling lava from Mount Rainier. These caverns are presently being used for the storage of natural gas.

The state park covers over 550 acres, and the forest here includes a stand of old growth Douglas-fir as well as western red cedar, western hemlock, Pacific yew, red alder and big-leaf maple. Native rhododendrons are part of the undergrowth. This dense forest would be an ideal place for wintering Varied Thrush and for woodpeckers year-round. Barn Owls, Black Bears and Douglas Squirrels are resident here.

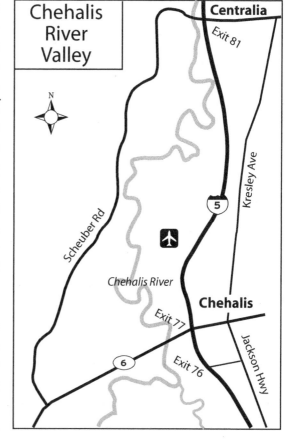

I-5 Exit 76. This is the exit for **Chehalis.** Roads that crisscross this valley may lead you to Great Egret, Short-eared Owl, White-tailed Kite, and

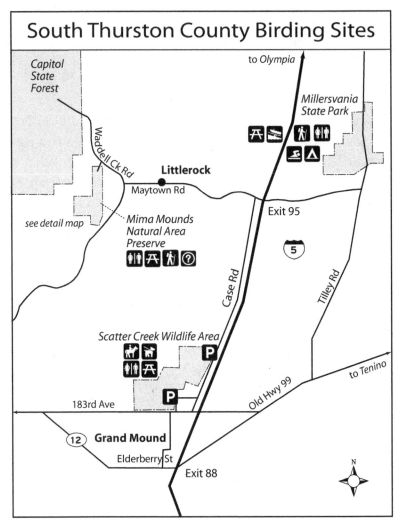

South Thurston County Birding Sites

even wintering Rough-legged hawk. See the map, and check listings on Washington State's Tweeters website.

I-5 Exit 81. Exit here for **Centralia,** where local birders have reported fall migrants such as Calliope Hummingbird and Wilson's Warbler. Best to check Washington State's Tweeters online listings for possible locations of any vagrants. Your online search engine will take you to the proper link for Tweeters messages.

I-5 Mile 85. This is the county line: Lewis County is to the south, Thurston County to the north.

I-5 Exit 88. Scatter Creek Wildlife Area. Go west on State Route 12 to Elderberry Street, then turn north to reach the state-run **Scatter Creek Wildlife Area.** What you'll find: A Discover Pass or Vehicle Access Pass is required, as on all properties managed by Washington's Department of Fish and Wildlife. This wildlife area's facilities include parking lots, picnic areas, toilets and trails. See *South Thurston County Birding Sites* map. Horseback riding, hunting, dog training, field trials, and dog walking are allowed. Leashes are required at certain times of year. Hunters may be about during pheasant season (October-December), when Washington State allows hunting of native and transplanted species, including Bobwhite and Ring-necked Pheasant.

Grasslands here are extensive and include a unique Idaho fescue/balsamroot short-grass prairie with a wide variety of wildflowers, including rare ones. Additional habitats are riparian forest along the creek, oak woodlands, wetlands and stands of Douglas-fir. There is an Oregon white oak community, which is uncommon north of the Columbia River. (Oregon white oak is also known as Garry oak.) The oaks' acorns support an abundance of wildlife. There are active beaver dams within the unit, as well as deer, fox, Bobcat, Coyote, hare, Raccoon, River Otter, Muskrat, American Mink, Black Bear, and the Western Gray Squirrel, a state threatened species.

Nearly 90 bird species are recorded for this location on eBird. The habitat mix affords a chance to see Scrub-Jay and Steller's Jay, Black-capped and Chestnut-backed Chickadee, Band-tailed Pigeon and Mourning Dove. Other species present in spring are three local vireos: Cassin's, Hutton's and Warbling. You might also spot Red-breasted Sapsucker, Pileated Woodpecker, Rufous Hummingbird, Violet-green Swallow, Bushtit, Swainson's Thrush near water, Western Tanager and Black-headed Grosbeak. In fall and winter, Evening Grosbeak may be seen here.

West of Scatter Creek is the relatively new **Black River National Wildlife Refuge**, a unit of Nisqually NWR. It's accessible now by canoe, but may eventually have visitor facilities.

If you go northeast on old WA 99 from Exit 88, you'll be headed toward Tenino. Along Gibson Road, about 5 miles from I-5, unusual low-elevation Mountain Bluebirds have been spotted a few times in past winters.

I-5 Exit 95. Three State-Owned Areas of Interest. From Exit 95, go west on Maytown Road to reach **Mima Mounds Natural Area Preserve** and **Capitol State Forest**. Mima Mounds is a 637-acre state property west of the village of Little Rock. It is an IBA. The main entrance is off Waddell Creek Road SW. What you'll find: toilets, picnic areas, information and trails. Dogs are not allowed. The Mima Prairie can also be viewed from Mima Road SW and from Bordeaux Road, which has one pullout on the south end of the preserve. See *South Thurston County Birding Sites* map.

Many theories exist as to how the Mounds were formed. What's known is that whatever happened took place millennia ago during the most recent Ice Age when glacial melt and a glacial lake ended up draining through this area. The water flowed southwest to join the Chehalis River, which runs generally westward to the Pacific Ocean. The soil drains quickly, is rich in gravel and supports a highly adapted flora. Wildflowers here are especially bold in May and June. In this grassland, the dominant plants include a Roemer's fescue and white-topped aster, Garry oak woodland and savannah. Similar habitat and birds can be found at the Scatter Creek Wildlife Area further south, near Exit 88 and described above. If you are coming from the north, you can reach Scatter

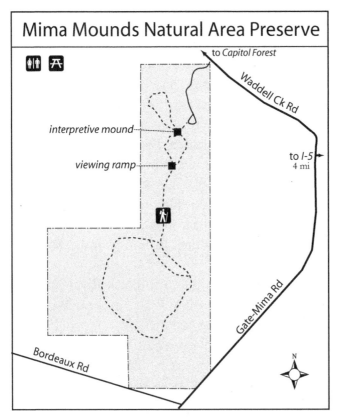

Creek from this exit, Exit 95.

Birds of the Mima Mounds include raptors like Harrier and White-tailed Kite. Other likely birds are Western Bluebirds, Rufous Hummingbird, Hutton's and Cassin's Vireo, White-crowned Sparrow and Evening Grosbeak. Spring is the best season to bird here. EBird shows over 70 species reported from this site.

Capitol State Forest. A few more miles to the west, beyond Mima Mounds, is **Capitol State Forest.** This working forest extends from Thurston County west into Grays Harbor County, covering over 91,000 acres southwest of Olympia. What you'll find: toilets, trails and campsites. There are two parts to the forest, one section accommodating vehicular recreation, the other reserved for non-motorized activities. Hunting, hiking, horseback riding, bicycles and off-road vehicles and mushroom picking are all accommodated. There is also on-going tree cutting for lumber. That can mean encounters with large timber-laden trucks on crooked and steep roads. Most of the 575 miles of road inside Capitol State Forest are gravel, not paved. There are eight entry points to the Capitol State Forest around its perimeter. The road complex inside the forest will require a map. A good trail and road map can be printed from the Washington State Department of Natural Resources website.

Here in Washington's Black Hills are nesting Hermit Warblers, lowland Mountain Quail coveys and even some Gray Jays. Despite steep topography, the two highest peaks—Larch Mountain and Capitol Peak—are both less than 2,700 feet in elevation. But less than 20 air miles away is Puget Sound and sea level.

Some species you could track down in Capitol State Forest include owls like Western Screech, Northern Pygmy and Northern Saw-whet. Unfortunately there are records of the invasive Barred Owl here as well. Other birds you could find most easily in spring include Rufous Hummingbird; Sooty and Ruffed Grouse that might give their location away by their wing ruffling during mating season; Red-breasted Sapsucker and Pileated Woodpecker; Olive-sided and Hammond's Flycatcher in mature woods; Pacific-slope Flycatcher along waterways; Cassin's Vireo; Swainson's, Hermit and Varied Thrush during breeding season; and MacGillivray's and Black-throated Gray Warbler. Townsend's Warblers appear during migration.

Millersylvania State Park. At Exit 95, if you go **east** 2.4 miles on Maytown Road SW, then north on Tilley for another mile, you'll arrive at **Millersylvania State Park**. What you'll find: toilets, picnic areas, campsites, a boat ramp, fishing, swimming and hiking trails. This densely forested park of 842 acres has more than a half-mile of shoreline on Deep Lake. The lake may once have been home to a unique, now extinct, species of freshwater crab. Park naturalists lead hikes in summer.

This is a good spot for Bald Eagle, Osprey in summer, Pileated Woodpecker and wintering Varied Thrush. Great Horned and Barn Owls nest here. Willow and Pacific-slope Flycatchers breed here. Ebird data is limited.

I-5 Exit 104. If you take Exit 104 onto Deschutes Way northbound, you can quickly reach the margins of **Capitol Lake** in Olympia. Much of the lake is bordered by a pedestrian pathway. On the southeast side the park borders the state capitol campus. Along the edge of the lake are several small parks. What you'll find: toilets, trails, picnic areas and a fishing dock. Little Brown Bats feed over the lake on summer nights.

There are plenty of birds, as well. Among the 130 species reported to eBird from here are Trumpeter Swan, Eurasian Wigeon, Redhead, Barrow's Goldeneye, Mew Gull, Thayer's Gull, Rufous Hummingbird in spring, Chestnut-backed Chickadee, and Evening Grosbeak in fall.

Further afield from Exit 104, if you take US 101 north, you will approach the two southwestern fingers of the **Puget Sound** complex of tidal inlets. In about 4 miles from I-5, US 101 begins to parallel the shore of Eld Inlet to the east. In another 4 miles you come to the **Kennedy Creek Estuary**. This is where Kennedy Creek empties into Oyster Bay, which is a finger of Totten Inlet, itself an arm of Puget Sound. See *Olympia Vicinity* map. This estuary and bay are part of an IBA that includes Little Skookum Inlet further north. All of these bodies of water are saltwater and tidal.

The two pullouts allow scoping of the mudflats for shorebirds, ducks and gulls. Birding is best in fall and winter at high tide or just before. EBird shows 85 species here, including Bald Eagle, Surf Scoter, Western Sandpiper, Lesser Yellowlegs, seven species of gull, Hutton's Vireo, Pacific Wren and Golden-crowned Sparrow.

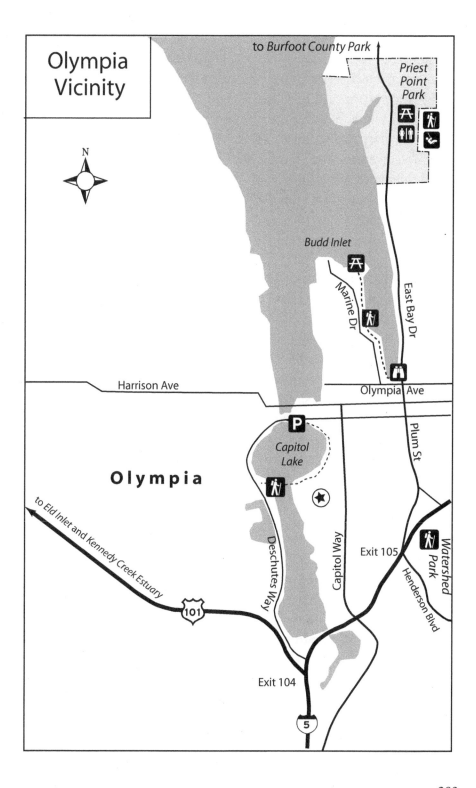

I-5 Exit 105. Exit here for some birding in the **Olympia** area. Olympia is the earthquake-prone capital city of Washington State. The city averages over 50 inches of rain per year, and winter floods are regular as it is low-lying and on the Deschutes River. Light snow falls occasionally in winter. Olympia has a higher proportion of overcast days (75%) than any other city in the Lower 48 States. July is the only month when Olympia averages less than an inch of rain. The climate is generally mild, with overnight lows from December through February at just about freezing, while winter daytime temperatures hit the forties. Even in "hot" August, the daily high averages less than 80 degrees.

Note that you can reach the north end of **Capitol Lake** from this exit (105).

Watershed City Park. If you go south on Henderson Boulevard, you will enter Watershed City Park. About 0.8 mile from Exit 105, you will see a small parking pullout on the left side of the road. This is a trailhead into Watershed Park. Another 0.3 mile downhill on Henderson is a second trailhead for a loop trail of 1.3 miles that will take you through a dense forest of western red cedar, bigleaf maple and heavy undergrowth of ferns, shrubs and mosses. The trail, sections of which are boardwalk, takes you through the **Moxlie Creek Spring Basin**. Water from this creek once supplied the town of Olympia. In addition to woodpeckers, there are Mule Deer and Western Gray Squirrels. The botanizing may be richer here than the birding.

Budd Inlet. If you go north on Henderson Boulevard, then north onto Plum, you're headed toward **Olympia Harbor**. Between the boatyards there are stretches of beach and mudflat plus an expanse of open water connected to the greater Puget Sound to the north. After a half mile, Plum intersects with Olympia Avenue NE. On your left (west) you will see a greensward along the edge of **Budd Inlet**. This inlet is a finger of East Bay, a part of the Puget Sound complex. You can park along Olympia Avenue east of the inlet or further north on Jefferson Street along the west side of the inlet. The inlet and the culvert bring fresh water into the saltwater of the Sound, providing good fishing for grebes, diving ducks and gulls. When the tide is out, expect shorebirds and Crows on the rocky flats. This can be especially rewarding in fall migration. The small-sized Crows here may not be true Northwestern

Crows but an intermediate variety. Their voices certainly sound different from that of the ordinary Common Crow found across much of the rest of the U.S. Probably only a DNA test of the population would truly settle the issue.

At the southeast corner of the inlet there are two viewing platforms. On the west side of the inlet, a trail goes north to the tip of the peninsula, over a mile away. There are no public toilets on this hike, but there are picnic tables at the north end. The trail provides good vantage for scoping the inlet and shoreline. Pelagic Cormorant can be expected on buoys and flotsam. Horned Grebe and Surf Scoter should be present in winter. Mew and Thayer's may be among the wintering gulls. Hooded Merganser may dive near the culvert at the south end of the inlet.

Priest Point Park. North of Olympia, Plum Street SE becomes East Bay Drive and will take you to **Priest Point Park,** 1.5 miles north. What you'll find: toilets, picnic areas, trails and a playground. The park is over 300 acres, mostly wooded. Coming from the south, the park entrance is on your right, and an overpass takes you to the west side, where you'll find trails with access to the beach. One trail takes you down to Ellis Creek, which runs into Ellis Cove. A second trail takes you to a flat beach facing onto Budd Inlet. The forest here is damp and dense — a perfect place to hunt for Varied Thrush in fall and winter. Other birds in the woods here are Red-breasted Nuthatch, Pacific Wren, Brown Creeper and Pileated Woodpecker. Offshore in winter you may find Surf Scoter, Red-breasted Merganser, both goldeneye, both scaup, Common Loon, Mew Gull and Pigeon Guillemot. EBird lists almost 90 species for the park.

Burfoot County Park. Continuing north on East Bay Drive, you will merge with Boston Harbor Road. About 4 miles from the intersection of Plum Street and Olympia Avenue, you will see Burfoot County Park on your left (west). What you'll find: playground, toilets, picnic areas, trails. The park is 50 acres with over a thousand feet of waterfront on Budd Inlet. This dense forest is good for woodpeckers and Varied Thrush in fall and winter. Two trails lead down to the edge of the water on Budd Inlet. Here you can look for ocean-going birds. You may find wintering species like Red-throated and Common Loon, Red-necked Grebe, Brandt's Cormorant and Pigeon Guillemot. In the woods are Pileated Woodpecker, Steller's Jay, Chestnut-backed Chickadee and Pacific-slope Flycatcher in the warm months.

Another half mile north on Boston Harbor Road and you are in the small town of **Boston Harbor**. Turn left toward the boat pier onto 73rd Avenue NE. In three blocks you will come to the store and boat dock. Park on the street for free or in the parking lots for a fee. Just west of the store, a boat ramp leads you down to the water. From here you can view a broad stretch of the bay. Loons, ocean-going ducks, alcids, grebes and gulls should all be present in fall and winter. Check for Red-necked Grebe (fall and winter), rotund little Cassin's Auklets and larger Rhino Auklets. Pigeon Guillemots can be present any time. The young birds in fall are very pale.

I-5 Exit 108. Exit here and drive north on Sleater-Kinney Road toward Henderson Inlet, a narrow finger of Puget Sound. Here you will find **Woodard Bay Natural Resource Conservation Area,** a state property about 5 miles north of I-5. Woodard Bay is on the west side of Henderson Inlet and a short drive east from Boston Harbor. What you'll find: entrance fee, toilets, trail, and boardwalk. This conservation area covers 600 acres of mostly second-growth forest and about 5 miles of shoreline. There are small patches of old growth trees, some more than 250 years old. Evergreens here are western red cedar, Douglas-fir, western hemlock and grand fir. There are also freshwater wetlands. Red alder and bigleaf maple grow in the lowlands. Understory plants include swordferns and salal, with spiraea in the wetlands at the north end of the conservation area.

This is a good place for spotting water birds. Cackling Goose, Surf and White-winged Scoter, all three mergansers, Common Loon and Horned Grebe have all been seen here—mostly in winter. Brandt's and Pelagic Cormorant may wander into the bay from more open water. Belted Kingfisher and Bald Eagle are year-round residents. Land birds here include Pileated Woodpeckers in the evergreens and Pacific Wren. Summer birds include Purple Martin, Violet-green Swallow, Pacific-slope Flycatcher, Chestnut-backed Chickadee, Wilson's Warbler and Swainson's Thrush. EBird has reports of over 90 species at Woodard

Bay. Other wildlife here are Northern River Otter and Harbor Seals. Olympia oysters are being raised in an area of habitat restoration near the mouth of Henderson Bay.

An abandoned lumber company railroad pier in Woodward Bay is used by nesting Yuma and Little Brown Bats. Hundreds of them breed here from May through August. These bats can be seen emerging at dusk and, if you have infrared viewers, you can watch their nighttime antics.

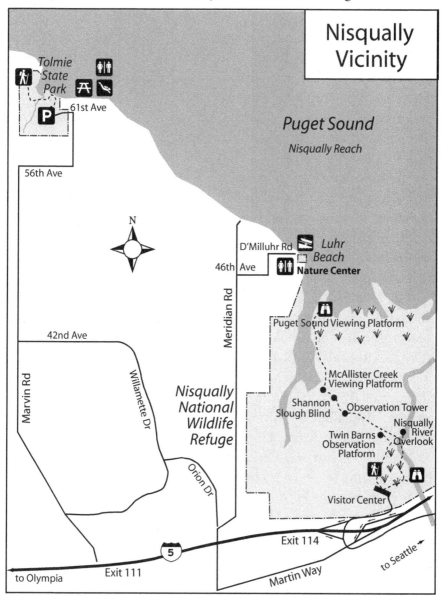

I-5 Exit 111. Tolmie State Park and **Luhr Beach.** Exit here and go north on Marvin Road NE to reach **Tolmie State Park.** This is the only Pacific Coast park I know of that is named for a naturalist. The park is closed on Mondays and Tuesdays in fall and winter. Otherwise it is open for daytime use. What you'll find: trails, toilets, scuba diving, picnic facilities and kitchen shelters that can be reserved. Dogs are allowed on leash.

The park covers more than a hundred acres. It sits in the deep woods at the southern end of a small bay off Nisqually Reach, which is itself a branch off Puget Sound. Flora here include red cedar, Douglas-fir, hemlock, yew, alder, bigleaf maple, foxglove and rhododendron. There is a nice sandy beach and a small salt marsh as well as the dense evergreen forest. The waves offshore are usually low and make for fine scoping from the beach. The creek entering Nisqually Reach in Tolmie Park is called Big Slough.

Tolmie State Park is named for Dr. William Fraser Tolmie (1812-1886). He was educated in his native Scotland and first came to the Columbia River area in 1833 as a doctor for the Hudson Bay Company. He later befriended Dr. James Kirk Townsend, an American doctor and naturalist also employed for awhile by the Hudson Bay Company. The two exchanged observations of and discoveries about local wildlife. Dr. Tolmie collected the first known specimen of the Black Oystercatcher, and he discovered several plant species that are named for him. In acknowledgement of Tolmie's expertise, Townsend gave the bird known as MacGillivray's Warbler the Latin binomial, *Oporornis tolmiei*. Dr. Tolmie remained in the Northwest his entire life. One of his sons was Premier of British Columbia from 1925 to 1933. After some years at Fort Nisqually, Dr. Tolmie moved to Vancouver Island, Canada. Townsend discovered his namesake warbler near Astoria, Oregon.

Land birds you may find at Tolmie State Park are Pileated Woodpecker, Pacific Wren and Varied Thrush (in winter). Waterfowl here include grebes, ducks, gulls and loons. You may expect Brant; Eurasian Wigeon; Barrow's Goldeneye; Long-tailed Duck; Red-breasted Merganser and White-winged Scoter; Pacific and Red-throated Loon; Eared, Horned and Red-necked Grebe; and Rhino Auklet and Pigeon Guillemot. Resident land birds include Steller's Jay, Hutton's Vireo, Chestnut-backed Chickadee, Golden-crowned Kinglet and Spotted

Towhee. EBird shows over 75 species reported from this park.

Luhr Beach is at 4949 D'Milluhr Drive. You can also reach it from I-5 Exit 114. See *Nisqually Vicinity* map. Go west on Martin Way, turn north onto Meridian Road NE which will take you across I-5 to the north. Next turn right on 46th Avenue NE, then north onto D'Milluhr.

This park is on the west side of the Nisqually River as it empties into the southern end of Puget Sound. What you'll find: toilets, parking, and the Nisqually Reach Nature Center. You must have a parking permit from Washington State Department of Fish and Wildlife to park here. This is a place for scoping the river and the sound.

Waterbirds are the specialty at Luhr Beach. Over 20 species of waterfowl, 3 loons and 4 grebes have been sighted here. Among them: Brant, Eurasian Wigeon, all three North American scoter species, all three possible mergansers, Pacific Loon and Red-necked Grebe. With open water to the north, you may find both Brandt's and Pelagic Cormorant as well. Gulls may include Mew (not in summer), Thayer's (winter) and Glaucous-winged. Pigeon Guillemot is a regular. Common Murre and Rhino Auklet are winter birds. Common Tern may pass in fall. A Snowy Owl has wintered here. Summer birds include Pacific-slope Flycatcher and Purple Martin along with the usual collection of rain forest species like Steller's Jay and Pacific Wren.

I-5 Exit 114. The entrance to the **Nisqually National Wildlife Refuge** is on the north side of I-5 about 0.8 mile from this exit. Nisqually covers 3,000 acres and it's only a two-minute drive from I-5 and one of the author's favorite stops. What you'll find: toilets, picnic tables, a 1.5-mile trail and boardwalk, and a visitors center with shop and gallery. An admission fee is charged. When the visitors center is open, the staff maintains a list of recent wildlife sightings.

This NWR includes the flat river delta of the north-flowing Nisqually River where it empties into the southern end of Puget Sound. The northern portion of the NWR is saltwater marsh, and the river itself is affected by tides. The NWR's website includes a tidal chart. Habitat here includes riparian forest, freshwater and saltwater marsh, grasslands, river and tidal estuary. The mature trees are covered with moss and ferns in this wet climate. The temperature is often below freezing here in the winter, and it's always damp. There's an annual Nisqually Watershed Festival in late September. The Tahoma Audubon Society in nearby Tacoma has a weekly birding walk at Nisqually.

EBird lists over 215 species for Nisqually NWR. The site is heavily birded, so rarities are likely to be found. The visitors center maintains a log of significant sightings. Among the unexpected species cataloged here are Yellow-billed Loon, White-faced Ibis, Red Knot, Gyrfalcon, Iceland Gull, Black Tern, Marbled Murrelet, and Pacific Golden-Plover, here regularly in small numbers, and a variety of shorebirds including Pectoral Sandpiper.

This NWR is a good place to find those wintering toughies like Northern Shrike, Eurasian Wigeon, Trumpeter and Tundra Swan, Rough-legged Hawk and Merlin. Snowy and Short-eared Owl can both be wintering birds here as well. In fall and winter there's usually a handful of Bald Eagles hunting, fishing and competing with one another. I've watched aerial chases where the eagle with a duck in its talons tries to escape from jealous fellows in loud pursuit.

Both kinglets are here in winter. In fall there can be huge flocks of Cackling Geese and large numbers of Pintail and Green-winged Teal. Summer breeders include Osprey, Pacific-slope Flycatcher in the forest, Red-breasted Sapsucker, Purple Martin, Violet-green Swallow, Swainson's Thrush, Wilson's Warbler and Black-headed Grosbeak. Year-round targets here include American Bittern, Pileated Woodpecker, Virginia Rail, Wilson's Snipe and Great Horned Owl. The riparian forest along the Nisqually River and just east of the visitors center can be good for Pileated Woodpecker.

Less than 5 miles from Exit 114 you can also reach **Luhr Beach,** at 4949 D'Milluhr Drive. See the discussion under Exit 111 entry. This park is on the west side of the Nisqually River mouth as it empties into the southern end of Puget Sound. This is a place for scoping the river and the sound. You must have a Washington State Dept. of Fish and Wildlife parking permit to park here.

I-5 Mile 115. This is the county line: Thurston County lies to the west, Pierce County to the east. The county line runs along the Nisqually River, so part of the Nisqually NWR east of the river is in Pierce County.

Puget Sound

The Puget Sound Complex is a rich mix of ocean water, tidal estuaries, salt marsh, rocky islands and shorelines with peninsulas and inlets ad infinitum. There are 2,500 miles of shoreline in the Puget Sound complex. 10,000 streams, including 14 major rivers drain into it. Hood Canal, Admiralty Inlet, Skagit Bay, Saratoga Passage, Possession Sound, Colvos Passage, Port Orchard–these are some of the larger portions of this complex. There are numerous smaller inlets that help make this a rich birding region. It is about 100 miles from Point Deception at the north end of Puget Sound to Olympia, WA, in the south.

Puget Sound and its neighboring inlets are an ideal place to find seabirds that are lured close to shore by schools of fish in water that may range from shallow to fairly deep–average depth is 450 feet. Currents can be swift as the whole area is tidal and can be subject to high winds in fall and winter. Here you can scope the water for loons including Yellow-billed, several species of alcids, at least ten gull species, terns in spring and summer, Brant flocks, ocean-going ducks and grebes. Puget Sound is far enough north that Harlequin, Long-tailed Duck, Red-necked Grebe, Pigeon Guillemot and Rhino Auklet can regularly be found in winter. Trumpeter Swans regularly winter in the lowlands along Puget Sound. A few hundred miles south along the Pacific Coast these species become much harder to find. If you've time a ride on one of the many Washington State Ferries can afford good birding in any season. You can get on board by car, foot or bicycle. Be aware that the ocean here is never warm and thus the wind is usually cool to freezing on a moving boat. Dress warmly even in summer and try birding from the stern, out of the wind.

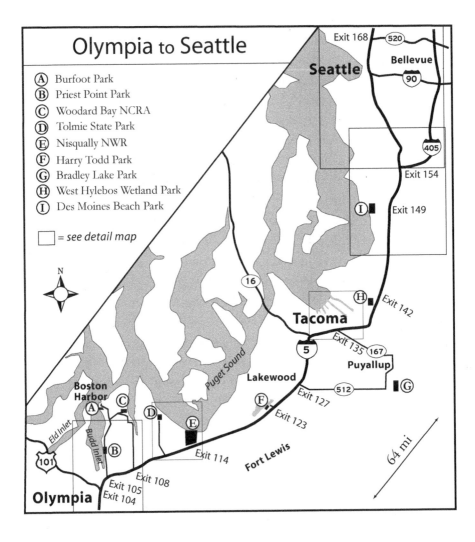

Olympia to Seattle

- (A) Burfoot Park
- (B) Priest Point Park
- (C) Woodard Bay NCRA
- (D) Tolmie State Park
- (E) Nisqually NWR
- (F) Harry Todd Park
- (G) Bradley Lake Park
- (H) West Hylebos Wetland Park
- (I) Des Moines Beach Park

☐ = *see detail map*

N

Seattle

Exit 168   520

Bellevue

90

405

Exit 154

(I)   Exit 149

16

(H)   Exit 142

Tacoma

Exit 135   167

5   Puyallup

Lakewood

Exit 127   512

(G)

Puget Sound

(F)   Exit 123

Boston Harbor

(C)

(A)   (D)   Exit 114   Fort Lewis

(E)

Eld Inlet   Budd Inlet

(B)

101

Exit 108

Exit 105
Exit 104

Olympia

64 mi

Chapter 12

Puget Sound Area, Tacoma and Seattle

I-5 and I-405
Pierce and King Counties

Pierce and King Counties are the northern-most limit of this book's coverage. Both counties are heavily urbanized so expect heavier traffic than you would encounter in more sparsely populated areas. Because there are so many active birders nearby unusual bird species are often discovered and their location shared on Washington State birders Tweeter website.

I-5 Exit 123. Harry Todd Park. Follow the map the short distance from this exit to **Harry Todd Park**, run by the city of Lakewood. What you'll find: picnic areas, playground and toilets. This small park, on the shore of American Lake, is a good place to scope for waterfowl, grebes, loons and gulls. A bit further west in Lakewood is a state maintained boat launch where you can also get a vantage point to bird the lake.

I-5 Exit 127. Bradley Lake Park. If you exit here onto WA 512 you can head east to **Bradley Lake Park** in the center of Puyallup. It's about 10 miles to the park from this exit. What you'll find: fishing, trails, toilets, a picnic area, two ball fields and a large playground. Bradley Lake Park covers about 60 acres and sports a 12-acre lake. In winter, a variety of ducks visit this small lake; a Tufted Duck wintered here recently. The eBird data for this site is limited.

I-5 Exit 132. Tacoma. The elevation in this city is generally just above 200 feet above sea level. The city gets an average of 39 inches precipitation per annum. Temperatures in Tacoma are mild with the average high in August only 78 degrees while winters bring only a few nights when the temperature drops below freezing.

Tacoma Nature Center. From Exit 132, take WA 16 west and then turn right (north) onto Tyler Street and into the Tacoma Nature Center. What you'll find: a visitors center, gift shop, toilets, a "discovery pond" for children, a 17-acre lake, and trails through 70 acres of forest and wetlands. Dogs and bicycles are not allowed. The woods include Garry oak, madrone and Douglas-fir. The lake is used by migrating ducks like Shoveler and Pintail. In the woods you may encounter Steller's Jay, Black-capped and Chestnut-backed Chickadee, Red-breasted Nuthatch and Brown Creeper. Violet-green Swallows can be seen over the lake in warm months.

Point Defiance Park. If you continue westward on WA 16 you can reach **Point Defiance Park.** If you can bird only one place around Tacoma, this is it. At the three-way intersection of WA 16, 6th Avenue and Pearl Street you need to take Pearl Street due north to Point Defiance. WA 16 here angles to the left toward the Tacoma Narrows Bridge (see *Tacoma Vicinity* map). What you'll find: toilets, picnic areas, trails, off-leash dog area, museum, ferryboat terminal, beach, zoo, aquarium and formal gardens. A fee is charged to visit the zoo and aquarium. This city park covers over 700 acres, including a precious patch of old-growth forest.

This park is on a peninsula, with The Narrows on one side and Commencement Bay on the other. Because of the narrow channel the tidal flows and currents here can be strong and dramatic. Birding can be the same, especially if you have a telescope.

Sixteen species of waterfowl have been reported here, including all three American scoter species and all three mergansers. Throw in Harlequin and Barrow's Goldeneye and you've got a ducky place in fall and winter. Red-necked Grebe (winter) and Pelagic and Brandt's Cormorant are also regular here. EBird shows a dozen gull species

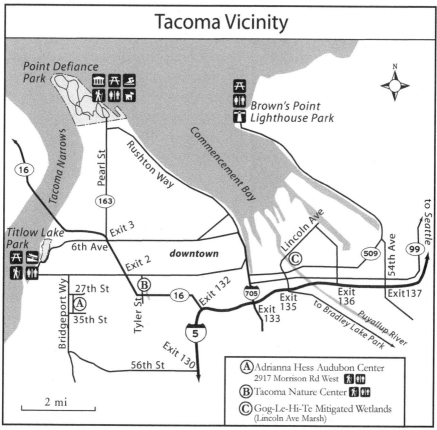

Tacoma Vicinity

Point Defiance Park

Brown's Point Lighthouse Park

Tacoma Narrows

16

Pearl St

Rushton Way

163

Commencement Bay

to Seattle

Titlow Lake Park

6th Ave

Exit 3

Exit 2

downtown

Lincoln Ave

509

54th Ave

99

Bridgeport Wy

27th St

35th St

Tyler St

B

16

Exit 132

705

C

Exit 135

Exit 133

Exit 136

Exit 137

to Bradley Lake Park

Puyallup River

A

56th St

Exit 130

5

2 mi

Ⓐ Adrianna Hess Audubon Center
2917 Morrison Rd West
Ⓑ Tacoma Nature Center
Ⓒ Gog-Le-Hi-Te Mitigated Wetlands
(Lincoln Ave Marsh)

found here, including Sabine's, Mew, Thayer's and Franklin's. Rhino Auklet and Pigeon Guillemot can be found any time of year. Marbled Murrelet may be passing through in spring and fall. Parasitic Jaeger and Common Tern are possible in fall. One winter a Black-tailed Gull showed up on the bay. It's a rare, medium-sized Asian vagrant.

If you tire of staring out to sea, or the waves give you *mal de mer*, try finding the Band-tailed Pigeon, Barred Owl, Anna's Hummingbird, Pileated Woodpecker, or Olive-sided Flycatcher (spring) that might be in the woods here. Land birds present all year include Bushtit, Chestnut-backed Chickadee, Brown Creeper, Bewick's and Pacific Wren, both kinglets, Spotted Towhee and Pine Siskin. EBird shows over 140 species reported from Point Defiance.

Mammals you might find here include California sea lion, harbor seal, Douglas' squirrel, and raccoons that are street smart. They may hit you up for food.

Titlow Park and Beach. Back at the three-way intersection of 6th Avenue, WA 16 and Pearl Street, you can continue west on 6th Avenue to Titlow Park. It's about 5 miles from I-5 via city streets. This city park of over 50 acres is at the west end of 6th Avenue, just south of the Tacoma Narrows Bridge. It faces onto The Narrows section of Puget Sound. What you'll find: picnic areas, trails, a boat launch, and access to the shore at adjacent Titlow Beach. This beach is popular for sunbathing, picnicking, launching kayaks and canoes, and as an entry point for scuba divers. There are evergreens growing down to the high tide line and Purple Martin boxes on old offshore pilings. This park has open seawater, freshwater ponds and a stream, plus the brackish habitat where the waters mix. That makes it ideal for birds who like open water and for those who prefer rich shoreline food supplies.

Titlow Park is a good place for spotting waterbirds including Common Loon, Pelagic and Brandt's Cormorant, ducks, gulls, alcids and grebes—especially in fall and winter. Bald Eagles are regular here but for shorebirds, it's usually just Killdeer. Some species reported to eBird from here: Brant, Harlequin, Barrow's Goldeneye, Eurasian Wigeon, all three likely mergansers, six species of grebe including Red-necked and Clark's, Rhino Auklet and Marbled Murrelet, Pileated Woodpecker, breeding Purple Martin, Pacific Wren (fall and winter), and Spotted Towhee. EBird shows 120 species reported here.

Adriana Hess Audubon Center is also reached from Exit 132 by taking WA 16 westbound. It's at 2917 Morrison Road West, about four miles from I-5 on city streets in the suburb of University Place. The center can also be reach from Exit 130 if you are northbound on I-5 (see *Tacoma Vicinity* map). It is located next to a small wetland. What you'll find: toilets, parking, a store, nature trails, and a pond.

The pond here hosts Great Blue Heron, Green Heron and Wood Duck. EBird shows 75 recorded species including Band-tailed Pigeon, Hooded Merganser, Glaucous Gull, Anna's and Rufous Hummingbird (summer), Hammond's Flycatcher, Hutton's Vireo, Purple Martin (summer), Chestnut-backed Chickadee, Bushtit and Townsend's Warbler (winter).

I-5 Exit 135. Gog-Le-Hi-Te Mitigated Wetlands. Exit here and head north to reach Gog-Le-Hi-Te Mitigated Wetlands in Tacoma. This small, restored wetland on the Puyallup River is known locally as Lincoln Avenue Marsh. It was restored by the Port of Tacoma. See *Tacoma Vicinity* map for its location.

EBird shows over 85 species reported here. Among unusual sightings here are Pectoral Sandpiper, Baird's Sandpiper, Glaucous and (rarely) a Slaty-backed Gull. Marsh Wren and Bald Eagle are residents. Salmon come into this marsh for food and shelter.

If you go south at Exit 135 and take WA 167, you can reach Bradley Lake Park in Puyallup (see map). It's about 7 miles through city traffic from Exit 135.

I-5 Exit 137. Browns Point Lighthouse Park. Exit here onto 54th Avenue East, then head north until you intersect WA 509. Turn right and go north on WA 509 to Browns Point Lighthouse Park. This is about 5 miles north of I-5. What you'll find: beach, toilet, and picnic areas. There is a restored historic lighthouse, which you can tour. Browns Point is a 7-acre Tacoma city park surrounded on three sides by saltwater.

Browns Point is a good place for Marbled Murrelet as it overlooks the open waters of Dalco Passage and Commencement Bay at this south end of Puget Sound. EBird reports almost 120 species, including Common Murrelet and an Ancient Murrelet in the autumn, all three scoter species, Harlequin and Long-tailed Duck in fall, Red-breasted Merganser, Red-throated and Pacific Loon, Red-necked Grebe, Pelagic and Brandt's Cormorant. Altogether this is a fine place for a convenient seawatch. Pigeon Guillemot are regular here. Ten gull species have been seen, most in winter. Red-necked Phalarope and Parasitic Jaeger may make appearances in August-September.

I-5 Mile 139. This is the county line, with Pierce County to the south, King County to the north.

I-5 Exit 142. West Hylebos Wetlands Park. Exit here for WA 18 West to get to West Hylebos Wetlands Park, a city park in Federal Way, only a mile from I-5 (see *South of Seattle* map). What you'll find:

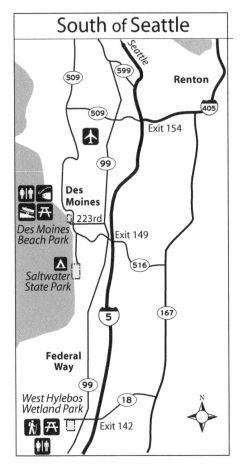

South of Seattle

parking, a picnic area, toilets, and a walking trail, including a boardwalk. Neither dogs nor bicycles are allowed on the trail or on the boardwalk. There are 120 acres here with wetlands, bog, streams and woodlands. Friends of West Hylebos describe the woods as follows: Douglas-fir, western hemlock, red cedar, and rare ancient Sitka spruce that began life around the time the Mayflower reached Plymouth Rock (1621).

Pileated Woodpeckers breed here. Birds in the wet forest include Steller's Jay, and even a Gray Jay at least once, Chestnut-backed Chickadee and Spotted Towhee. Among the other wildlife are mink, weasel, American Beaver, Douglas' Squirrel and Townsend's Mole.

I-5 Exit 149. Des Moines Marina and Beach Park. Exit here onto WA 516 heading west toward the town of Des Moines and Puget Sound. WA 516 merges with WA 509, which is a north/south highway. Go right (north) on WA 509. When you come to South 223rd Street, turn left (west) toward the **Des Moines Beach Park** (see the map). What you'll find: beach, playground, picnic areas and toilets. This is a spot for water birders. The park covers almost 20 acres, and the **Des Moines Marina** is a few blocks south of the beach and park. The marina affords the best birding from its third mile-long fishing pier.

EBird shows 17 species of ducks reported plus three loons, including Pacific, who prefer open seas. Wintering birds you may see include all three scoter species, both scaup and both goldeneye, Red-necked

Grebe and all three local cormorants. You should also find a selection of the local gulls and alcids along with fishing Bald Eagle and Belted Kingfisher. Harlequin show up here in fall and winter, and occasionally more pelagic birds appear, like Pacific Loon. EBird shows over 80 species seen at the marina. The land birds in the park north of the marina are the ones you expect in Northwestern evergreen stands above the beach. Varied Thrush and Golden-crowned Sparrows can be expected in winter, Northern Flicker, Pacific Wren and Song Sparrow will be in residence.

Saltwater State Park is about 2 miles south of Des Moines, also on the shore of Puget Sound. Go south on South Marina Drive, then follow the *South of Seattle* map.

What you'll find: camp sites, picnic areas, scuba diving, a swimming beach, toilets and trails. A Discover Pass is required for vehicle entry, and fees are charged for camping. The park features tide pools and marine life, including salmon spawning in McSorley Creek. There is an underwater artificial reef for scuba divers. The park covers over 85 acres, including the wooded canyon of McSorley Creek, eastward from the beach. Be aware that the park is on the flight path for nearby Sea-Tac Airport and that the park is heavily used.

Saltwater State Park affords good scoping of the open sound for waterbirds from ducks to loons. Among the 100 birds reported to eBird from here are Brant; Trumpeter Swan; all three merganser species; all three scoter species; three loon species, including Red-throated, who prefer open water; Red-necked Grebe; and seven gull species. A variety of woodland birds are here as well.

Interstate 405 Corridor

I-5 Exit 154. This will put you onto I-405 at its Sound end. This route takes you along the eastern edge of metropolitan Seattle and along the eastern shore of Lake Washington, then continues northward from King into Snohomish County where it rejoins I-5 several miles north of central Seattle.

I-405 Exit 14. Exit here onto WA 520 to reach **Marymoor Park** in Redmond. This park, on the north shore of Lake Sammamish, is about 5 miles from I-405 and is operated by King County Parks. From Seattle, go east on WA 520 to the West Lake Sammamish Parkway exit, then follow the signs. The main entrance to the park is one block south of the exit.

What you'll find: toilets, a velodrome, a museum, picnic areas, playing fields, bike roads and free bikes, and over 40 acres of off-leash tennis courts, cafe, dog area, and a tranquil "pet garden." The off-leash dog area includes tall grass and swimming areas on a quiet slough. A parking fee is charged. Habitat at Marymoor includes a broad expanse of grassy playing fields plus riparian forest along the Sammamish River. The park covers 640 acres. There is a boardwalk in the wetlands and a viewing platform on the lakeshore, and weekly bird walks are conducted at Marymoor.

If you continue on West Lake Sammamish Parkway NE, you'll will come to the south entrance to the park, which gives you access to the west side of the Sammamish River. This western section of Marymoor offers some different birding possibilities. Park at the rowing club parking lot off West Lake Sammamish Parkway (at about 48th Street), and walk to the river. Along the path are three ponds, which may shelter shy ducks that prefer shorelines with plenty of cover. Barrow's Goldeneye will occasionally winter here.

Birders have seen about 220 species in this park. Mountain Bluebirds have been seen here in spring. Other possible birds of passage are Common Loon, Merlin, Short-eared Owl, Say's Phoebe, Ash-throated Flycatcher and Lazuli Bunting.

Breeding birds here include Pied-billed Grebe, Wood Duck, Bald Eagle, Red-tailed Hawk, Barn Owl, Virginia Rail, Rufous Hummingbird, Willow Flycatcher, Red-eyed and Warbling Vireo, Bewick's and Marsh Wren, Swainson's Thrush, Cedar Waxwing, Yellow Warbler, Common Yellowthroat, Savannah Sparrow and Black-headed Grosbeak.

I-405 Exit 17. Bridle Trails State Park. Turn east after you exit I-405 to reach **Bridle Trails State Park.** See *I-405 Corridor* map. What you'll find: picnic areas, toilets, horseback riding, 28 miles of trails serving

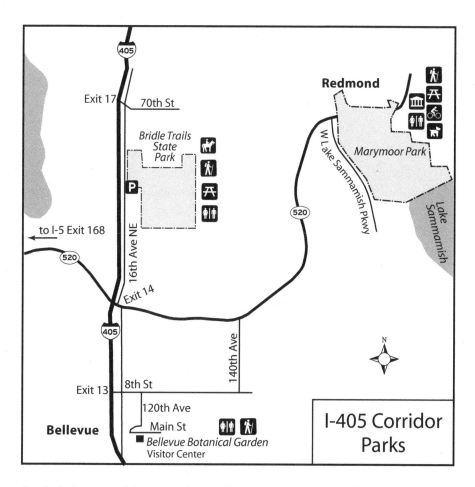

both hikers and horses, dogs allowed on leash. The park closes at night. Bridle Trails Park covers more than 400 acres of forest. Some of the Douglas-fir are over 200 years old, though much of the park was logged in the 1920s. There is little bird data for this park, but Pileated Woodpecker and American Dipper nest here, and once a great Gray Owl was found here in winter. It is home to Aplodontia and Douglas' Squirrel.

Seattle

The Seattle Audubon Society is currently conducting regular bird surveys in nine city parks. You can contact them for data on those parks, listed on the society's website. Seattle offers many and varied birding spots. The city maintains more than 400 parks and open areas, and park lands cover more than 6,200 acres. I haven't tried to cover them all, but below you'll find information about some selected birding sites in Seattle.

Alki Point. One spring there were two Red-faced Cormorants off Alki Point. That alone is reason enough to visit and to bring your scope. Pelagic and Brandt's Cormorant are regular wintering birds here. Over 110 other species have been reported to eBird from Alki Point and adjacent Alki Beach. Brant, Harlequin and Surf Scoter are abundant here. Black and White-winged Scoter, both goldeneyes and all three merganser species can be seen here. Also possible in winter: three loon species, including Pacific, and six grebe species, including Clark's and Red-necked. Pigeon Guillemot and Rhino Auklet are regular here in fall and winter.

Bellevue Botanical Garden. With its wide range of native plants, including ferns, rhododendrons, and dwarf conifers, the botanical garden offers birds a wide range of flowers. Try the fuchsia garden when it's in full bloom for glimpses of hummingbirds, including Anna's, Black-chinned, Calliope and Rufous. Also to be found here: Hutton's Vireo, Pileated Woodpecker, Steller's Jay, Chestnut-backed Chickadee, Bushtit, and Varied Thrush (winter).

Golden Gardens Park. For shoreline bird spotting, try Golden Gardens Park, right on Puget Sound. Ducks and geese favor this park for resting on their migratory treks. Birds may include American Coot, Black Oystercatcher and Black Scoter. You may see Bald Eagles nesting on the cliffs. As a bonus, California sea lions may be visible, gathered on the rock jetty near the marina. Venturing north along the beach or east into the wetlands area will yield plenty of bird-spotting opportunities. Heading down into Ballard along the locks you may glimpse a Belted Kingfisher.

Interlaken Park. There are over 50 acres of forest in this city park. Among resident birds here are Pileated Woodpecker, Hutton's Vireo and Spotted Towhee.

Magnuson Park. Formerly known as Sand Point Park, on the site of a former U.S. Navy air base, Magnuson runs along a splendid mile of Lake Washington's shoreline in northeastern Seattle. At 350 acres, it's Seattle's second largest park.

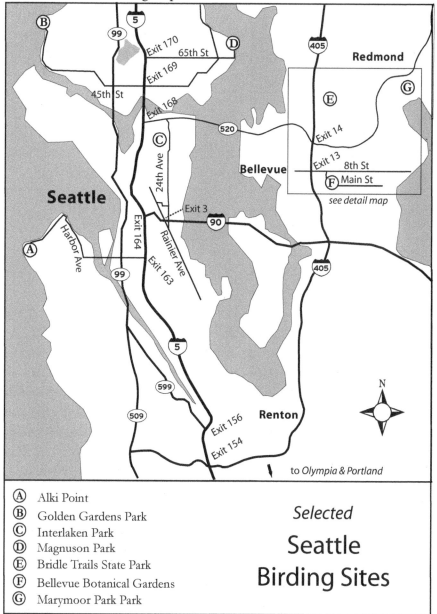

Ⓐ Alki Point
Ⓑ Golden Gardens Park
Ⓒ Interlaken Park
Ⓓ Magnuson Park
Ⓔ Bridle Trails State Park
Ⓕ Bellevue Botanical Gardens
Ⓖ Marymoor Park Park

Selected

Seattle Birding Sites

What you'll find: boating, swimming, toilets, kite flying, sports fields, walking paths, natural areas, and a historic campus. EBird shows about 175 species recorded here, including most expected waterbirds from scoters to loons to grebes. Uncommon birds sighted here include Trumpeter Swan, Redhead, Red-breasted Merganser, White-winged Scoter and Pacific Loon. Red-necked Grebe are regular winter visitors to Lake Washington and can be seen along this park's shoreline. Over a dozen species of shorebird have been reported and eight gull species, plus the usual assortment of northwestern hybrids to challenge your eye and brain. If you put much attention to gulls you will know that Western X Glaucous-winged, or Herring X almost-anybody are just the tip of the iceberg of hybrid gulls possible along the northern Pacific Coast. In fall you may find Wilson's and Black-throated Gray Warbler, Horned Grebe, Swainson's and Varied Thrush, Pacific Wren and Barn Owl.

Range Change

A study of Christmas Bird Counts over the past four decades has shown just how quickly some American bird species are changing their winter range. Purple Finches now winter more than 400 miles north of where they were found 50 years ago. There's ample evidence to show how some species are also moving northward for breeding. Anna's Hummingbird, Hooded Oriole, Northern Cardinal and Northern Mockingbird are far more northern now than they were half a century ago.

In the West, White-tailed Kite, Red-shouldered Hawk, Great-tailed Grackle, Black Phoebe and Chestnut-backed Chickadee are among those species pushing their range to the north. In 1953, *Birds of Washington State* did not list Anna's Hummingbird, Red-shouldered hawk, White-tailed Kite or Black Phoebe as residents. An 1892 report of a Black Phoebe at Chehalis was rejected as unsubstantiated. All four species are now established in southwestern Washington State. A century ago they would have been considered "California birds." In 1953 the European Starling was still considered rare in Washington State; it had only recently moved northward from California and begun to spread around Oregon. The invasion of the Pacific Coast by the Barred Owl shows clearly how some species will take advantage of changes brought about by man and nature. Range change is often an unintended consequence of human activity.

Some range evolution is due to habitat change, some to climate change or a combination. It is expected that "lowland" birds will expand their range upslope as global warming continues. This will put pressure on those species limited to higher elevation habitats, like Rosy-Finches and Clark's Nutcracker.

A number of species have taken advantage of human-altered habitat to expand their range and population. Canada Goose, Wild Turkey (not a Pacific Coast native species), Ring-necked Pheasant, Cattle Egret, Red-shouldered Hawk, Rock Pigeon, Barred Owl, Anna's Hummingbird, Northern Mockingbird, American Robin, European Starling, Hooded Oriole, and Brown-headed Cowbird were more limited in range 200 years ago. The Eurasian Collared-Dove didn't even breed in North America until the 1980s. It arrived in Florida and then conquered North America within less than 40 years. Breeding parrot and parakeet populations can be found in Los Angeles, Miami, San Francisco and other cities. Rare bird alerts and annual counts like the Christmas Bird Count, Backyard Bird Count and FeederWatch are showing the continual flux in bird species' ranges.

Conservation often plays a role in the resurgence of decimated populations within their historic ranges. In the first half of the 20th century, herons and egrets were rare across their pre-colonial breeding range, including the San Francisco Bay Area. Once the United States banned market hunting for these birds' feathers, their populations rebounded. Now it is easy for birders in the Bay Area to find Great Blue Heron, Black-crowned Night-Heron, Great Egret and Snowy Egret. Another good example of this kind of thing is the California Condor. After nearly disappearing from the Earth, this bird is successfully breeding in the wild again and could soon be showing up in warm months along the California section of Interstate 5 covered by this book. Over 200 years ago the Lewis a and Clark Expedition killed a California Condor soaring over the Columbia River. Who will make the first sighting of a Condor in Oregon in the 21st Century?

Chapter 13

Specialty Species

This is a guide to habitat, behavior and seasonal activities of some of the limited-range species you can find in the area covered by this book.

Trumpeter Swan. Uncommon south of Puget Sound, this swan may be found some winters in the Willamette Valley or on Sauvie Island. It is drawn to flat, damp grasslands or marshy areas.

Tundra Swan. A regular wintering bird in Sacramento River Valley, Willamette Valley and lowlands of western Washington, this swan is drawn to marshlands.

Brant. A gregarious goose that normally feeds on eelgrass in saltwater, the Brant is rare away from ocean inlets. It frequents arms of Puget Sound.

Emperor Goose. An occasional winter vagrant from Asia, this goose may be found grazing with Canada or other wintering geese.

Ross's Goose. Much of the world's population of this petite white goose winters in the Sacramento River Valley. The best place to see large numbers is the Sacramento Wildlife Refuge driving loop, I-5 Exit 585 in California, where it is easily identified next to the larger, abundant Snow Goose. Ross's migrate northeast from there to North-central Canada, passing over eastern Oregon and Washington State. Thus they are rare further north along I-5.

Eurasian Wigeon. An annual winter vagrant on the Pacific Slope, the Eurasian Wigeon can turn up in any flock of American Wigeons, which concentrate on quieter, inland waters. Almost a sure thing in the winter at Nisqually NWR, WA.

Cinnamon Teal. A common, but shy, resident bird in most areas covered by this book. The Cinnamon Teal is most likely in the Sacramento River Valley in sheltered ponds and marshes, near heavy cover. This is not a bird to be seen far from a lakeshore or in salt water.

Common Teal. A vagrant winter visitor. European science considers the Common Teal a separate species from our Green-winged Teal. The Common Teal male lacks the white vertical shoulder stripe. This bird may turn up wherever Green-winged Teal can be found in sheltered coves and ponds. I've had good luck on Sauvie's Island, OR.

Tufted Duck. Another Asian vagrant, the Tufted Duck can be found with wintering flocks of Ring-necked Duck or scaup in small lakes or other waters suitable for diving ducks.

Harlequin Duck. This beauty usually winters in rough offshore waters, but can be found around the perimeter of Puget Sound complex. Occasionally Harlequins are seen on the Columbia River or other large bodies of water.

Long-tailed Duck (formerly Oldsquaw). This duck is most at home in the open ocean or large bays, but may be seen in reservoirs or estuaries like the Columbia's.

Scoters. All three species are pelagic. The Surf Scoter is most abundant and most likely to show up in Portland or around Puget Sound, even on inland lakes. The White-winged is less abundant but more likely as you travel northward in winter. The Black is increasingly scarce. The best chance of finding these scoter species inland is right after a major storm blows in off the ocean.

Barrow's Goldeneye. This duck winters on fast streams or on windblown open water. It is not to be found in a quiet cattail marsh. The further north you go, the more likely the Barrow's Goldeneye is to be found with other diving ducks. It's a regular around Puget Sound.

Red-throated Loon. Wandering or storm-blown individuals may turn up in large rivers or estuaries some distance from the actual coast, but this loon usually winters in offshore or near shore ocean waters. It's not going to show up in a small pond.

Pacific Loon. This bird is larger, darker and more pelagic than the Red-throated. Still, occasionally an individual will end up in a large reservoir or estuary far from the open ocean. Sightings are most likely around Puget Sound.

Pelagic Cormorant. This small, slender ocean-going cormorant will sometimes follow estuaries or narrow inlets well inland. It's most likely on the Columbia River or in Puget Sound.

Brandt's Cormorant. Larger and more pelagic than the Pelagic, Brand's Cormorant may occasionally drift or be wind-blown into estuaries.

White-tailed Kite. This pale, slender, elegant raptor is hard to miss in its preferred open grasslands. In all seasons it likes hunting in pairs, and prefers lowland with plenty of voles. This kite was almost wiped out in California in 1930s, but has rebounded well. It first colonized Oregon in 1970s, and now can be found north into western Washington as well. However, it is not common north of Eugene, OR.

Northern Goshawk. This is a bird of montane forests. The best place to look for it along the I-5 is in Jackson County, Oregon. It soars much more easily than smaller accipiters.

Red-shouldered Hawk. Now considered a subspecies, this Western hawk may become a separate species in the future. The Red-shouldered has spread northward from California and now can be found north of Portland. It was first noted regularly in Oregon starting in the 1970s. Now it breeds in the Rogue and Willamette river valleys. A rodent specialist, it hunts from a perch in a tree next to open ground. This hawk does well around farms and towns.

Swainson's Hawk. A breeding bird in Sacramento River Valley, this hawk winters in South America. Not every buteo you see above I-5 in California is a Red-tailed Hawk. It specializes in eating large insects and thus has a small gape.

Ferruginous Hawk. This scarce migrant and wintering bird may be seen in the grassy valleys along I-5. It's most likely in the area north of Mount Shasta in California and wintering in the Rogue Valley of Oregon.

Rough-legged Hawk. This migrant from the Arctic winters in windy grasslands. It's often seen on the ground. Most winters it can be found in the Willamette Valley in Oregon or in other open areas along I-5 from Sacramento to Seattle. The Rough-legged is abundant in winter in the Klamath Basin, which is east of the area covered by this book.

Mountain Quail. Larger and more elusive than California Quail, this bird is rarely found below 3,000 feet elevation. Your best hope for this bird along I-5 is in the mountains around Jackson County, Oregon. It likes steep, inaccessible slopes covered with manzanita, ceanothus or other dense growth. Learn the call before you go searching. The males are often heard in spring.

Sooty Grouse. This large, sedentary bird is best found on Mount Ashland or along the Cascade Mountain Loop. Sometimes the hen will perch on a boulder to keep her eye on chicks feeding in the meadow below. In spring males will thrum from the tops of Douglas firs or other conifers.

Common Gallinule (formerly Moorhen). This bird is common in the marshes of the Sacramento River Valley, but shy — and rare north of there.

Clapper Rail. The San Francisco Bay is the north end of this rare bird's range, so seek it in Marin or Solano County. This bird can be seen at highest tide in pickleweed or other salt marsh plants. In spring the males "clap" their large beaks as part of courtship and territory defense. This is not a freshwater bird like the Sora or Virginia Rail.

Black Rail. This small nocturnal bird is the most secretive of all the rails. Grizzly Island, CA, at night is your best hope. Sightings are unlikely anywhere north of that point.

Mountain Plover. An uncommon but regular wintering bird in the grassy hills along I-505 in California. Often found with Killdeer, blackbirds, Horned Larks and other short-grass denizens.

Black Turnstone, Wandering Tattler, Surfbird. These three shorebirds are often lumped together as "rockpipers." They all like rocky coastlines on the ocean or bays. The turnstone and Surfbird generally overwinter all along the coast, including Puget Sound. They often form mixed flocks. The more solitary Tattler generally winters south of the area of this book, so it's most easily found in August-September and again in May.

Red-necked Phalarope. A regular fall migrant through the Willamette and Sacramento River Valleys, the Red-Necked Phalarope can be found swirling in even tiny irrigation ponds in August and September.

Red Phalarope. Best seen on a winter pelagic trip about 20 miles offshore, but the Red Phalarope can become briefly abundant inland after an extremely windy winter storm. The storm-tossed birds feed in flooded fields and in ponds and reservoirs until the weather allows them to return to the Pacific.

Mew Gull. This delicate-looking gull is normally coastal, and can be found along San Francisco Bay and Puget Sound. It is present only in late fall and winter, breeding much further north.

Ring-billed Gull, California Gull. These two medium-sized gulls are often found inland. Study the field marks as they seem similar but actually are different. The two gulls even show up at rest stops along I-5, sometimes in the same flock. The California Gull is the larger and darker of the two, and lacks the yellow eye of adult Ring-billed.

Thayer's Gull. The first time you go looking for this gull, try to go with a local expert. Thayer's is tough to ID. It is a regular wintering bird along the coast, however, and so can be found in San Francisco, Marin, Portland and around Puget Sound. In California it is mostly likely you'll encounter first- or second-year Thayer's. Try Lake Merced in San Francisco.

Western Gull. This large dark-mantled gull is most common in California, near or at the coast, but uncommon inland. The Western frequently crossbreeds with the Glaucous-winged Gull. It is a common breeding gull on the San Francisco and Marin coastline.

Glaucous-winged Gull. This hefty gull has no black feathers. It is mostly coastal in California but is found in the Willamette Valley and other inland areas north of there. In the Puget Sound area, the Glaucous-winged X Western hybrids are known locally as "Olympic Gulls" for the Olympic Peninsula, where they are abundant. The further north you go the more common this gull becomes and it breeds around Puget Sound.

Heermann's Gull. A medium-sized dark gull with a red beak, the Heermann's Gull is usually seen along the coast, but rarely inland. This gull is present in large numbers in Northern California from May to December, to coincide with the presence of Brown Pelicans. Both species breed further south in late winter.

Pigeon Guillemot. Found near shore from April to August in the San Francisco Bay Area, the Pigeon Guillemot breeds on rocky cliffs on islands or on the mainland. In the Puget Sound area, it can be found on open bays all winter; often a first-year offspring and its male parent will be seen together.

Common Murre. This bird can often be seen within easy scoping distance of shore in San Francisco Bay and Puget Sound. It breeds primarily on offshore islands but often feeds near shore.

Rhinoceros Auklet. This little bird prefers open bays, but it may wander into the narrow fingers of Puget Sound. It can often be seen from ferries in that area.

Band-tailed Pigeon. This rather bulky pigeon nests in old growth forests, but it may feed in pastures and crop land. This pigeon is never found far from large trees. The Band-Tailed Pigeon tends to be more coastal in winter. Sightings are most likely in the mountains between Redding, CA, and Eugene, OR.

Great Gray Owl. There's a small breeding population in the Cascades of Jackson County, OR. In the evening, this large owl hunts from snags or stumps along the edge of a mountain meadow. It's not migratory and is our longest bodied owl in North America.

Western Screech-Owl. Often found around farms and small towns, this small owl hunts moths in the street lights in summer. It is non-migratory. Human residents often know where this owl roosts, so contact local birders. This bird will nap during the day in a small owl box or in a hole in a tree trunk about 20 feet off the ground.

Northern Pygmy-Owl. This tiny, elusive, diurnal bird hunter frequents open and mixed forests in the mountains of California, Oregon and Washington. Learn to imitate the call as it is the best way to lure one into view. A frequent target of mobbing by small birds up to jay size, the Northern Pygmy-Owl usually perches in mid-canopy, not in treetops.

Spotted Owl. This owl is nocturnal and difficult to locate. An endangered deep-forest dweller of the northwest, the Spotted Owl is now under territorial invasion from its near relative, the Barred Owl.   It's fate is still the subject of heated and angry political debate in the West so if you inquire locally, do so with care and discretion.

Burrowing Owl. Sadly, this charming little diurnal owl is increasingly rare as we plow, pave and exploit its native prairies in the west. Not treated kindlhy by users of pesticides. Burrowing Owl colonies are constantly being demolished or depopulated by human activities, so it's best to check recent local birding data. The open areas around Davis, CA, can sometimes be rewarding in the search for this photogenic fellow.

Vaux's Swift. This small dark bird is the tiniest swift in North America. Vaux's Swift is abundant in forests of southwestern Oregon and across much of Washington State. Several fall communal roost sites are well known and draw large audiences of admiring humans for the returning birds, late on a summer evening. This bird is present May through September from Ashland northward through the Willamette Valley. Vaux's Swift often hunts over ponds with swallows, but is much faster and appears all dark in good light.

Black Swift. This scarce bird is best found at Burney Falls State Park, CA, about an hour's drive east from I-5 near Mount Shasta. Inquire before going as this species is sometimes not present until mid-June. There are also known nesting sites in the Cascades, a couple hours' drive east of Eugene, OR.

Anna's Hummingbird. A year-round resident in most parts of the I-5 corridor below 2,500 feet elevation, Anna's Hummingbird prefers nesting at the forest's edge and in brushland. Males seem especially loath to migrate, instead going into torpor when temperatures drop below 37 degrees. This bird loves hummingbird feeders. It's often found in gardens and city parks.

Calliope Hummingbird. This is the smallest bird in North America. The Calliope breeds on mountain slopes where blooming bushes like manzanita and ceanothus provide food. Along I-5, the Siskiyous in southern Oregon are the likeliest spot for this bird.

Rufous Hummingbird. The Rufous is a migrant in September along the I-5 corridor and through the San Francisco Bay Area. It nests in the Willamette Valley and western Oregon. Can be found at feeders and from town to forest but it breeds mostly in forests with heavy canopy and dense underbrush. The Rufous is very similar to the more southerly and more coastal Allen's Hummingbird, which is found in Northern California and along the Oregon Coast from February to August.

Acorn Woodpecker. The name says it all. Look for oak woodlands and listen for this bird's laughing call. The Acorn Woodpecker can be found in town and country, a colonial nester and communal bird all year round. All of a colony's eggs go into a single nest. The colony stores thousands of acorns in holes drilled into dead oaks or soft-barked conifers. These birds tend to be very sedentary. Not found from Portland northward.

Lewis's Woodpecker. An unpredictable cousin of the Acorn, this bird disperses from breeding territory to similar oak habitat in winter. Presumably it is moving for slightly warmer winter weather. It definitely breeds along the Klamath River in the Siskiyou Mountains of Northern California. Some winters it is common in Jackson County, Oregon, to the north. This woodpecker often flycatches and can look like a crow at a distance. It has no white feathers.

Red-breasted Sapsucker. Generally a mountain breeder, this bird usually moves down into wooded valleys and coastal forests in winter. It drills lines of sap wells in some soft-barked trees. It is not found in the Cascades.

Williamson's Sapsucker. Found mostly in the Cascades and eastward, Williamson's likes a tall conifer forest. Two good spots for this species can be found on the Cascade Mountain Loop.

Nuttall's Woodpecker. Only slightly bigger than a Downy, this ladder-backed Woodpecker likes oak forests and riparian corridors. It is confined to the lowlands of California including the Sacramento River Valley. Do not expect to find this bird north of Redding, CA.

White-headed Woodpecker. This strongly marked mountain bird is the same size as a Hairy Woodpecker. It's found in both the Siskiyou and Cascade Mountains, rarely below 4000' elevation. It feeds largely on ponderosa pine seeds. So if you're seeking this bird it's good to recognize the six-inch long dull green needles in bunches of three that indicate a ponderosa. This bird does not migrate but may move downslope in winter.

Pileated Woodpecker. A sparse but permanent resident of forests north of Redding. Can be in both mountain and lowland forests. Best place to look is along the Nisqually River in the Nisqually NWR, WA, or in nearby Tolmie State Park. Many large, dead trees are a requirement for this, our largest surviving woodpecker in North America.

Olive-sided Flycatcher. A treetop bird of conifer or mixed woods. Song is said to be "quick three beers." The size of a phoebe but nearly always fifty feet or more above the ground.   Check mountain forests north of Redding.

Western Wood-Pewee. Tolerant of dry summers as long as there are big trees or brush. Often feed in middle of canopy, rarely near the ground. Never secretive. Its wheezy call is commonly heard all spring and summer in many habitat types along I-5. Never in grassland.

Empidonax. There are four likely Empids nesting in this area. The widespread Willow Flycatcher is found in forests along the route. Pacific-slope like damp thickets and brushy stream margins. This is the only Empid in this area that nests near sea-level. Dusky like forest edges in the mountains but arrive in valleys before snow melts in May, then move up. Ditto the Hammond's which likes a deep conifer forest for breeding. Finally, the Gray Flycatcher nests primarily east of the Cascades summit but is a regular migrant along the western slope of those mountains.

Phoebes. Two species possible along I-5 in winter. The black-and-white Black Phoebe is a common year-round resident as far north as Jackson County, Oregon. It likes open water margins in freezing weather, often fly-catching on the surface. It does not migrate. Say's Phoebe brings its brighter colors west to the I-5 corridor from the Great Basin. It is present in small numbers along the Sacramento River Valley and into Oregon from October through April. It is most likely over open grasslands at low to moderate elevations in winter.

Ash-throated Flycatcher. This bird favors dry slopes with open oak forest. Often seen in areas with Oak Titmouse and White-breasted Nutnatches. It is larger than a phoebe, smaller than a kingbird. Its dry lowland habitat is not often used by other flycatchers, though it may border open grasslands where Western Kingbirds hunt.

Northern Shrike. A possible wintering bird in valleys north of Mt. Shasta. Likes open, cold, windy grasslands. I have never seen this bird in forest but it will perch in lone trees in open land. Frequently found on Christmas counts in OR and WA.

Hutton's Vireo. A small vireo that can make you think you have a sluggish Ruby-crowned Kinglet. Likes mixed forest, usually with some oak. Primarily a coastal species it can be found in Marin and Sonoma Counties of CA and in winter in the Rogue River Valley. Also found in hills west of Portland and in forests along Puget Sound. Disperses in fall but non-migratory.

Cassin's Vireo. In spring and summer the insistent, repetitive call of this bird can be heard in mountain conifer woods. Best located by voice as it is usually well up in a dense evergreen and doesn't usually fly-catch, gleaning branches slowly and carefully.

Gray Jay. A mountain bird along I-5 that occurs from the Siskiyou Mountains northward. Along I-5 it prefers higher elevations. Usually in small flock and can be vocal as it forages through conifers. From Eureka, CA, northward along the coast this bird can be found near sea level.

Clark's Nutcracker. A pine seed specialist, this large Corvid is found in small numbers along the Cascades Ridge. Best sure locations for the bird: Crater Lake National Park and Mt. Hood east of Portland, both two hours from I-5. Some experts say this bird will suffer much from global warming because of its narrow habitat and food preferences.

Magpies. The widespread Black-billed is not common as far west as I-5 but it does inhabit the Shasta Valley area from Mt. Shasta to Weed. Occasionally small number winters along the Cascade Mountain Loop in Oregon. One of two California endemics, the Yellow-billed Magpie has a very small range. There are locations along I-80 and I-5 in the Sacramento River valley where the bird is abundant and obvious when present. Can't mistake that tail. The Yellow-billed will not be found north of Redding, CA.

Northwestern Crow. A problematic species but the voices and diminutive size of crows around Puget Sound make you think you've seen a Northwestern. Some local birders there say you have to go to Canada for the real thing as it hybridizes with American Crow.

Violet-Green Swallow. A beautiful swallow that's a cavity nester like the Tree. Found all along I-5 where there are good stands of trees. Not a colonial bird like Cave, Cliff or Bank Swallows. Often migrates with Tree Swallows.

A few thousand Tree Swallows over-winter in the Sacramento Valley each year. One or two stray Violet-greens may be in with them.

Oak Titmouse. The name defines this bird's habitat. Dry oak forests as far north as Jackson County, OR. Resident year- round and often calls while feeding in winter flock of gleaners. Emigrant Lake near Ashland, OR, is almost guaranteed spot for this bird as is Deer Island in Marin County, CA.

Bushtit. A gregarious gray bird with a long tail that weaves a teardrop shaped bag nest, unlike orioles' nest that has double attachments to limbs. After breeding, Bushtits form nervous troops that constantly move through willows and brush, twittering softly as they go. Rarely high in canopy, never seen on the ground. They will flock to suet feeders in winter but rarely linger. Found all along the route of this book in open forest and brushland.

Chestnut-backed Chickadee. The only low elevation chickadee in central California. Smallest of the three chickadee species in this area. Range overlaps with widely found Black-capped in Oregon and Washington. Likes damp forests. Non-migratory and often in mixed gleaner flocks in winter.

Mountain Chickadee. Breeds in mountain conifers above 3000' but may drop into nearby valleys during especially severe mountain winter. Larger than other chickadees and equally vocal. Can be found in forests between Redding, CA, and Grants Pass, OR. Common on Mount Ashland. Further north it is found in Cascades and eastward only.

Bewick's Wren. A year-round resident and singer, this bird likes brushy habitat and riparian forest with dense underbush. Not a montane species nor does it migrate.

Pacific Wren (formerly Winter Wren). The darker and damper the habitat, the happier this bird will be. Found in shaded mountain gorges and dense, wet underbrush in winter. Mostly in mountains in summer. Winters in San Francisco, Marin, Multnomah and Seattle area.

Rock Wren, Canyon Wren. The habitat in the Klamath River Canyon west of I-5 in northern California is good for both these birds.

American Dipper. This is a bird that loves mountain water. Can be found along upper Sacramento River above Shasta Lake, CA, and on streams around Ashland, OR, including creek running through Lithia Park and in the center of town.

Wrentit. This secretive, sedentary little brown bird is America's only species of babbler. Pairs are together year round in their brushy redoubt.

Their bouncing ball call is diagnostic but they can still be hard to spot. Never more than few feet above the ground. Found in Sacramento, Rogue, Umpqua and upper Willamette Valleys as well as brushy habitat in Marin Headlands. Range becomes coastal north of Eugene. Never at high elevation.

Mountain Bluebird. Generally nest above 4500' and found from Mt. Shasta northward in montane openings. Migrates mostly east of the Cascades so extremely rare in valleys along I-5 even in fall.

Townsend's Solitaire. Common gray thrush of mountain conifer forests. Likes juniper berries in fall and winter, often congregating in large flocks like Robins.

Varied Thrush. This secretive shade lover often feeds along a road in heavily wooded, damp areas. Comes down into valleys in winter but is irruptive and thus erratic for one year to the next. Sometimes in large flocks and may feed on ground with Robins, but always shyer, quicker to fly away. When spooked, will often fly up into tree and freeze on a limb thinking its color has made it disappear. Local birders will know if this species is present as it is much admired.

California Thrasher. Found only in California and Baja, very sedentary and hard to find after singing season is over. Prefers brushy habitat, neither grassland nor dense conifer forest. There is a resident population along Klamath River west of I-5. Extremely rare north of that point.

Black-throated Gray Warbler. This western warbler is an early migrant arriving in California and Oregon in April. It nests in all three states mostly in medium density woodlands or regenerating forests in a wide variety of trees from oak to spruce. They also frequent chaparral with scattered oak and madrone. They don't nest in the Sacramento Valley but otherwise may be found all along Interstate 5 and into British Columbia.

Townsend's Warbler. Winters along the northern California Coast, uncommon inland. In San Francisco Bay Area it's usually second most abundant Christmas Count warbler behind Yellow-rumped. Migrates through lowlands as well as along mountain ridges. Breeds in Siskiyous and Cascades and higher Sierra. May be replacing Hermit Warbler in some areas where ranges overlap. The two species also interbreed.

Hermit Warbler. This heavy-looking yellow-headed warbler is a bird of dense conifer forest where it prefers the higher branches. Should be easily found on Mt. Ashland, OR, in spring. Its range is in coastal mountains and Siskiyous and Cascades. Migrant only in river valleys along I-5.

Western Tanager. In spring it feeds in valley forests. Then moves upslope to nest in mountains. It prefers forest with some conifers and does not nest in Sacramento River Valley but can be found in spring or summer in woods north of Redding, CA, all the way to Seattle. Migrates in large flocks in spring.

Black-headed Grosbeak. Another forest lover and in spring a non-stop singer. Both genders sing in spring. Especially abundant along streams where trees are dense. Common feeder bird in its nesting range. Usually doesn't feed on the ground.

Blue Grosbeak. A scarce breeding bird in the Sacramento River Valley. Not likely north of Red Bluff. Found in brushy habitat near irrigation canals or natural streams. Far more common in eastern U.S.

Lazuli Bunting. This beauty is found in brush and chaparral, open forests and along streams from near sea level to 6500' or more. The males often sing from conifer treetops in spring. They do not feed on the ground or flycatch like bluebirds.

Spotted Towhee. An adaptable and abundant breeding bird all along this section of I-5. Prefers brush, streamside growth or forest edge. Usually near the ground, even when singing in spring. Fairly sedentary though mountain birds may move downslope to escape winter snow. Found in valleys and mountain slopes but not alpine habitat. Not expected above 4000'. Often found on ground beneath bird feeders. Frequents some rest stops with good brush thickets. Non-migratory.

California Towhee. Abundant in Bay Area and Sacramento Valley. Uncommon in Jackson County, OR, and not expected north of there. A lowland bird of town, gardens and brushy habitat. Pairs stay together year round. Non-migratory. Its loud "chink" warning call is diagnostic.

Green-tailed Towhee. This handsome towhee with the melodic song is a mountain bird, even migrates generally along mountain ranges. Can be found in Cascades and Siskiyous. Likes mountain meadows and brushy slopes, not forest. Can be found in Siskiyou County, CA, and Jackson County, OR.

Golden-crowned Sparrow. This large, dark-breasted Sparrow is an abundant fall and winter bird all along this section of Interstate 5. It frequents hedgerows, brushy areas, high weedy fields and streamsides. Often feeds on ground in mixed sparrow flocks and this bird frequently scratches like a chicken. Appears at numerous I-5 rest stops.

Black-throated Sparrow. This is a scarce breeding bird in Siskiyou and Jackson Counties. Prefers arid slopes that face south but are covered with dense brush. Present only in warm months.

Tricolored Blackbird. This blackbird is often in mixed feeding flocks with Brewer's and Red-winged Blackbirds in winter. Watch for the bright white wing bar in flight. Highly gregarious, its nesting colonies are often in wetlands near large herds of cows. Tricolors used to follow the elk herds. They can be found with luck in the Sacramento Valley and Shasta Valley of California as well as Rogue Valley in Oregon. This bird is in decline in its limited range but it does now breed in selected parts of southern Oregon as well as California. In winter it flocks with other blackbird species

Cassin's Finch. This reddish finch has a heavier beak than Purple or House. The male often shows a slight crest. Wing extension is longer than either House or Purple Finch. It's a mountain species that only occasionally ventures into valleys during bad winter weather. Breeds in ponderosa, juniper, even aspen woods with some openings. Mostly confined to Cascade but may be seen on Mt. Ashland, tallest of the Siskiyous in southern Oregon.

Lesser Goldfinch. This smallest goldfinch prefers dry grasslands and unmown weeds. It's hardy enough to winter in southwestern Oregon. Abundant at winter feeding stations in its territory, sometimes along with Pine Siskins who've left the mountains. Male Lesser keeps his bright yellow plumage in all phases unlike larger American Goldfinch. Found along Interstate 5 year-round from Sacramento north to Portland, rare north of there. May nest as high as 7000'.

Lawrence's Goldfinch. A scarce and erratic lowland or foothill bird that prefers arid habitat and a bush called chemise. May nest up to 3500' in right habitat. Does not always return to same nesting area each year. In spring it may migrate with other goldfinch species in Sacramento River Valley. Not expected north of Redding, CA. May turn up along any brushy side roads in Northern California. Does not overwinter in this area as do American and Lesser Goldfinches.   Sometimes caused to wander by late summer brushfires.

Evening Grosbeak. Our largest finch, this gregarious species moves around the mountain forests of the west. It may move into town over the winter or in spring before establishing a nesting locale by humans. Best to inquire locally as you would with Cedar Waxwing or Varied Thrush. "Seen any lately?"

Bird Festivals and Walks

Bird festivals can be a good way for a visitor or newly arrived resident to get acquainted with an area's birds and with other birders. Field trips led by local experts who know the terrain and the birds are always part of the festivals. Here are some that are on or near the area covered by this book:

State List

California:
   Snow Goose Festival, Chico, CA - January
   San Francisco Bay Flyway Festival, Vallejo, CA - February
   California Duck Days, Davis, CA - February
   Point Reyes Birding and Nature Festival, Point Reyes Station,
      CA - April or May
   Sandhill Crane Festival, Lodi, CA - November

Oregon:
   Winter Wings, Klamath Falls, OR - February
   Festival of the Birds, Portland, OR - May
   Tualatin River Bird Festival, Tualatin, OR - May
   Ashland Mountain Bird Festival, Ashland, OR - late May

Washington:

Nisqually Watershed Festival, Nisqually NWR, WA - September
Puget Sound Bird Fest, Edmonds, WA - September
Birdfest and Bluegrass, Ridgefield, WA - October

Date List

January – February

California Duck Days, Davis, CA
San Francisco Bay Flyway Festival, Vallejo, CA
Snow Goose Festival, Chico, CA
Winter Wings, Klamath Falls, OR

April – May

Festival of the Birds, Portland, OR
Point Reyes Birding and Nature Festival, Point Reyes Station, CA
Tualatin River Bird Festival, Tualatin, OR
Ashland Mountain Bird Festival, Ashland, OR

September

Nisqually Watershed Festival, Nisqually NWR, WA
Puget Sound Bird Fest, Edmonds, WA

October

Birdfest and Bluegrass, Ridgefield, WA

November

Sandhill Crane Festival, Lodi, CA

Groups and Organizations that Sponsor Bird Walks

Locally led bird walks can often be the best and most informative way to find local birds if you are visiting an unfamiliar area. Check before you arrive. Most organizations and parks have websites that will list time and place of field trips of all sorts. Here are some suggestions of specific bird walk providers along our route between San Francisco and Seattle.

Audubon Societies. Local groups generally listed under home county. There are Audubon Centers in Portland and Tacoma.

BLM and US Forest Service properties designated for camping or recreational use

Christmas Bird Counts. Nearly every population center has one or more, Dec. 15 - Jan. 15.

Klamath Bird Observatory, Ashland, Oregon

National Wildlife Refuges

Nature Centers in Ashland, Corvallis, and Eugene, Oregon, also Tacoma, Washington

Nature Conservancy properties

Numerous **National, City and State Parks**

Point Reyes Bird Observatory, Point Reyes, California

Bibliography

"A Birder's Guide to Driving Routes in Siskiyou County". Map. Natural Resource Geospatial, 2005.

"Birds of Shasta County" checklist. Wintu Audubon Society, 2005.

California Atlas and Gazetteer. DeLorme Mapping Company, Freeport, Maine, 2010.

Claypole, Bob. *Klamath River Bird Finder.* Living Gold Press, Klamath River, California, 2004.

Contreras, Alan. *Northwest Birds in Winter.* Oregon State University Press, Corvallis, 1997.

Eder, Tamara. *Mammals of Washington and Oregon.* Lone Pine Publishing, Edmonton, Canada, 2002.

Evanich, Joseph Jr. *The Birder's Guide to Oregon.* Portland Audubon Society, Portland, Oregon, 1990.

Evens, Jules and Ian Tait. *Introduction to California Bird Life.* University of California Press, Berkeley, 2005.

Fitchen, John. *Birding Portland and Multnomah County.* Catalyst Publications, Portland, Oregon, 2004.

Herlyn, Hendrik and Alan Contreras. *Handbook of Oregon Birds.* Oregon State University Press, Corvallis, 2009.

Houck, Michael C. and M.J. Cody, editors. *Wild in the City: Exploring the Intertwine.* Oregon State University Press, Corvallis, 2011.

Jewett, Stanley, Walter Taylor, William Shaw, John Aldrich. *Birds of Washington State.* University of Washington Press, Seattle, 1953.

Kemper, John. *Birding Northern California.* Falcon Publishing, Helena, Montana, 1999.

Krickenberg, Arthur. *Natural History of Puget Sound Country.* University of Washington Press, Seattle, 1991.

Massey, Barbara and Dennis Vroman. *Guide to Birds of the Rogue Valley.* Oregon Field Ornithologists, 2003.

McNair-Huff, Rob and Natalie. *Birding Washington.* Falcon Publishing, Helena, Montana, 2005.

Morse, Rob, Tom Aversa, Hal Opperman, R.W. Morse. *Birds of the Puget Sound Region.* R. W. Morse Company, Olympia, WA, 2003.

Opperman, Hal. A *Birder's Guide to Washington.* American Birding Association, Colorado Springs, 2003.

Oregon Road and Recreation Atlas. Benchmark Maps, Medford, Oregon, 2006.

Peters, Hans. *Owls of California and the West.* University of California Press, Berkeley, 2007.

Rakestraw, John. *Birding Oregon.* Falcon Publishing, Helena, Montana, 2007.

"The Great Washington State Birding Trail" maps. Audubon Washington, Seattle, dates unknown. (This is a series of seven birding maps, two of which ("Puget Sound Loop" and "Southwest Loop") cover areas discussed in this book.

Tualatin Riverkeepers. *Exploring the Tualatin River Basin.* Oregon State University Press, Corvallis, 2002.

Wallace, David Raines. *Klamath Knot: Exploration of Myth and Evolution.* University of California Press, Berkeley, 2003.

"Western Washington Interstate 5 Wildlife Viewing Map." Washington Dept. of Fish and Wildlife, Seattle, 2009.

Westrich, LoLo and Jim. *Birder's Guide to Northern California.* Gulf Publishing, Houston, 1991.

Willamette Riverkeeper. "Willamette River Trail Guide". Available for print or purchase at www.willamettewatertrail.org.

Williams, David. *Street Smart Naturalist: Field Notes from Seattle.* West Winds Press, Seattle, 2005.

Zimmer, Kevin. *Birding in the American West.* Cornell University Press, Ithaca, NY, 2000.

Index

Red-shouldered Hawk © Dan Elster www.elsterphotography.com